The Idea of a Theater

Pensa, lettor, s' io mi maravigliava
quando vedea la cosa in se star queta,
e nell' idolo suo si trasmutava.
                —*Purgatorio*, CANTO XXXI

THE IDEA
OF A THEATER

A Study of Ten Plays
The Art of Drama
in Changing Perspective

BY

FRANCIS FERGUSSON

PRINCETON, NEW JERSEY
PRINCETON UNIVERSITY PRESS

TO MARION CROWNE FERGUSSON

CONTENTS

CONTENTS

CONTENTS

ACKNOWLEDGMENTS

MUCH of the material in this book has appeared, in different form, in *Accent, The Hudson Review, The Kenyon Review,* and *The Partisan Review,* and I wish to thank the editors of those magazines for permission to use it here.

Permission has very kindly been granted me to quote from the following published works: *The Purgatorio of Dante Alighieri* (London: J. M. Dent and Sons, Ltd., 1926); *The Complete Works of William Shakespeare* (New York: Oxford University Press); *Selected Essays, 1917-1932,* by T. S. Eliot (New York: Harcourt Brace and Co., 1932), *Murder in the Cathedral,* by T. S. Eliot (New York: Harcourt Brace and Co., 1935). The quotations in Chapter V are taken from *The Cherry Orchard,* by Anton Chekhov, translated by Stark Young (New York: Samuel French, 1941). The excerpts from Aristotle's *Poetics* are taken from *Aristotle's Theory of Poetry and Fine Art* with a *Critical Text and Translation of the Poetics,* by S. H. Butcher, M.P. (London: Macmillan and Co., Ltd., 1932. 4th edn.).

I also wish to record my debt to several individuals and institutions, for instruction and rare opportunities to study the theater: to The American Laboratory Theater, especially its founder, the late Miriam K. Stockton; Madame Maria Ouspenskaya; the late Richard Boleslavsky; and my wife; to Bennington College, and my former students in the Theater Studio there; and to Dr. J. Robert Oppenheimer, Director of the Institute for Advanced Study, for the year's appointment as a member of the Institute, which enabled me to complete the writing of this book.

Miss Margot Cutter and Miss Gladys Fornell, of Princeton University Press, have given invaluable help.

Because of the analytical table of contents and the extensive use of cross-references in the text, an index has been dispensed with.

F. F.

PART I

THE IDEA OF A THEATER

INTRODUCTION

THE IDEA OF A THEATER

" . . . The purpose of playing, whose end, both at first and now, was and is, to hold, as 'twere, the mirror up to nature; to show virtue her own feature, scorn her own image, and the very age and body of the time his form and pressure."

HAMLET's charge to the players expresses the perennial need for a direct and significant imitation of human life and action which can be played as music is played. But though we may assent to Hamlet's definition, if we read it attentively, we shrug it off the next moment, thinking of Broadway or Hollywood, feeling that drama in this sense is not for us. Hamlet was referring to the drama he knew, and to the theater in which it had its life. He assumed the symbolic stage of the Elizabethans and, behind it, the traditional scene of human life which the stage itself represented; the starry firmament above, the stagehouse façade which could indicate various versions of the human City—market-place or court or castle; and the platform for the players, from which the trap-door opened down into Hell or the cellar. If he could ask the players to hold the mirror up to nature, it was because the Elizabethan theater was itself a mirror which had been formed at the center of the culture of its time, and at the center of the life and awareness of the community. We know now that such a mirror is rarely formed. We doubt that our time has an age, a body, a form, or a pressure; we are more apt to think of it as a wilderness which is without form. Human nature seems to us a hopelessly elusive and uncandid entity, and our playwrights (like hunters with camera and flash-bulbs in the depths of the Belgian Congo) are lucky if they can fix it, at rare intervals, in one of its momentary postures, and in a single bright, exclusive angle of vision. Thus the very *idea* of a theater,

1

as Hamlet assumed it, gets lost; and the art of drama, having no place of its own in contemporary life, is confused with lyric poetry or pure music on one side, or with editorializing and gossip on the other.

I do not mean to imply that we lack superb playwrights: on the contrary, the modern theater can show many images of human life which are both beautiful and revealing; triumphs of the stealthy hunt in the jungle. The centerless diversity of our theater may be interpreted as wealth. And we do not wish to relinquish any of it: neither Lorca nor Eliot, neither Chekhov nor Cocteau. But, thinking of such masters together, we cannot tell what to make of them. We cannot understand the arts and the visions of particular playwrights, nor the limited perfection of minor dramatic genres, without some more catholic conception of the art in general. Thus the pious effort to appreciate contemporary playwrights leads behind and beyond them. It leads, I think, to the dramatic art of Shakespeare and the dramatic art of Sophocles, both of which were developed in theaters which focused, at the center of the life of the community, the complementary insights of the whole culture. We do not have such a theater, nor do we see how to get it. But we need the "Idea of a Theater," both to understand the masterpieces of drama at its best, and to get our bearings in our own time.

I have selected *Oedipus Rex*, Racine's *Bérénice*, Wagner's *Tristan und Isolde*, and *Hamlet*, as landmarks in the study of drama; and they are the subject of the first four chapters. Behind these masterpieces of the theater lies the *Divine Comedy:* not written for the stage, yet presenting the most complete imitation of action, and the most developed idea of the theater of human life, to be found in the tradition. I wish to indicate briefly how I place these works, and what use I propose to make of them.

Oedipus Rex, near the beginning of the tradition, and *Hamlet,* on the threshold of the modern world, have been called artistic failures almost as often as they have been called supreme masterpieces. They are sphinxes of literature, with the disconcerting property of showing up those who would interpret them. Nevertheless, the instinct which leads students of drama (and, indeed, of the whole tradition) to question them again and again, is sound. Mysterious they are and will remain; but we can see that they mirror human life and action, both with extraordinary directness, and from many angles at once, catching the creature in the very act of inventing those partial rationalizations which make the whole substance of lesser dramas. In short, they are sources and landmarks which an inquiry of this kind cannot avoid. If there is an art of drama in its own right, not derived from the more highly developed arts and philosophies, but based upon a uniquely direct sense of life, then *Oedipus Rex* and *Hamlet* are crucial instances of it.

The chapters on Racine's *Bérénice* and Wagner's *Tristan und Isolde* are intended as companion-pieces to the chapter on *Oedipus Rex*. Both Racine and Wagner thought they understood and accepted the essential principles of Greek tragedy, and realized them anew in their own works. And their purposes were like those of Sophocles, "to mirror human nature." But they lacked the tragic theater which Sophocles found to write for, a natural growth in his community. The theaters of Racine and Wagner are, by comparison, arbitrary inventions, and the images they reflect—images of reason or passion—are artificially limited, and thus in a sense even false. But it is this drastic limitation of view which makes possible the ideal perfection of Racine's art, and also of Wagner's very different art. Both were purer artists than Sophocles, as the best modern critics have taught us to understand that idea. Their artistic principles still guide the best contemporary dramatists, and get in the way of our understanding of Sophocles' dramaturgy, more realist in the Aristotelian sense, and inspired by a less idealist conception of form. In the three chapters following I endeavor to elucidate these distinctions, and to propose the view that Racine and Wagner can only be understood with reference to Sophocles, rather than the other way round.

Hamlet, as I remarked, is on the threshold of modern times, and touches us with special intimacy. But many recent studies have shown that the Elizabethan theater had not quite broken with the Middle Ages: it was, like older forms of Medieval art, popular, traditional, and ritualistic. Partly for this reason, the tradition of the Greeks is alive in it. Shakespeare's plays echo

Plato and Aristotle in a thousand ways—in the social and moral order which they assume as natural; in their realism, and their continuity with the common sense of the community; and in their dramaturgy, which is closely akin to the dramatic forms of the Platonic dialogues. Thus I take *Hamlet* as a parallel to *Oedipus:* not an idealized derivation of Greek principles like *Bérénice* and *Tristan,* but as a later, more elaborate, and more skeptical masterpiece in the same great tradition.

"Tragedy," says Aristotle, thinking of *Oedipus Rex,* "is the imitation of an action." The definition applies by analogy to *Bérénice* and *Tristan* also, and indeed to all forms of drama, including comedy. Coleridge widens its application still further when he writes that unity of action "is not properly a rule, but in itself the great end, not only of the drama, but of the epic, lyric, even to the candle-flame of an epigram—not only of poetry, but of poesy in general, as the proper generic term inclusive of all the fine arts, as its species." But though the notion of the imitation of action says so much, it tells us on the other hand almost nothing, unless we think of particular works; for we depend upon the dramatists both to discover the infinitely various modes of human action, and to devise the cognate forms whereby they show them to us on the stage. There is only one work intended to exhaust the possibilities in Aristotle's definition: to imitate all the modes of human action in ordered and rhythmic relationship. That work, of course, is the *Divine Comedy*.

Dante was not writing for the stage; and my purpose is to study the drama which is played before an audience in a real theater. If we had a theater like Hamlet's, focusing all the available insights—historical, ethical, religious—upon "two boards and a passion," we should not be impelled to question Dante. Since we do not, we try to recover the ancient understanding of dramatic art, and the idea of a theater which it assumes. So we are led beyond the stage itself to the *Divine Comedy:* the very pattern of the imitation of action—mirroring the greatest height and depth of human experience, as Eliot says—in the most comprehensive scene-of-human-life to be found in our tradition.

Though I note that Dante is there, I make no attempt to investigate his work for itself. I wish rather to assume it, and to refer to it, from time to time, for clues to the analogies between various forms of drama proper. For this purpose the *Purgatorio* is particularly useful. The *Purgatorio*, a transition, presents the endless forms of moral change; and in this it is close to the human-centered realm of Sophocles and Shakespeare, who imitate the tragic rhythm of human life in a world which, though mysterious, is felt to be real. The literal scene of the *Purgatorio* is like the natural world of common sense, subject to the changing lights of day and night, and to the changing perspectives of our various modes of thought and feeling. In this part of the *Divine Comedy* especially it is evident that, though Dante was not writing to be acted on a stage, he appeals, like the great dramatists, to the histrionic sensibility, i.e., our direct sense of the changing life of the psyche.

The scenes of the *Inferno* are more like those which the most elegant modern drama reveals: each is complete in itself; each is formed by the idolatry of a particular mode of thought and feeling; each has its own esthetic clarity and perfection, and its own dead-end finality.

The *Paradiso*, of course, is centered in a finality beyond the human altogether; and for this reason the *Paradiso* is not very directly related to drama as we actually find it in the theaters, even the great ones. Drama flourishes best in the center of the life of its time; and no community, as a whole, is ever engaged in "the occupation of a saint." The ultimate object of faith is assumed by great drama as Dante assumes it in the *Purgatorio*, at the outer edge of the human situation; but it is never made the center of the play, as the God of Christian Revelation is the center of the *Paradiso*. It is true that the *Inferno* and the *Purgatorio* are not complete in themselves, and can only be finally grasped with reference to the *Paradiso*. No doubt the forms our lives take do in fact depend upon what we believe to be real, both moment by moment, and over longer periods. Great drama shows this; but the realm of experience it takes for its own is the contingent, fallible, changing one which is this side of final truth, and in constant touch with common sense. The *Divine Comedy* is useful for my purposes because it throws light upon *this* realm, and upon our theaters as more or less adequate means of representing man as we know him here below. Mr Eliot, in his essay on Dante, offers a very interesting discussion of I. A. Richards' notion of the "suspension of disbelief" whereby we are able to read a poet without either accepting or rejecting his theology. Mr. Eliot concludes that we may accept the *Divine Comedy* without being Christian as Dante was, or perhaps Christian at all; elsewhere he describes this masterpiece as an "organization of the sensibility." Professor Auerbach points out* that though Dante's fictive journey is in the timeless realm beyond the grave, the effect of this setting is to reveal his characters as we know them in their earthly beings, but more completely and clearly. "The beyond becomes a theater of men and of their passions," he writes; "their eternal situation in the divine order is only known to us as a show-place, whose irrevocability (Unwiderruflichkeit) further heightens the effect of their humanity, which is thus preserved in all its force."† It is the humanity of the *Divine Comedy* which reaches us directly, whatever our beliefs; and when I refer to it I am thinking of it in this way: not as theology or metaphysics, but as a type (the best available) of that art of imitating action which is realized, in various ways, in the changing theaters of our tradition.

*Mimesis, by Erich Auerbach. Dargestellte Wirklichkeit in der Abendländischen Literatur. Eine Geschichte des abendländischen Realismus als Ausdruck der Wandlungen in der Selbstanschuung des Menschen. (Reality represented in western literature. A history of western realism as an expression of the transformations in man's intuition of himself.) A. Francke Verlag, Bern, 1946. As the title indicates, Professor Auerbach's purpose is similar to mine, though he does not confine himself to any one literary form, and covers vastly more territory. I have made as much use of his book as I could, especially his elucidations of Medieval Realism.

†Page 195.

~~~~~~

The very vastness of the subject leaves a possibility that
one may have something to say worth saying.

—Eliot's essay on Dante

~~~~~~

THE selection of plays which I have made is necessarily arbitrary. It is intended to limit the scope of the inquiry, and to
suggest a certain notion of drama. My purpose is not to make a
history; and the method of sampling precludes any sort of completeness. There are many kinds of drama of great intrinsic
interest which I do not even mention. But the plays which I
have selected are themselves critical *causes célèbres*. The concept of drama, as we get it from the great plays, has interested
contemporary writers in many fields, perhaps because it seems
to offer a way of comprehending (short of actually solving) the
tragic issues of our skeptical and divided age; and when we
come to look at the plays themselves we are aware of a bewildering wealth of meanings. Critics of poetry and fiction,
even of music or sculpture, use the notion of "the dramatic" to
clarify the intention of the artist and the form of his work.
Students of history, of ideas, of social and political forms, resort
to drama both for factual evidence and for understanding. In
short, a great deal is known about the drama, and many tools of
analysis are available if one could use them. The question is, at
what point may one hope to join so thorny a discussion? I wish
to indicate the contemporary works on which I have depended,
and then to specify my own purpose in examining the plays
selected.

"The poet must be aware," Mr. Eliot writes, in *Tradition and
the Individual Talent*, "that the mind of Europe—the mind of
his own country—a mind which he learns in time to be much
more important than his own private mind—is a mind which
changes, and that this change is a development which abandons
nothing *en route*, which does not superannuate either Shakespeare, or Homer, or the rock drawing of the Magdalenian
draughtsmen." This conception of tradition, suggesting an ideal

of understanding which one may at least recognize, exercises a great and continuing influence upon the study of literature. My attempt to distinguish a few landmarks by which to grasp the changing art of drama, is a corollary of it. Moreover, any study of drama must discover a more particular debt to Eliot: he has been over this ground before; he is one of very few contemporary writers in English who are directly concerned with drama as a serious art. The view which I propose is, I think, quite unlike Eliot's; I attempt to extend Aristotle's definition to subsequent forms, and to cling to Hamlet's view of drama as an art of playing, while Mr. Eliot, coming to the drama from lyric poetry, starts rather with the Idealist conception of art as formally prior to the theater itself. But he has surveyed the terrain, raised the crucial questions, and shown by his example both the need and possibility of such a study.

Modern literary criticism, by which I mean the writers discussed by Mr. John Crowe Ransom in his *The New Criticism*, has done much to make the arts of letters understandable, especially the art of lyric verse. The close textual analyses of this criticism often point to the dramatic basis of poetry—to the "dramatic situation" in which the poet speaks or sings; or to the histrionic basis of language itself, as in Mr. Blackmur's phrase, "language as gesture." A few of these critics have been led, through the arts of language, to problems of purely dramatic form, notably Mr. William Empson. In his *Versions of Pastoral* he applied his notions of ambiguity (originally derived from the study of the language of poets) to the analysis of the double plot—the characteristic form of British drama until the middle of the eighteenth-century. In general, the new critics have taught us to read any literature with more understanding; and, since we lack a theater, we need their lore in order to read dramatic literature also. But a drama, as distinguished from a lyric, is not primarily a composition in the verbal medium; the words result, as one might put it, from the underlying structure of incident and character. As Aristotle remarks, "the poet, or 'maker' should be the maker of plots rather than of verses; since he is a poet because he imitates, and what he imitates are actions." This distinction shows where my intention diverges from that of the properly *literary* critic: I am in search of that dramatic art which, in all real plays, underlies the more highly evolved arts of language.

This idea of drama, as an art which eventuates in words, but which in its own essence is at once more primitive, more subtle, and more direct than either word or concept—the irreducible idea of the dramatic—appears in a number of contemporary writers who are students of culture rather than literary critics. Unamuno's phrase, "the tragic sense of life," expresses it. Professor Scott Buchanan, in his *Poetry and Mathematics*, remarks that drama at its best "undercuts" both scientific and theological modes of understanding the life of the psyche. Mr. Kenneth Burke has devised what he calls a "dramatistic vocabulary" for classifying the various forms of discourse, from lyric poetry at one end of the spectrum to the most abstract prose at the other. He regards all the verbal arts as types of symbolic action; and so he elaborates the Aristotelian notion of the imitation of action, applying it to forms which are not ostensibly dramatic at all. The reader will soon see how much this study owes to Mr. Burke's analyses, especially when it is concerned with the relation between the underlying dramatic form of a play, and the words and concepts in which it is realized in detail. But though these writers suggest a fundamental idea of drama, they seldom study particular plays directly. They all, I think, assume that notion of drama which we owe to the Cambridge School of Classical Anthropologists. Cornford, Harrison, Murray, and others of this school have given us a new understanding of Greek tragedy by demonstrating its roots in myth and ritual, its implication in the whole culture of its time. They suggest that drama is prior to the arts, the sciences of man, and the philosophies, of modern civilization; and that the tragic form offers a clue to the relationships of cultural forms which we now know as merely divergent, divisive, and mutually exclusive. It is this very general conception of drama, as a mode of understanding and a reflection of culture, which is assumed in so much contemporary thought and criticism.

The conception of this book depends upon the converging lines of thought and research which reveal the suggestiveness and the centrality of drama at its best. But the wealth of the materials raises the problem of criticism in its most acute form; the critic who wishes to study particular works of art of various periods needs the work of scholars and historians, but he cannot be responsible for it, nor presume to judge it as scholarship or history. He must be allowed to use it for his own limited purpose—the elucidation of the particular work—and to judge it solely for its value in helping us to grasp the artist's vision and the form in which it is presented. In short, the critics must assume that works of art, even those of the remote past and of foreign cultures, are in some sense directly understandable; and that what we learn about them may modify or deepen, but can never replace, our immediate acquaintance with them.

Because drama is written to be played, it both offers and requires a peculiarly immediate understanding. Olivier's performance as Oedipus—the hit of the London season in 1944 and after that a success in New York also—may serve to illustrate this point. Mr. Olivier's audiences cannot have depended upon much knowledge of the Festival of Dionysos, for which the play was first written, or of the meanings of the tragic form as modern writers expound it. I do not suppose that the Irish speech-rhythms of Yeats' translation helped them very much either. They must have been moved by the perennial vitality of the great role itself, which Olivier discovered by way of the plot and the words, and then communicated by his own stage life. If the chorus, the other characters, and the rhythms of the play as a whole had been equally well understood, we might have enjoyed a direct perception of Sophocles' *play:* i.e., the performable rhythm of life and action which may still touch us though originally realized in the customs, beliefs, and ritual forms of antiquity. Sophocles, like Hamlet, thought of his art as basically playing—"imitation of action *in the form of action,*" as Aristotle puts it. Writing for real performers in a real theater, he appeals to the histrionic sensibility first, and then further elaborates with words and concepts. And the histrionic sensibility, like the ear for music, is a natural virtue. By means of it—by a direct, mimetic response—we get a play as such; and if we understand a play we must understand it as performable.

Unfortunately the histrionic sensibility is seldom recognized, as the ear for music is. Ear-training is required wherever music is studied, but the actor's sensibility is supposed to be incorrigible. Perhaps that is because we are all actors so much of the time—imitating ourselves or others; feeling our way histrionically through the tangle of personal relationships; trying to judge people by our direct sense of their motivations, while discounting the rationalizations they offer. We recognize the histrionic talent of diagnosticians, children, and practical politicians; but we think of it as a completely unintelligible gift. Nevertheless the histrionic sensibility can be trained. The great continental reportory theaters of the last generation—the Vieux Colombier, Reinhardt's theaters, the Moscow Art Theater—required of their actors a discipline of the feelings and the imagination as conscious and severe as the physical disciplines of ballet. The purpose of this discipline was to free the actor's emotions and cultivate his perceptions, so that he could make-believe the situations invented by the playwrights and then respond mimetically with his whole being. An actor or director trained in this way reads a play as a composition to be performed, just as a trained musician reads a score as a composition of sounds and rhythms. It is this kind of understanding of drama which one must seek; and insofar as one reaches it, one has direct access to the plays of other cultures.

The process of becoming acquainted with a play is like that of becoming acquainted with a person. It is an empirical and inductive process; it starts with the observable facts; but it instinctively aims at a grasp of the very life of the machine which is both deeper and, oddly enough, more immediate than the surface appearances offer. We seek to grasp the quality of a man's life, by an imaginative effort, *through* his appearances, his words, and his deeds:

senza operar non è sentita, / ne si dimostra ma che per effetto, / come per verdi fronde in pianta vita,

it is not perceived save in operation, nor manifested except by its effects, as life [is manifested] in a plant by the green leaves, as Virgil explains to Dante (*Purgatorio*, Canto xviii). We grasp the stagelife of a play through the plot, characters, and words which manifest it; and if we are successful we can then act it, on the stage, or privately and silently. By such make-believe we come to understand the theater which the genius of the playwright has used to fix his vision. Beyond that we more vaguely discern the further mysteries: the picture of the human situation which the whole culture embodies and which the stage itself represents. At this point the studies of historians, theologians, and anthropologists are useful, for they may help to free us from some of our provincial habits of mind; and they provide a way of correcting and amplifying direct impressions. But the present study is focused upon the life and form of the play itself—or rather of a few exemplary plays, landmarks in the changing theaters of the tradition.

CHAPTER I

OEDIPUS REX: THE TRAGIC RHYTHM
OF ACTION

... quel secondo regno
dove l'umano spirito si purga.
—*Purgatorio,* CANTO I

I SUPPOSE there can be little doubt that *Oedipus Rex* is a crucial instance of drama, if not *the* play which best exemplifies this art in its essential nature and its completeness. It owes its position partly to the fact that Aristotle founded his definitions upon it. But since the time of Aristotle it has been imitated, rewritten, and discussed by many different generations, not only of dramatists, but also of moralists, psychologists, historians, and other students of human nature and destiny.

Though the play is thus generally recognized as an archetype, there has been little agreement about its meaning or its form. It seems to beget, in every period, a different interpretation and a different dramaturgy. From the seventeenth century until the end of the eighteenth, a Neoclassic and rationalistic interpretation of *Oedipus,* of Greek tragedy, and of Aristotle, was generally accepted; and upon this interpretation was based the dramaturgy of Corneille and Racine. Nietzsche, under the inspiration of Wagner's *Tristan und Isolde,* developed a totally different view of it, and thence a different theory of drama. These two views of Greek tragedy, Racine's and Nietzsche's, still provide indispensable perspectives upon *Oedipus.* They show a great deal about modern principles of dramatic composition; and they show, when compared, how central and how essential Sophocles' drama is. In the two essays following, the attempt is made to develop the analogies, the similarities and differences, between these three conceptions of drama.

In our day a conception of *Oedipus* seems to be developing which is neither that of Racine nor that of Nietzsche. This view is based upon the studies which the Cambridge School, Fraser, Cornford, Harrison, Murray, made of the ritual origins of Greek tragedy. It also owes a great deal to the current interest in myth as a way of ordering human experience. *Oedipus*, we now see, is both myth and ritual. It assumes and employs these two ancient ways of understanding and representing human experience, which are prior to the arts and sciences and philosophies of modern times. To understand it (it now appears) we must endeavor to recapture the habit of significant make-believe, of the direct perception of action, which underlies Sophocles' theater.

If *Oedipus* is to be understood in this way, then we shall have to revise our ideas of Sophocles' dramaturgy. The notion of Aristotle's theory of drama, and hence of Greek dramaturgy, which still prevails (in spite of such studies as Butcher's of the *Poetics*) is largely colored by Neoclassic taste and rationalistic habits of mind. If we are to take it that Sophocles was imitating action before theory, instead of after it, like Racine, then both the elements and the form of his composition appear in a new light.

In the present essay the attempt is made to draw the deductions, for Sophocles' theater and dramaturgy, which the present view of *Oedipus* implies. We shall find that the various traditional views of this play are not so much wrong as partial.

Oedipus, Myth and Play

When Sophocles came to write his play he had the myth of Oedipus to start with. Laius and Jocasta, King and Queen of Thebes, are told by the oracle that their son will grow up to kill his father and marry his mother. The infant, his feet pierced, is left on Mount Kitharon to die. But a shepherd finds him and takes care of him; at last gives him to another shepherd, who takes him to Corinth, and there the King and Queen bring him up as their own son. But Oedipus—"Clubfoot"— is plagued in his turn by the oracle; he hears that he is fated to kill his father and marry his mother; and to escape that fate he leaves Corinth never to return. On his journey he meets an old man with his servants; gets into a dispute with him, and kills him and all his followers. He comes to Thebes at the time when the Sphinx is preying upon that City; solves the riddle which the Sphinx propounds, and saves the City. He marries the widowed Queen, Jocasta; has several children by her; rules prosperously for many years. But, when Thebes is suffering under a plague and a drought, the oracle reports that the gods are angry because Laius' slayer is unpunished. Oedipus, as King, undertakes to find him; discovers that he is himself the culprit and that Jocasta is his own mother. He blinds himself and goes into exile. From this time forth he becomes a sort of sacred relic, like the bones of a saint; perilous, but "good medicine" for the community that possesses him. He dies, at last, at Athens, in a grove sacred to the Eumenides, female spirits of fertility and night.

It is obvious, even from this sketch, that the myth, which covers several generations, has as much narrative material as *Gone with the Wind*. We do not know what versions of the story Sophocles used. It is the way of myths that they generate whole progenies of elaborations and varying versions. They are so suggestive, seem to say so much, yet so mysteriously, that the mind cannot rest content with any single form, but must add, or interpret, or simplify—reduce to terms which the reason can accept. Mr. William Troy suggests that "what is possibly most in order at the moment is a thoroughgoing refurbishment of the medieval four-fold method of interpretation, which was first developed, it will be recalled, for just such a purpose—to make at least partially available to the reason that complex of human problems which are embedded, deep and imponderable, in the Myth."[*] It appears that Sophocles, in his play, succeeded in preserving the suggestive mystery of the Oedipus myth, while presenting it in a wonderfully unified dramatic form; and this drama has all the dimensions which the fourfold method was intended to explore.

Everyone knows that when Sophocles planned the plot of the play itself, he started almost at the end of the story, when the plague descends upon the City of Thebes which Oedipus and

[*] "Myth, Method and the Future," by William Troy. *Chimera*, spring, 1946.

Jocasta had been ruling with great success for a number of years. The action of the play takes less than a day, and consists of Oedipus' quest for Laius' slayer—his consulting the Oracle of Apollo, his examination of the Prophet, Tiresias, and of a series of witnesses, ending with the old Shepherd who gave him to the King and Queen of Corinth. The play ends when Oedipus is unmistakably revealed as himself the culprit.

At this literal level, the play is intelligible as a murder mystery. Oedipus takes the role of District Attorney; and when he at last convicts himself, we have a twist, a *coup de théâtre*, of unparalleled excitement. But no one who sees or reads the play can rest content with its literal coherence. Questions as to its meaning arise at once: Is Oedipus really guilty, or simply a victim of the gods, of his famous complex, of fate, of original sin? How much did he know, all along? How much did Jocasta know? The first, and most deeply instinctive effort of the mind, when confronted with this play, is to endeavor to reduce its meanings to some set of rational categories.

The critics of the Age of Reason tried to understand it as a fable of the enlightened moral will, in accordance with the philosophy of that time. Voltaire's version of the play, following Corneille, and his comments upon it, may be taken as typical. He sees it as essentially a struggle between a strong and righteous Oedipus, and the malicious and very human gods, aided and abetted by the corrupt priest Tiresias; he makes it an antireligious tract, with an unmistakable moral to satisfy the needs of the discursive intellect. In order to make Oedipus "sympathetic" to his audience, he elides, as much as possible, the incest motif; and he adds an irrelevant love story. He was aware that his version and interpretation were not those of Sophocles but, with the complacent provinciality of his period, he attributes the difference to the darkness of the age in which *Sophocles* lived.

Other attempts to rationalize *Oedipus Rex* are subtler than Voltaire's, and take us further toward an understanding of the play. Freud's reduction of the play to the concepts of his psychology reveals a great deal, opens up perspectives which we are still exploring. If one reads *Oedipus* in the light of Fustel de Coulanges' *The Ancient City*, one may see it as the expression of the ancient patriarchal religion of the Greeks. And other interpretations of the play, theological, philosophical, historical, are available, none of them wrong, but all partial, all reductions of Sophocles' masterpiece to an alien set of categories. For the peculiar virtue of Sophocles' presentation of the myth is that it preserves the ultimate mystery by focusing upon the tragic human at a level beneath, or prior to any rationalization whatever. The plot is so arranged that we see the action, as it were, illumined from many sides at once.

By starting the play at the end of the story, and showing on-stage only the last crucial episode in Oedipus' life, the past and present action of the protagonist are revealed together; and, in each other's light, are at last felt as one. Oedipus' quest for the slayer of Laius becomes a quest for the hidden reality of his own past; and as that slowly comes into focus, like repressed material under psychoanalysis—with sensory and emotional immediacy, yet in the light of acceptance and understanding—his immediate quest also reaches its end: he comes to see himself (the Savior of the City) and the guilty one, the plague of Thebes, at once and at one.

This presentation of the myth of Oedipus constitutes, in one sense, an "interpretation" of it. What Sophocles saw as the essence of Oedipus' nature and destiny, is not what Seneca or Dryden or Cocteau saw; and one may grant that even Sophocles did not exhaust the possibilities in the materials of the myth. But Sophocles' version of the myth does not constitute a "reduction" in the same sense as the rest.

I have said that the action which Sophocles shows is a quest, the quest for Laius' slayer; and that as Oedipus' past is unrolled before us his whole life is seen as a kind of quest for his true nature and destiny. But since the object of this quest is not clear until the end, the seeking action takes many forms, as its object appears in different lights. The object, indeed, the final perception, the "truth," looks so different at the end from what it did at the beginning that Oedipus' action itself may seem not a quest, but its opposite, a flight. Thus it would be hard to say, simply, that Oedipus either succeeds or fails. He succeeds; but his success is his undoing. He fails to find what, in one way, he sought; yet from another point of view his search is brilliantly successful. The same ambiguities surround his effort to discover who and what he is. He seems to find that he is nothing; yet thereby finds himself. And what of his relation to the gods? His quest may be regarded as a heroic attempt to escape their decrees, or as an attempt, based upon some deep natural faith, to discover what their wishes are, and what true obedience would be. In one sense Oedipus suffers forces he can neither control nor understand, the puppet of fate; yet at the same time he wills and intelligently intends his every move.

The meaning, or spiritual content of the play, is not to be sought by trying to resolve such ambiguities as these. The spiritual content of the play is the tragic action which Sophocles directly presents; and this action is in its essence *zweideutig:* triumph and destruction, darkness and enlightenment, mourning and rejoicing, at any moment we care to consider it. But this action has also a shape: a beginning, middle, and end, in time. It starts with the reasoned purpose of finding Laius' slayer. But this aim meets unforeseen difficulties, evidences which do not fit, and therefore shake the purpose as it was first understood; and so the characters suffer the piteous and terrible sense of the mystery of the human situation. From this suffering or passion, with its shifting visions, a new perception of the situation emerges; and on that basis the purpose of the action is redefined, and a new movement starts. This movement, or *tragic rhythm of action*, constitutes the shape of the play as a whole; it is also the shape of each episode, each discussion between principals with the chorus following. Mr. Kenneth Burke has studied the tragic rhythm in his *Philosophy of Literary Form*, and also in *A Grammar of Motives*, where he gives the three moments traditional designations which are very suggestive: *Poiema, Pathema, Mathema*. They may also be called, for convenience, Purpose, Passion (or Suffering) and Perception. It is this tragic rhythm of action which is the substance or spiritual content of the play, and the clue to its extraordinarily comprehensive form.

In order to illustrate these points in more detail, it is convenient to examine the scene between Oedipus and Tiresias with the chorus following it. This episode, being early in the play (the

first big agon), presents, as it were, a preview of the whole
action and constitutes a clear and complete example of action in
the tragic rhythm.

Hero and Scapegoat: The Agon between Oedipus and Tiresias

The scene between Oedipus and Tiresias comes after the
opening sections of the play. We have seen the citizens of
Thebes beseeching their King to find some way to lift the
plague which is on the City. We have had Oedipus' entrance
(majestic, but for his tell-tale limp) to reassure them, and we
have heard the report which Creon brings from the Delphic
Oracle: that the cause of the plague is the unpunished murder of
Laius, the former king. Oedipus offers rewards to anyone who
will reveal the culprit, and he threatens with dire punishment
anyone who conceals or protects him. In the meantime, he de-
cides, with the enthusiastic assent of the chorus, to summon
Tiresias as the first witness.

Tiresias is that suffering seer whom Sophocles uses in *Antigone* also to reveal a truth which other mortals find it hard and
uncomfortable to see. He is physically blind, but Oedipus and
chorus alike assume that if anyone can see who the culprit is, it
is Tiresias, with his uncanny inner vision of the future. As
Tiresias enters, led by a boy, the chorus greets him in these
words: *

> CHORUS. But the man to convict him is here. Look: they are
> bringing the one human being in whom the truth is native,
> the godlike seer.

Oedipus is, at this point in the play, at the opposite pole of
experience from Tiresias: he is hero, monarch, helmsman of the
state; the solver of the Sphinx's riddle, the triumphant being. He
explains his purpose in the following proud clear terms:

> OEDIPUS. O Tiresias, you know all things: what may be told,
> and the unspeakable: things of earth and things of heaven.

*I am responsible for the English of this scene. The reader is referred to
Oedipus Rex, translated by Dudley Fitts and Robert Fitzgerald (New York:
Harcourt, Brace and Co., 1949), a very handsome version of the whole play.

You understand the City (though you do not see it) in its present mortal illness—from which to save us and protect us, we find, Lord, none but you. For you must know, in case you haven't heard it from the messengers, that Apollo, when we asked him, told us there was one way only with this plague: to discover Laius' slayers, and put them to death or send them into exile. Therefore you must not jealously withhold your omens, whether of birds or other visionary ·way, but save yourself and the City—save me, save all of us—from the defilement of the dead. In your hand we are. There is no handsomer work for a man, than to bring, with what he has, what help he can.

This speech is the prologue of the scene, and the basis of the agon or struggle which follows. This struggle in effect analyzes Oedipus' purpose; places it in a wider context, reveals it as faulty and dubious. At the end of the scene Oedipus loses his original purpose altogether, and suffers a wave of rage and fear, which will have to be rationalized in its turn before he can "pull himself together" and act again with a clear purpose.

In the first part of the struggle, Oedipus takes the initiative, while Tiresias, on the defensive, tries to avoid replying:

TIRESIAS. Oh, oh. How terrible to know, when nothing can come of knowing! Indeed, I had lost the vision of these things, or I should never have come.

OEDIPUS. What things? . . . In what discouragement have you come to us here!

TIR. Let me go home. I shall endure this most easily, and so will you, if you do as I say.

OED. But what you ask is not right. To refuse your word is disloyalty to the City that has fed you.

TIR. But I see that your demands are exorbitant, and lest I too suffer such a—

OED. For the sake of the gods, if you know, don't turn away! Speak to us, we are your suppliants here.

TIR. None of you understands. But I—I never will tell my misery. Or yours.

OED. What are you saying? You know, but tell us nothing?

You intend treachery to us, and death to the City?

TIR. I intend to grieve neither myself nor you. Why then do you try to know? You will never learn from me.

OED. Ah, evil old man! You would anger a stone! You will say *nothing?* Stand futile, speechless before us?

TIR. You curse my temper, but you don't see the one that dwells in you; no, you must blame me.

OED. And who would *not* lose his temper, if he heard you utter your scorn of the City?

TIR. It will come. Silent though I be.

OED. Since it will come, it is your duty to inform me.

TIR. I shall say no more. Now, if you like, rage to your bitter heart's content.

OED. Very well: in my "rage" I shall hold back nothing which I now begin to see. I think you planned that deed, even performed it, though not with your own hands. If you could see, I should say that the work was yours alone.

In the last speech quoted, Oedipus changes his tack, specifying his purpose differently; he accuses Tiresias, and that makes Tiresias attack. In the next part of the fight the opponents trade blow for blow:

TIR. You would? I charge you, abide by the decree you uttered: from this day forth, speak neither to these present, nor to me, unclean as you are, polluter of the earth!

OED. You have the impudence to speak out words like these! And now how do you expect to escape?

TIR. I have escaped. The truth strengthens and sustains me.

OED. Who taught you the truth? Not your prophet's art.

TIR. You did; you force me against my will to speak.

OED. Speak what? Speak again, that I may understand better.

TIR. *Didn't* you understand? Or are you goading me?

OED. I can't say I really grasp it: speak again.

TIR. I say you are the murderer of the man whose murderer you seek.

OED. You won't be glad to have uttered that curse twice.

TIR. Must I say more, so you may rage the more?

OED. As much as you like—all is senseless.

TIR. I say you do not know your own wretchedness, nor see in what shame you live with those you love.

OED. Do you think you can say that forever with impunity?

TIR. If the truth has power.

OED. It has, with all but you: helpless is truth with you: for you are blind, in eye, in ear, in mind.

TIR. You are the impotent one: you utter slanders which every man here will apply to you.

OED. You have your being only in the night; you couldn't hurt me or any man who sees the sun.

TIR. No. Your doom is not to fall by me. Apollo suffices for that, he will bring it about.

OED. Are these inventions yours, or Creon's?

TIR. Your wretchedness is not Creon's, it is yours.

OED. O wealth, and power, and skill—which skill, in emulous life, brings low—what envy eyes you! if for this kingly power which the City gave into my hands, unsought—if for *this* the faithful Creon, my friend from the first, has stalked me in secret, yearning to supplant me! if he has bribed this juggling wizard, this deceitful beggar, who discerns his profit only, blind in his own art!

Tell me now, tell me where you have proved a true diviner? Why, when the song-singing sphinx was near, did you not speak deliverance to the people? Her riddles were not for any comer to solve, but for the mantic art, and you were apparently instructed neither by birds nor by any sign from the gods. Yet when I came, I, Oedipus, all innocent, I stopped her song. No birds taught me, by my own wit I found the answer. And it is I whom you wish to banish, thinking that you will then stand close to Creon's throne.

You and your ally will weep, I think, for this attempt; and in fact, if you didn't seem to be an old man, you would already have learned, in pain, of your presumption.

In this part the beliefs, the visions, and hence the purposes of the antagonists are directly contrasted. Because both identify themselves so completely with their visions and purposes, the fight descends from the level of dialectic to a level below the rational altogether: it becomes cruelly *ad hominem*. We are made to see the absurd incommensurability of the very beings of Oedipus and Tiresias; they shrink from one another as from the uncanny. At the end of the round, it is Oedipus who has received the deeper wound; and his great speech, "O wealth and power," is a far more lyric utterance than the ordered exposition with which he began.

The end of this part of the fight is marked by the intervention of the chorus, which endeavors to recall the antagonists to the most general version of purpose which they supposedly share: the discovery of the truth and the service of the gods:

> CHORUS. To us it appears that this man's words were uttered in anger, and yours too, Oedipus. No need for that: consider how best to discharge the mandate of the god.

The last part of the struggle shows Tiresias presenting his whole vision, and Oedipus, on the defensive, shaken to the depths:

> TIR. Although you rule, we have equally the right to reply; in that I too have power. Indeed, I live to serve, not you, but Apollo; and I shall not be enrolled under Creon, either. Therefore I say, since you have insulted even my blindness, that though you have eyesight, you do not see what misery you are in, nor where you are living, nor with whom. Do you know whence you came? No, nor that you are the enemy of your own family, the living and the dead. The double prayer of mother and father shall from this land hound you in horror—who now see clearly, but then in darkness.
>
> Where then will your cry be bounded? What part of Kitharon not echo it quickly back, when you shall come to understand that marriage, to which you sailed on so fair a wind, homelessly home? And many other evils which you do not see will bring you to yourself at last, your children's equal.
>
> Scorn Creon, therefore, and my words: you will be struck down more terribly than any mortal.

Oed. Can I really hear such things from him? Are you not gone? To death? To punishment? Not fled from this house?

Tir. I should never have come if you hadn't called me.

Oed. I didn't know how mad you would sound, or it would have been a long time before I asked you here to my house.

Tir. This is what I am; foolish, as it seems to you; but wise, to the parents who gave you birth.

Oed. To whom? Wait: *who* gave me birth?

Tir. This day shall give you birth, and death.

Oed. In what dark riddles you always speak.

Tir. Aren't you the best diviner of riddles?

Oed. Very well: mock that gift, which, you will find, is mine.

Tir. That very gift was your undoing.

Oed. But if I saved the City, what does it matter?

Tir. So be it. I am going. Come, boy, lead me.

Oed. Take him away. Your presence impedes and trips me; once you are gone, you can do no harm.

Tir. I shall go when I have done my errand without fear of your frowns, for they can't hurt me. I tell you, then, that the man whom you have long been seeking, with threats and proclamations, Laius' slayer, is here. He is thought to be an alien, but will appear a native Theban, and this circumstance will not please him. Blind, who once could see; destitute, who once was rich, leaning on a staff, he will make his way through a strange land. He will be revealed as brother and father of his own children; of the woman who bore him, both son and husband; sharer of his father's bed; his father's killer.

Go in and ponder this. If you find it wrong, say then I do not understand the prophetic vision.

Oedipus rushes off-stage, his clear purpose gone, his being shaken with fear and anger. Tiresias departs, led by his boy. The chorus is left to move and chant, suffering the mixed and ambivalent feelings, the suggestive but mysterious images, which the passion in which the agon eventuated produces in them:

CHORUS

Strophe I. Who is it that the god's voice from the Rock of
　　Delphi says
　　Accomplished the unspeakable with murderous hands?
　　Time now that windswift
　　Stronger than horses
　　His feet take flight.
　　In panoply of fire and lightning
　　Now springs upon him the son of Zeus
　　Whom the dread follow,
　　The Fates unappeasable.

Antistrophe I. New word, like light, from snowy Parnassus:
　　Over all the earth trail the unseen one.
　　For in rough wood,
　　In cave or rocks,
　　Like bull bereft—stampeded, futile
　　He goes, seeking with futile foot to
　　Flee the ultimate
　　Doom, which ever
　　Lives and flies over him.

Strophe II. In awe now, and soul's disorder, I neither accept
　　The augur's wisdom, nor deny: I know not what to say.
　　I hover in hope, see neither present nor future.
　　Between the House of Laius
　　And Oedipus, I do not hear, have never heard, of any feud:
　　I cannot confirm the public charge against him, to help
　　Avenge the dark murder.

Antistrophe II. Zeus and Apollo are wise, and all that is mortal
　　They know: but whether that human seer knows more
　　　　than I
　　There is no way of telling surely, though in wisdom
　　A man may excel.
　　Ah, never could I, till I see that word confirmed, consent
　　　　to blame him!
　　Before all eyes the wingèd songstress, once, assailed him;
　　Wise showed he in that test, and to the City, tender; in my
　　　　heart
　　I will call him evil never.

The chorus is considered in more detail below. At this point I merely wish to point out that Oedipus and Tiresias show, in their agon, the "purpose" part of the tragic rhythm; that this turns to "passion," and that the chorus presents the passion and also the new perception which follows. This new perception is that of Oedipus as the possible culprit. But his outlines are vague; perhaps the vision itself is illusory, a bad dream. The chorus has not yet reached the end of its quest; that will come only when Oedipus, in the flesh before them, is unmistakably seen as the guilty one. We have reached merely a provisional resting-place, the end of the first figure in which the tragic rhythm is presented. But this figure is a reduced version of the shape of the play as a whole, and the fleeting and unwelcome image of Oedipus as guilty corresponds to the final perception or epiphany, the full-stop, with which the play ends.

Oedipus: Ritual and Play

The Cambridge School of Classical Anthropologists has shown in great detail that the form of Greek tragedy follows the form of a very ancient ritual, that of the *Enniautos-Daimon*, or seasonal god.* This was one of the most influential discoveries of the last few generations, and it gives us new insights into *Oedipus* which I think are not yet completely explored. The clue to Sophocles' dramatizing of the myth of Oedipus is to be found in this ancient ritual, which had a similar form and meaning—that is, it also moved in the "tragic rhythm."

Experts in classical anthropology, like experts in other fields, dispute innumerable questions of fact and of interpretation which the layman can only pass over in respectful silence. One of the thornier questions seems to be whether myth or ritual came first. Is the ancient ceremony merely an enactment of the Ur-Myth of the year-god—Attis, or Adonis, or Osiris, or the "Fisher-King"—in any case that Hero-King-Father-High-Priest who fights with his rival, is slain and dismembered, then rises anew with the spring season? Or did the innumerable myths of

*See especially Jane Ellen Harrison's *Ancient Art and Ritual,* and her *Themis* which contains an "Excursus on the ritual forms preserved in Greek Tragedy" by Professor Gilbert Murray.

this kind arise to "explain" a ritual which was perhaps mimed or danced or sung to celebrate the annual change of season?

For the purpose of understanding the form and meaning of *Oedipus*, it is not necessary to worry about the answer to this question of historic fact. The figure of Oedipus himself fulfills all the requirements of the scapegoat, the dismembered king or god-figure. The situation in which Thebes is presented at the beginning of the play—in peril of its life; its crops, its herds, its women mysteriously infertile, signs of a mortal disease of the City, and the disfavor of the gods—is like the withering which winter brings, and calls, in the same way, for struggle, dismemberment, death, and renewal. And this tragic sequence is the substance of the play. It is enough to know that myth and ritual are close together in their genesis, two direct imitations of the perennial experience of the race.

But when one considers *Oedipus* as a ritual one understands it in ways which one cannot by thinking of it merely as a dramatization of a story, even that story. Harrison has shown that the Festival of Dionysos, based ultimately upon the yearly vegetation ceremonies, included *rites de passage*, like that celebrating the assumption of adulthood—celebrations of the mystery of individual growth and development. At the same time, it was a prayer for the welfare of the whole City; and this welfare was understood not only as material prosperity, but also as the natural order of the family, the ancestors, the present members, and the generations still to come, and, by the same token, obedience to the gods who were jealous, each in his own province, of this natural and divinely sanctioned order and proportion.

We must suppose that Sophocles' audience (the whole population of the City) came early, prepared to spend the day in the bleachers. At their feet was the semicircular dancing-ground for the chorus, and the thrones for the priests, and the altar. Behind that was the raised platform for the principal actors, backed by the all-purpose, emblematic façade, which would presently be taken to represent Oedipus' palace in Thebes. The actors were not professionals in our sense, but citizens selected for a religious office, and Sophocles himself had trained them and the chorus.

This crowd must have had as much appetite for thrills and diversion as the crowds who assemble in our day for football games and musical comedies, and Sophocles certainly holds the attention with an exciting show. At the same time his audience must have been alert for the fine points of poetry and dramaturgy, for *Oedipus* is being offered in competition with other plays on the same bill. But the element which distinguishes this theater, giving it its unique directness and depth, is the *ritual expectancy* which Sophocles assumed in his audience. The nearest thing we have to this ritual sense of theater is, I suppose, to be found at an Easter performance of the *Mattias Passion*. We also can observe something similar in the dances and ritual mummery of the Pueblo Indians. Sophocles' audience must have been prepared, like the Indians standing around their plaza, to consider the playing, the make-believe it was about to see—the choral invocations, with dancing and chanting; the reasoned discourses and the terrible combats of the protagonists; the mourning, the rejoicing, and the contemplation of the final stage-picture or epiphany—as imitating and celebrating the mystery of human nature and destiny. And this mystery was at once that of individual growth and development, and that of the precarious life of the human City.

I have indicated how Sophocles presents the life of the mythic Oedipus in the tragic rhythm, the mysterious quest of life. Oedipus is shown seeking his own true being; but at the same time and by the same token, the welfare of the City. When one considers the ritual form of the whole play, it becomes evident that it presents the tragic but perennial, even normal, quest of the whole City for its well-being. In this larger action, Oedipus is only the protagonist, the first and most important champion. This tragic quest is realized by all the characters in their various ways; but in the development of the action as a whole it is the chorus alone that plays a part as important as that of Oedipus; its counterpart, in fact. The chorus holds the balance between Oedipus and his antagonists, marks the progress of their struggles, and restates the main theme, and its new variation, after each dialogue or agon. The ancient ritual was probably performed by a chorus alone without individual developments and variations, and the chorus, in *Oedipus*, is still the element that throws most light on the ritual form of the play as a whole.

The chorus consists of twelve or fifteen "Elders of Thebes." This group is not intended to represent literally all of the citizens either of Thebes or of Athens. The play opens with a large delegation of Theban citizens before Oedipus' palace, and the chorus proper does not enter until after the prologue. Nor does the chorus speak directly for the Athenian audience; we are asked throughout to make-believe that the theater is the agora at Thebes; and at the same time Sophocles' audience is witnessing a ritual. It would, I think, be more accurate to say that the chorus represents the point of view and the faith of Thebes as a whole, and, by analogy, of the Athenian audience. Their errand before Oedipus' palace is like that of Sophocles' audience in the theater: they are watching a sacred combat, in the issue of which they have an all-important and official stake. Thus they represent the audience and the citizens in a particular way—not as a mob formed in response to some momentary feeling, but rather as an organ of a highly self-conscious community: something closer to the "conscience of the race" than to the overheated affectivity of a mob.

According to Aristotle, a Sophoclean chorus is a character that takes an important role in the action of the play, instead of merely making incidental music between the scenes, as in the plays of Euripides. The chorus may be described as a group personality, like an old Parliament. It has its own traditions, habits of thought and feeling, and mode of being. It exists, in a sense, as a living entity, but not with the sharp actuality of an individual. It perceives; but its perception is at once wider and vaguer than that of a single man. It shares, in its way, the seeking action of the play as a whole; but it cannot act in all the modes; it depends upon the chief agonists to invent and try out the detail of policy, just as a rather helpless but critical Parliament depends upon the Prime Minister to act but, in its less specific form of life, survives his destruction.

When the chorus enters after the prologue, with its questions, its invocation of the various gods, and its focus upon the hidden and jeopardized welfare of the City—Athens or Thebes—the list of essential *dramatis personae*, as well as the elements needed to celebrate the ritual, is complete, and the main action can begin. It is the function of the chorus to mark the stages of this action, and to perform the suffering and perceiving part of the tragic rhythm. The protagonist and his antagonists develop the "purpose" with which the tragic sequence begins; the chorus, with its less than individual being, broods over the agons, marks their stages with a word (like that of the chorus leader in the middle of the Tiresias scene), and (expressing its emotions and visions in song and dance) suffers the results, and the new perception at the end of the fight.

The choral odes are lyrics but they are not to be understood as poetry, the art of words, only, for they are intended also to be danced and sung. And though each chorus has its own shape, like that of a discrete lyric—its beginning, middle, and end—it represents also one passion or pathos in the changing action of the whole. This passion, like the other moments in the tragic rhythm, is felt at so general or, rather, so deep a level that it seems to contain both the mob ferocity that Nietzsche felt in it and, at the other extreme, the patience of prayer. It is informed by faith in the unseen order of nature and the gods, and moves through a sequence of modes of suffering. This may be illustrated from the chorus I have quoted at the end of the Tiresias scene.

It begins (close to the savage emotion of the end of the fight) with images suggesting that cruel "Bacchic frenzy" which is supposed to be the common root of tragedy and of the "old" comedy: "In panoply of fire and lightning / The son of Zeus now springs upon him." In the first antistrophe these images come together more clearly as we relish the chase; and the fleeing culprit, as we imagine him, begins to resemble Oedipus, who is lame, and always associated with the rough wilderness of Kitharon. But in the second strophe, as though appalled by its ambivalent feelings and the imagined possibilities, the chorus sinks back into a more dark and patient posture of suffering, "in awe," "hovering in hope." In the second antistrophe this is developed into something like the orthodox Christian attitude of prayer, based on faith, and assuming the possibility of a hitherto unimaginable truth and answer: "Zeus and Apollo are wise," etc. The whole chorus then ends with a new vision of Oedipus, of the culprit, and of the direction in which the welfare of the City is to be sought. This vision is still colored by the chorus's human love of Oedipus as Hero, for the chorus has still its own purgation to complete, cannot as yet accept completely either the suffering in store for it, or Oedipus as scapegoat. But it marks the end of the first complete "purpose-passion-perception" unit, and lays the basis for the new purpose which will begin the next unit.

It is also to be noted that the chorus changes the scene which we, as audience, are to imagine. During the agon between Oedipus and Tiresias, our attention is fixed upon their clash, and the scene is literal, close, and immediate: before Oedipus' palace. When the fighters depart and the choral music starts, the focus suddenly widens, as though we had been removed to a distance. We become aware of the interested City around the bright arena; and beyond that, still more dimly, of Nature, sacred to the hidden gods. Mr. Burke has expounded the fertile notion that human action may be understood in terms of the scene in which it occurs, and vice versa: the scene is defined by the mode of action. The chorus's action is not limited by the sharp, rationalized purposes of the protagonist; its mode of action, more patient, less sharply realized, is cognate with a wider, if less accurate, awareness of the scene of human life. But the chorus's action, as I have remarked, is not that of passion itself (Nietzsche's cosmic void of night) but suffering informed by the faith of the tribe in a human and a divinely sanctioned natural order: "If such deeds as these are honored," the chorus asks after Jocasta's impiety, "why should I dance and sing?" (lines 894, 895). Thus it is one of the most important functions of the chorus to reveal, in its widest and most mysterious extent, the theater of human life which the play, and indeed the whole Festival of Dionysos, assumed. Even when the chorus does not speak, but only watches, it maintains this theme and this perspective—ready to take the whole stage when the fighters depart.

If one thinks of the movement of the play, it appears that the tragic rhythm analyzes human action temporally into successive modes, as a crystal analyzes a white beam of light spatially into the colored bands of the spectrum. The chorus, always present, represents one of these modes, and at the recurrent moments when reasoned purpose is gone, it takes the stage with its faith-informed passion, moving through an ordered succession of modes of suffering, to a new perception of the immediate situation.

Sophocles and Euripides, the Rationalist

Oedipus Rex is a changing image of human life and action which could have been formed only in the mirror of the tragic theater of the Festival of Dionysos. The perspectives of the myth, of the rituals, and of the traditional *hodos*, the way of life of the City—"habits of thought and feeling" which consti-tute the traditional wisdom of the race—were all required to make this play possible. That is why we have to try to regain these perspectives if we are to understand the written play which has come down to us: the analysis of the play leads to an analysis of the theater in which it was formed.

But though the theater was there, everyone could not use it to the full: Sophocles was required. This becomes clear if one considers the very different use which Euripides, Sophocles' contemporary, makes of the tragic theater and its ritual forms.

Professor Gilbert Murray has explained in detail how the tragic form is derived from the ritual form; and he has demon-strated the ritual forms which are preserved in each of the ex-tant Greek tragedies. In general, the ritual had its agon, or sacred combat, between the old King, or god or hero, and the new, corresponding to the agons in the tragedies, and the clear "purpose" moment of the tragic rhythm. It had its *Sparagmos*, in which the royal victim was literally or symbolically torn asunder, followed by the lamentation and/or rejoicing of the chorus: elements which correspond to the moments of "passion." The ritual had its messenger, its recognition scene, and its epipha-ny; various plot devices for representing the moment of "per-ception" which follows the "pathos." Professor Murray, in a word, studies the art of tragedy in the light of ritual forms, and thus, throws a really new light upon Aristotle's *Poetics*. The parts of the ritual would appear to correspond to parts of the plot, like recognitions and scenes of suffering, which Aristotle mentions, but, in the text which has come down to us, fails to expound completely. In this view, both the ritual and the more highly elaborated and individualized art of tragedy would be "imitating" action in the tragic rhythm; the parts of the ritual, and the parts of the plot, would both be devices for showing forth the three moments of this rhythm.

Professor Murray, however, does not make precisely these deductions. Unlike Aristotle, he takes the plays of Euripides, rather than Sophocles' *Oedipus,* as the patterns of the tragic form. That is because his attitude to the ritual forms is like Euripides' own: he responds to their purely theatrical effectiveness, but has no interest or belief in the prerational image of human nature and destiny which the ritual conveyed; which Sophocles felt as still alive and significant for his generation, and presented once more in *Oedipus*. Professor Murray shows that Euripides restored the literal ritual much more accurately than Sophocles— his epiphanies, for example, are usually the bodily showing-forth of a very human god, who cynically expounds his cruel part in the proceedings; while the "epiphany" in *Oedipus*, the final tableau of the blind old man with his incestuous brood, merely conveys the moral truth which underlay the action, and implies the anagoge: human dependence upon a mysterious and divine order of nature. Perhaps these distinctions may be summarized as follows: Professor Murray is interested in the ritual forms in abstraction from all content; Sophocles saw also the spiritual content of the old forms: understood them at a level deeper than the literal, as imitations of an action still "true" to life in his sophisticated age.

Though Euripides and Sophocles wrote at the same time and for the same theater, one cannot understand either the form or the meaning of Euripides' plays on the basis of Sophocles' dramaturgy. The beautiful lyrics sung by Euripides' choruses are, as I have said, incidental music rather than organic parts of the action; they are not based upon the feeling that all have a stake in the common way of life and therefore in the issue of the present action. Euripides' individualistic heroes find no light in their suffering, and bring no renewal to the moral life of the community: they are at war with the very clear, human, and malicious gods, and what they suffer, they suffer unjustly and to no good end. Where Sophocles' celebrated irony seems to envisage the *condition humaine* itself—the plight of the psyche in a world which is ultimately mysterious to it—Euripides' ironies are all aimed at the incredible "gods" and at the superstitions of those who believe in them. In short, if these two writers both used the tragic theater, they did so in very different ways.

Verral's *Euripides the Rationalist* shows very clearly what the basis of Euripides' dramaturgy is. His use of myth and ritual is like that which Cocteau or, still more exactly, Sartre makes of them—for parody or satirical exposition, but without any belief in their meaning. If Euripides presents the plight of Electra in realistic detail, it is because he wants us to feel the suffering of the individual without benefit of any objective moral or cosmic order—with an almost sensational immediacy: he does not see the myth, as a whole, as significant as such. If he brings Apollo, in the flesh, before us, it is not because he "believes" in Apollo, but because he disbelieves in him, and wishes to reveal this figment of the Greek imagination as, literally, incredible. He depends as much as Sophocles upon the common heritage of ritual and myth: but he "reduces" its form and images to the uses of parody and metaphorical illustration, in the manner of Ovid and of the French Neoclassic tradition. And the human action he reveals is the extremely modern one of the psyche caught in the categories its reason invents, responding with unmitigated sharpness to the feeling of the moment, but cut off from the deepest level of experience, where the mysterious world is yet felt as real and prior to our inventions, demands, and criticisms.

Though Sophocles was not using the myths and ritual forms of the tragic theater for parody and to satirize their tradition, it does not appear that he had any more naïve belief in their literal validity than Euripides did. He would not, for his purpose, have had to ask himself whether the myth of Oedipus conveyed any historic facts. He would not have had to believe that the performance of *Oedipus*, or even the Festival of Dionysos itself, would assure the Athenians a good crop of children and olives.

On the contrary he must have felt that the tragic rhythm of action which he discerned in the myth, which he felt as underlying the forms of the ritual, and which he realized in so many ways in his play, was a deeper version of human life than any particular manifestation of it, or any conceptual understanding of it, whether scientific and rationalistic, or theological; yet potentially including them all. If one takes Mr. Troy's suggestion, one might say, using the Medieval notion of fourfold symbolism, that Sophocles might well have taken myth and ritual as literally "fictions," yet still have accepted their deeper meanings—trope, allegory, and anagoge—as valid.

Oedipus: The Imitation of an Action

The general notion we used to compare the forms and spiritual content of tragedy and of ancient ritual was the "imitation of action." Ritual imitates action in one way, tragedy in another; and Sophocles' use of ritual forms indicates that he sensed the tragic rhythm common to both.

But the language, plot, characters of the play may also be understood in more detail and in relation to each other as imitations, in their various media, of the one action. I have already quoted Coleridge on the unity of action: "not properly a rule," he calls it, "but in itself the great end, not only of the drama, but of the epic, lyric, even to the candle-flame cone of an epigram —not only of poetry, but of poesy in general, as the proper generic term inclusive of all the fine arts, as its species."* Probably the influence of Coleridge partly accounts for the revival of this notion of action which underlies the recent studies of poetry which I have mentioned. Mr. Burke's phrase, "language as symbolic action," expresses the idea, and so does his dictum: "The poet spontaneously knows that 'beauty *is* as beauty *does*' (that the 'state' must be embodied in an 'actualization')." (*Four Tropes.*)

This idea of action, and of the play as the imitation of an action, is ultimately derived from the *Poetics*. This derivation is explained in the Appendix. At this point I wish to show how the complex form of *Oedipus*—its plot, characters, and discourse

*The essay on *Othello*.

--may be understood as the imitation of a certain action.

The action of the play is the quest for Laius' slayer. That is the over-all aim which informs it—"to find the culprit in order to purify human life," as it may be put. Sophocles must have seen this seeking action as the real life of the Oedipus myth, discerning it through the personages and events as one discerns "life in a plant through the green leaves." Moreover, he must have seen this particular action as a type, or crucial instance, of human life in general; and hence he was able to present it in the form of the ancient ritual which also presents and celebrates the perennial mystery of human life and action. Thus by "action" I do not mean the events of the story but the focus or aim of psychic life from which the events, in that situation, result.

If Sophocles was imitating action in this sense, one may schematically imagine his work of composition in three stages, three mimetic acts: 1. He makes the plot: i.e., arranges the events of the story in such a way as to reveal the seeking action from which they come. 2. He develops the characters of the story as individualized forms of "quest." 3. He expresses or realizes their actions by means of the words they utter in the various situations of the plot. This scheme, of course, has nothing to do with the temporal order which the poet may really have followed in elaborating his composition, nor to the order we follow in becoming acquainted with it; we start with the words, the "green leaves." The scheme refers to the "hierarchy of actualizations" which we may eventually learn to see in the completed work.

1. The first act of imitation consists in making the plot or arrangement of incidents. Aristotle says that the tragic poet is primarily a maker of plots, for the plot is the "soul of a tragedy," its formal cause. The arrangement which Sophocles made of the events of the story—starting near the end, and rehearsing the past in relation to what is happening now—already to some degree actualizes the tragic quest he wishes to show, even before we sense the characters as individuals or hear them speak and sing.

(The reader must be warned that this conception of the plot is rather unfamiliar to us. Usually we do not distinguish between the plot as the form of the play and the plot as producing a certain effect upon the audience—excitement, "interest," suspense, and the like. Aristotle also uses "plot" in this second sense. The mimicry of art has a further purpose, or final—as distinguished from its formal—cause, i.e., to reach the audience. Thinking of the Athenian theater, he describes the plot as intended to show the "universal," or to rouse and purge the emotions of pity and terror. These two meanings of the word—the form of the action, and the device for reaching the audience—are also further explained in the Appendix. At this point I am using the word *plot* in the first sense: as the form, the first actualization, of the tragic action.)

2. The characters, or agents, are the second actualization of the action. According to Aristotle, "the agents are imitated mainly with a view to the action"—i.e., the soul of the tragedy is there already in the order of events, the tragic rhythm of the life of Oedipus and Thebes; but this action may be more sharply realized and more elaborately shown forth by developing individual variations upon it. It was with this principle in mind that Ibsen wrote to his publisher, after two years' of work on *The Wild Duck*, that the play was nearly complete, and he could now proceed to "the more energetic individuation of the characters."

If one considers the Oedipus-Tiresias scene which I have quoted, one can see how the characters serve to realize the action of the whole. They reveal, at any moment, a "spectrum of action" like that which the tragic rhythm spread before us in temporal succession, at the same time offering concrete instances of almost photographic sharpness. Thus Tiresias "suffers" in the darkness of his blindness while Oedipus pursues his reasoned "purpose"; and then Tiresias effectuates his "purpose" of serving his mantic vision of the truth, while Oedipus "suffers" a blinding passion of fear and anger. The agents also serve to move the action ahead, develop it in time, through their conflicts. The chorus meanwhile, in some respects between, in others deeper, than the antagonists, represents the interests of that resolution, that final chord of feeling, in which the end of the action, seen ironically and sympathetically as one, will be realized.

3. The third actualization is in the words of the play. The

seeking action which is the substance of the play is imitated first in the plot, second in the characters, and third in the words, concepts, and forms of discourse wherein the characters "actualize" their psychic life in its shifting forms, in response to the everchanging situations of the play. If one thinks of plotting, characterization, and poetry as successive "acts of imitation" by the author, one may also say that they constitute, in the completed work, a hierarchy of forms; and that the words of the play are its "highest individuation." They are the "green leaves" which we actually perceive; the product and the sign of the one "life of the plant" which, by an imaginative effort, one may divine behind them all.

At this point one encounters again Mr. Burke's theory of "language as symbolic action," and the many contemporary studies of the arts of poetry which have been made from this point of view. It would be appropriate to offer a detailed study of Sophocles' language, using the modern tools of analysis, to substantiate my main point. But this would require the kind of knowledge of Greek which a Jebb spent his life to acquire; and I must be content to try to show, in very general terms, that the varied forms of the poetry of *Oedipus* can only be understood on a histrionic basis: i.e., as coming out of a direct sense of the tragic rhythm of *action.*

In the Oedipus-Tiresias scene, there is a "spectrum of the forms of discourse" corresponding to the "spectrum of action" which I have described. It extends from Oedipus' opening speech—a reasoned exposition not, of course, without feeling but based essentially upon clear ideas and a logical order—to the choral chant, based upon sensuous imagery and the "logic of feeling." Thus it employs, in the beginning, the principle of composition which Mr. Burke calls "syllogistic progression," and, at the other end of the spectrum, Mr. Burke's "progression by association and contrast." When the Neoclassic and rationalistic critics of the seventeenth century read *Oedipus*, they saw only the order of reason; they did not know what to make of the chorus. Hence Racine's drama of "Action as Rational": a drama of static situations, of clear concepts and merely illustrative images. Nietzsche, on the other hand, saw only the passion of the chorus; for his insight was based on *Tristan*, which is composed essentially in sensuous images, and moves by association and contrast according to the logic of feeling: the drama which takes "action as passion." Neither point of view enables one to see how the scene, as a whole, hangs together.

If the speeches of the characters and the songs of the chorus are only the foliage of the plant, this is as much as to say that the life and meaning of the whole is never literally and completely present in any one formulation. It takes *all* of the elements—the shifting situation, the changing and developing characters, and their reasoned or lyric utterances, to indicate, in the round, the action Sophocles wishes to convey. Because this action takes the form of reason as well as passion, and of contemplation by way of symbols; because it is essentially moving (in the tragic rhythm); and because it is shared in different ways by all the characters, the play has neither literal unity nor the rational unity of the truly abstract idea, or "univocal concept." Its parts and its moments are one only "by analogy"; and just as the Saints warn us that we must believe in order to understand, so we must "make believe," by a sympathetic and imitative act of the histrionic sensibility, in order to get what Sophocles intended by his play.

It is the histrionic basis of Sophocles' art which makes it mysterious to us, with our demands for conceptual clarity, or for the luxury of yielding to a stream of feeling and subjective imagery. But it is this also which makes it so crucial an instance of the art of the theater in its completeness, as though the author understood "song, spectacle, thought, and diction" in their primitive and subtle roots. And it is the histrionic basis of drama which "undercuts theology and science."

Analogues of the "Tragic Rhythm"

In the present study I propose to use *Oedipus* as a landmark, and to relate subsequent forms of drama to it. For it presents a moving image at the nascent moment of highest valency, of a way of life and action which is still at the root of our culture.

Professor Buchanan remarks, in *Poetry and Mathematics*, that the deepest and most elaborate development of the tragic rhythm is to be found in the *Divine Comedy*. The *Purgatorio* especially, though an epic and not a drama, evidently moves in the tragic rhythm, both as a whole and in detail. The daylight climb up the mountain, by moral effort, and in the light of natural reason, corresponds to the first moment, that of "purpose." The night, under the sign of Faith, Hope and Charity, when the Pilgrim can do nothing by his own unaided efforts, corresponds to the moments of passion and perception. The Pilgrim, as he pauses, mulls over the thoughts and experiences of the day; he sleeps and dreams, seeing ambivalent images from the mythic dreaming of the race, which refer, also, both to his own "suppressed desires" and to his own deepest aspirations. These images gradually solidify and clarify, giving place to a new perception of his situation. This rhythm, repeated in varied forms, carries the Pilgrim from the superficial but whole-hearted motivations of childhood, in the Antipurgatorio, through the divided counsels of the growing soul, to the new innocence, freedom, and integrity of the Terrestrial Paradise—the realm of *The Tempest* or of *Oedipus at Colonos*. The same rhythmic conception governs also the detail of the work, down to the *terza rima* itself—that verse-form which is clear at any moment in its literal fiction yet essentially moving ahead and pointing to deeper meanings.

Because Dante keeps his eye always upon the tragic moving of the psyche itself, his vision, like that of Sophocles, is not limited by any of the forms of thought whereby we seek to fix our experience—in which we are idolatrously expiring, like the coral animal in its shell. But Professor Buchanan shows that the abstract shape, at least, of the tragic rhythm is to be recognized in other and more limited or specialized cultural forms as well. "This pattern," he writes, "is the Greek view of life. It is the method of their and our science, history and philosophy. . . . The Greek employment of it had been humanistic in the main. . . . The late Middle Ages and the Renaissance substituted natural objects for the heroes of vicarious tragedies, the experiments in the laboratory. They put such objects under controlled conditions, introduced artificial complications, and waited for the answering pronouncement of fate. The crucial experiment is the crisis of an attempt to rationalize experience, that is, to force it into our analogies. Purgation and recognition are now called elimination of false hypotheses and verification. The shift is significant, but the essential tragic pattern of tragedy is still there."

The tragic rhythm is, in a sense, the shape of Racinian tragedy, even though Racine was imitating action as essentially rational, and would have called the moments of the rhythm exposition, complication, crisis, and denouement, to satisfy the reason. It is in a way the shape of *Tristan*, though action in that play is reduced to passion, the principles of composition to the logic of feeling. Even the over-all shape of *Hamlet* is similar, though the sense of pathos predominates, and the whole is elaborated in such subtle profusion as can only be explained with reference to Dante and the Middle Ages.

The next two chapters are devoted respectively to *Bérénice* and *Tristan*. It is true that neither Racine nor Wagner understood the dramatic art in the exact spirit of Aristotle's definition, "the *imitation* of action." Wagner was rather expressing an emotion, and Racine was *demonstrating* an essence. But expression of emotion and rational demonstration may themselves be regarded as modes of action, each analogous to one moment in Sophocles' tragic rhythm.

CHAPTER II

BÉRÉNICE: THE ACTION AND
THEATER OF REASON

Zénon! Cruel Zénon! Zénon d' Élée!
M'as-tu percé de cette flèche ailée
Qui vibre, vole, et ne vole pas!
Le son m'enfante et la flèche me tue.
Ah! Le Soleil! . . . Quelle ombre de tortue
Pour l'âme, Achille immobile à grands, pas!*
　　　　　　　　　　　　—*Le Cimetière Marin*

The Tragedy of Reason: *Bérénice*, Act I

THIS stanza by Valéry, at the latter end of that rationalist tradition which had its beginnings in the age of Racine, puts very beautifully the abstract and timeless situation of the soul as reasoning. Zeno's famous paradox of the arrow's flight, though a triumph of the reason viewing itself, nevertheless pierces the soul; the arrow kills, though the music of its winged flight wakes the soul to its own life. It is like the other parable of Zeno's: the very brilliance of the demonstration (in Zeno's rational terms) that Achilles can never overtake the tortoise casts a shadow upon the soul in the act of reason. In the clarity with which the metaphysical tragedy of reason is thus conceived; in the use of illustrative metaphor, and in the musical effects—the plucked string, the vibrant stillness—one may recognize the action and the form of Racinian tragedy.

I have selected *Bérénice* to illustrate the tragedy of reason and the peculiar properties of the Baroque theater. It is true that

*Zeno! Cruel Zeno! Elean Zeno! / You have transfixed me with that wingéd arrow / Which vibrates, flies, and does not fly! / My birth is that sound and my death that arrow. / Ah! The brilliant Sun! . . . What tortoise-shadow / On the soul, Achilles motionless in stride!

some of Racine's contemporaries and some subsequent critics*
deny that this play is really a tragedy at all. The passion in it
is only that of love; the catastrophe only the separation of
Antiochus from Bérénice, whom he loves, and of Bérénice and
Titus, who are in love, from each other. But Racine himself
thought it one of his most perfect tragedies: "It is not necessary," he writes in his preface, "for there to be blood and
corpses in a tragedy: it is enough that its action be great, its
actors heroic, that the passions be excited in it; and that the
whole give that experience of majestic sadness in which the
whole pleasure of tragedy resides." Racine was right: *Bérénice*
lacks the complicated intrigue and the off-stage violence which
one so often finds in Corneille's tragedies; but this is the sign of
its formal and intellectual integrity. It never lapses from the high
plane which the idea of Neoclassic tragedy demands; and in it,
therefore, one can see this idea very clearly.

The story which Racine used is simple. Antiochus, King of
Comagene, is in love with Bérénice, Queen of Palestine. But
Bérénice has dismissed Antiochus because she is in love with
Titus, as he is in love with her. When the play opens Titus
is about to be made Emperor of Rome, and Antiochus and
Bérénice (tributary monarchs like nobles at the court of Louis
XIV) are in Rome for the coronation ceremonies. It is assumed
that Titus will presently marry Bérénice; but there is one possible hitch: the Roman Senate may object on constitutional
grounds to his marrying a foreign queen. Thus there is implicit
in the situation a conflict between the love and the reasonable
duty of each of the three monarchs. Antiochus' duty is to con-
ceal and renounce his love for the Queen, unless her feelings
and Titus' have changed. It will be Titus' duty to sacrifice his
love for Bérénice to his duty to Rome, unless the Senate relents.
And Bérénice will have to stifle her love for Titus, both because of her own regal integrity and because of the regard
for *Titus'* duty which reason demands. When we have learned
that Bérénice's feelings are unchanged, and that the Senate is
adamant—when all the facts are in hand, and all the possibilities
explored—the passionate monarchs part forever, in obedience to

*Cf. *The Classical Moment*, by Martin Turnell, for example.

their sad and separate duties.

Thus we have, in this play, a tragedy exactly as the textbooks define it: "Une action héroique, accomplie par des personnages ayant pour idéal le triomphe de la volonté sur l'instinct." Moreover, the situation of the three monarchs, in which Rome is identified with both reason and duty, is the metaphysical situation of the rational soul which Valéry's stanza presents. This basic situation is clear in advance; and though it is explored with the orderly thoroughness of logic, it never changes: Reason reveals with triumphant clarity its own tragic incommensurability with the merely actual world of the senses and the emotions; the soul realizes its timeless life in reason by the same moral-intellectual act which kills its temporal life. Voltaire marveled that Racine was able to make five acts out of so single a theme and so simple a situation. He concluded that only Racine understood the human heart well enough for such virtuosity; and he might have added that only Racine understood the Baroque theater— the theater of reason—well enough to use it with such perfect consistency.

The art by which Racine makes his story seem to move, though a most difficult technical achievement, is fundamentally very simple. He withholds until the very end, from one or more of his three main characters, some crucial fact of that character's situation, and so forces them all to explore every logical possibility, and ring all the changes upon hope and despair. Neither the basic situation, nor their principles, change; but the available facts are shifted like the pieces on a chessboard. Thus at the beginning of the play Antiochus does not know beyond doubt how Bérénice feels about him now; and neither he nor Bérénice knows that the Senate will forbid Bérénice's marriage to Titus. This is the first situation; and Act I analyzes its uncertainties and tantalizing possibilities. But, in order to show how this works, one must try to get a little closer to the actual play, and to the consistent basis of Racine's peculiar make-believe.

The difficulty we have with Racine seems to be due to the fact that we do not want to accept as "really" tragic the single moment of experience and the single angle of vision upon which the whole drama is based. We instinctively demand the shifting perspectives, comic and tragic in alternation, which Shakespeare's wider stage provides—or else we simply refuse to relinquish the cosier and more slovenly habits of mind of modern naturalism. If we are to perceive Racine's tragedy at all, we must abstract such moral integrity as we possess from all qualifying circumstance and boldly contemplate *it*. In the very beginning of the play Racine directs our attention to this intimate yet abstract moment of experience, this timeless theater of life and action. Antiochus addresses Arsace, his indispensable *confident:*

> Arrêtons un moment: la pompe de ces lieux,
> Je le vois bien, Arsace, est nouvelle à tes yeux.
> Souvent ce cabinet, superbe et solitaire,
> Des secrets de Titus est le dépositaire:
> C'est ici quelquefois qu'il se cache à sa cour,
> Lorsqu'il vient à la Reine expliquer son amour.
> De son apartement cette porte est prochaine,
> Et cette autre conduit dans celui de la reine.

> (Let us pause a moment: the pomp of this place,
> I plainly see, is new to you, Arsace.
> Often this chamber, in its lonely pride,
> Receives the secrets which Titus would hide;
> Sometimes it is his refuge from the court,
> When he shows the queen the feelings in his heart.
> His own apartments are beyond that door,
> And this one leads to the queen's lodgings here.)*

The ringing words (in French) establish not only the stage itself, with its two significant doors, its lusters, and its polished floor, but the spiritual locus also: the *pureté* and *clarté* of the enlightened moral consciousness. For all its *pompe,* this region is sad, being shadowed by the mortal peril of love. It is shared (for all its secrecy) by the Emperor Titus, by Queen Bérénice, and by Antiochus, since he now, in wig, breastplate, and ruffles, gravely takes it for his own. We in the audience must pull ourselves together, for it is assumed that we too can live up to these

*I am responsible for this English. Racine is notoriously untranslatable; and yet a literal prose version gives a hopelessly distorted impression.

rigors, both in their searching intimacy, and in their visible, ceremonial, full-dress solemnity.

In a sense, this scene is the whole matter of the play: Racine makes a bull's eye at the first shot. But as we shall see, he can play many variations within the one vibrant mode of awareness.

Arsace departs to summon Bérénice, and Antiochus is left to *expliquer* his love for the Queen, in terms of his present situation, as Titus so often does in this very place. His tirade is a firm, light structure of parallels and antitheses. Shall he hope, or despair? Shall he speak, or be silent? Offend the queen, or do an injustice to his own constancy? Every possible formulation of his situation is explored, and every possible result of the forthcoming interview; his strict intelligence follows every subterfuge of his suffering heart, and politely lays it bare for us. Racine says that the passions must be excited; but they are roused only to enter the inimical realm of the mind. The action of the whole tirade occurs on that thin and cutting edge where rationality meets its opposite. For all the tremors of his inner being, Antiochus is firmly planted on the very point of hopelessness itself; and so we are never far from the ultimate statement of the tragic split which is the single matter of the play. Antiochus puts it very musically at the highest lyrical point of the tirade, just before we modulate into the more prosaic key of his forthcoming scene with Arsace:

> Example infortuné d'une longue constance,
> Après cinq ans d'amour et d'espoir superflus,
> Je pars, fidèle encor quand je n'espère plus.

> (An ill-fated instance of long constancy,
> After five years of love and hope in vain,
> I go, still faithful, with nothing more to gain.)

When Arsace returns, after we have learned that Bérénice will see Antiochus presently, the excitement drops for the scene between Arsace and Antiochus. We are farther from the inner being of Antiochus, where the soul-as-reason has its imperiled life; we descend from reason-intuiting-itself to the plane of the discursive reason. Here we develop the corollaries which follow from Antiochus' integrity; the policies to be followed, the machinery of the "intrigue" of the play. The scene is in the dialectical form of question and answer. Arsace does not see Antiochus' integrity itself; but he very shrewdly asks all the practical questions, such as, "Why do you owe the Queen anything?" Thus he gives Antiochus an opportunity to demonstrate the logical impeccability of his tragic position. When Arsace has been silenced, and the mind satisfied, we are back to the crux of reason and passion, just in time for Bérénice's entrance.

The scene with Bérénice reaches greater intensity, with richer musical effects, than Antiochus' tirade. Bérénice is contemplating, in the steady light of reason and duty, but in ignorance of Rome's opposition, the beautiful prospect of her love for Titus, while Antiochus contemplates his renounced but living love for her. Thus the subject of Antiochus' solo is resumed as a duet, and Antiochus (closer to the painful reality than Bérénice, because she lacks one fact) brings it to a close as he had his solo:

> Surtout ne craigniez point qu'une aveugle douleur
> Remplisse l'univers du bruit de mon malheur:
> Madame, le seul bruit d'une mort que j'implore
> Vous fera souvenir que je vivais encore.

> (Above all, have no fear that my blind sorrowing
> Could ever make the world hear of my suffering:
> Only the rumor of my longed-for death
> Will remind you, then, that I once drew breath.)

On this perfectly controlled scheme, Racine continues to demonstrate the variety in unity, and the unity always in the variety of his play. He moves majestically from the concentrated intensity of the tirade—which he sometimes develops at more length as a duet or trio—to the more relaxed discursive analysis of the dialogue scenes. But the peculiarity of this dramatic form is that all of the developments may so easily be reduced to the one identical theme. The characters, for instance, have little individual being. Arsace is essentially a voice in Antiochus' conversation with himself; the same is true of Bérénice's and Titus' *confidents*. As for the three monarchs themselves,

Bérénice is a woman and a queen, Titus the emperor of Rome, and Antiochus a tributary king, but the tragic life of reason which they share is one, just as the proud and solitary scene where it performs its sad feat of perpetual self-demonstration is one. At the end of the trio which closes the play, Bérénice's single voice can convey their common triumph and lament:

> Adieu, Servons tous trois d'example à l'univers
> De l'amour la plus tendre et la plus malheureuse
> Dont il puisse garder l'histoire douleureuse.

> (Good-bye. Let us, all three, be emblems for the world
> Of love, the saddest love and the most tender
> Of all the stories that the world remembers.)

If one looks at this play from an alien angle of vision, deviating ever so slightly from the point of view which Racine maintains and demands from the audience, the whole crystalline structure may appear lifeless and absurd. But if one brings the play into focus in the mirror of reason (the underlying idea of the Baroque theater) one sees an intense, inescapable, and intimate moment of human life. By limiting himself so strictly to this moment, or mode of psychic being, and to its resources of expression, Racine defines a histrionic, and thence a verbal, medium almost as abstract as that of musical sound. Like music, it may touch us with surprising depth precisely because it is so purified; and, again like music, it is the abstractness of the medium which makes possible such economical and controlled actualizations of the poet's idea: such literally perfect form: such intellectual and esthetic univocity.

These points may be made a little clearer by considering how the principles of Racine's dramaturgy are derived from his strict and final sense of human life and action.

The Rational Imitation of Action: Principles of Racine's Dramaturgy

In the chapter on Sophocles' *Oedipus*, we endeavored to find our way through the words, characters, and changing events of the play to the one action which Sophocles was imitating; and this action was seen as the clue to the coherence of the whole complex structure. It then appeared that one might think of the life, or hidden essence of the tragedy, as having been realized in the poet's successive acts of imitation: in plot, in character, in reasoned exposition and dialogue, and in the choric odes. So Sophocles would have adumbrated the one essence, basing his art upon the primitive and subtle histrionic sensibility and the ceremonial make-believe of the Greek tragic theater.

It is very clear that Racine and Corneille did not understand the art of drama as the imitation of action in just this way, though they thought their plays were tragedies in the Greek sense, and obeyed Aristotle's principles. Corneille's *Trois Discours* and Racine's prefaces frequently mention the imitation of action; but "action" in these contexts does not suggest the notion which I have attributed to Aristotle and used in the analysis of *Oedipus*. As Racine and Corneille use the word, it does not mean action so much as its results: not the movement or focus of the soul which actualizes its essence moment by moment but the overt deeds, chains of events reportable as facts, which action produces. Thus when they say "action" they usually mean the concatenated incidents of the rationalized plot, or "intrigue" as they call it.

One must not conclude from this that Racine and Corneille did not sense action at all. They did not make the distinction between action and deed, nor between the plot as the formal cause or "soul" of tragedy and plot as a rationalized series of incidents, intended to satisfy the discursive reason.* But the life of their drama *is* the rational mode of action. When Racine says of his Phèdre, "Her crime is rather a punishment of the gods than a *movement of her will*," he has his eye upon the action of that character, as I understand the word, though only action in the rational mode. They assumed this mode of action as self-evidently the one shape and substance of truly human life. They assumed that the audience assumed it; and so they took the art of drama to be, not that of imitating and celebrating action as a central mystery, in various modes and from various angles of vision, but rather that of demonstrating with the utmost clarity, economy, and harmony, an essence already given and accepted.

*The reader is referred to the Appendix for a discussion of this distinction.

Thus if one wishes to study the histrionic basis of the art of Baroque drama, one gets no help from Neoclassic theory, though so much of it is ostensibly an elucidation of the *Poetics*. One must look at the wonderfully single action of the plays themselves; in that light one can understand the rules which the dramatists and the critics thought they had taken from Aristotle.

The action of *Bérénice* (using an infinitive to suggest if not to define it) is "to demonstrate the tragic life of the soul-as-rational in the situation of the three passionate monarchs." It is this demonstration which the audience is invited to see, which the three principal characters perform, and which Racine makes, first in his rational plot, then in his reasonable presentation of character (kings and queens as they logically would be by conventional agreement); and finally and above all, in the logical and musical order of his language.

But I must attempt to make a little clearer what I mean by Racine's art of plotting as rational demonstration. In Book VI of the *Ethics* Aristotle points out that fully conscious choice has the implicit form of the syllogism. The facts of the concrete situation (Rome forbids Titus's marriage to a foreign queen) constitute the minor premise. The general principle to be obeyed (rationality itself; the categorical imperative) is the major premise. I have only to recognize the voice of Rome as that of reason-duty itself, and my action follows by a series of connected syllogisms: i.e., as though by pure logic. If one now endeavors to imagine, not the completed plot, but the author as he makes the plot, one can see that plot-making must itself have appeared to him to be essentially logical, and to have as its purpose the satisfaction of the mind. The essence he wishes to demonstrate is the tragic life of the soul as reasoning. Reason is the sole value: reason is always to be obeyed. From this both the selection, and the arrangements of the facts of the story, follow deductively. Such facts will be chosen as will best illustrate the eternal nature of the reasoning soul: i.e., its life as a conflict with passion. And they will be arranged in such a way as to demonstrate, again and again, the logical inevitability of its choices. So in his plot-making Racine (like one of his own heroes) seeks the cruelest constraints of passion in order to demonstrate to the mind of the audience that essence, that rational mode of action, which he politely assumes we share.

In Racine's dramaturgy, the situation, static in the eye of the mind, and illustrating the eternal plight of reason, is the basic unit of composition; in Sophocles' the basic unit is the tragic rhythm, in which the mysterious human essence, never completely or finally realized, is manifested in successive and varied modes of action. Is there any analogy between the timeless tragedy of reason, and the temporal *change* from one realization of the human essence to another which the tragic rhythm shows?

If you consider the succession of situations in the five acts of *Bérénice*, you can see a shape which has an abstract resemblance to that of the Sophoclean tragic rhythm. In the first three acts the characters are acquiring and ordering the facts of their situation, as these become available; dialogue scenes predominate; and this part of the play corresponds to the moment of "purpose" in the tragic rhythm, represented (in *Oedipus*) by the agon. In Act IV, with all the facts clear to all, the rational soul suffers a more direct intuition of its plight; there are no discursive dialectical analyses, but only the tirades of Bérénice and Titus, and their duet; and this act corresponds to the pathos, which Sophocles represents by means of the chorus. Act V corresponds to the moment of perception which ends the tragic rhythm. The three monarchs accept the outcome of their situation—their eternal separation: the triumph of duty and the sacrifice of love —as the clear, distinct, and final illustration of the tragedy of reason. The action of reason in this situation has its beginning, middle, and end. But the full scope of the tragic rhythm as we find it in Sophocles, which spreads as it were a whole spectrum of modes of action before us by varying acts of imitation—this scope we do not find in Racine's tragedy of purely ethical motivation.

It is revealing to look more closely at the traces which are left, in Racine's plot, of the parts of the Sophoclean plot: the agon, or conflict; the scene of suffering or pathos, with its chorus; and the new perception or epiphany, with its messenger, or its visible stage tableau, and its awe-struck contemplation.

The scenes of dialogue correspond to the agons; but the polite exchange between Arsace and Antiochus, in the first act, is far from the terrible conflict between Oedipus and Tiresias, wherein the moral beings of the antagonists are at stake. Arsace is best understood as merely one voice in Antiochus' polite discussion with himself: the moral being is unmistakable and impossible to lose while the stage life continues at all. And this is true also of those more painful discussions between principals: the very possibility of the interchange depends upon the authority of reason, which secures the moral being in any contingency. Even when the Baroque hero is very angry (like Thésée in *Phèdre*, and many of Corneille's heroes) he bases his anger upon the congested sense of outraged rationality, and one is reminded of Aristotle's dictum that anger is the passion which does least violence to reason and is most easily cured thereby. But if the moral being is *ex hypothesi* secure, the very basis of the whole make-believe of the play, there cannot be a *pathos* in the Sophoclean sense at all. The pathos pictured by the Sophoclean chorus is a moment of change in the moral being: it includes the breakdown of one rationalized, moral *persona*; the suffering of feelings and images suggesting a human essence capable of both good and evil, and always underlying the individual with his desperate reasons and his fragile integrity. The Sophoclean pathos can only be conveyed by the chorus, with its less than individual mode of being; its musical and kinesthetic mimicry, and its sensuous dreamlike imagery, precisely because it has to convey a change in the highly realized and rationalized individual moral being. With this in mind, it is easy to see why Corneille and Racine had no idea what to make of the chorus: it is based upon a mode of action (an attitude toward suffering) which the theater of reason cannot mirror. And for the same reason they did not understand, or try to use, the epiphany or new perception with which the Sophoclean tragic rhythm ends.

And yet it is clear that Racinian tragedy as a whole is a kind of epiphany. The direct intuition of the life of reason, upon which all is based, is (though abstracted from experience) like the intuition in which a Sophoclean chorus, or a Sophoclean tragedy, ends. Racine feels that this abstracted moment of action contains by implication all the rest: that this mode of being *is* the human essence. He sees it as so abstracted, so clear and distinct, so final, that he senses no analogies whatever between it and other modes of being: the less definable "conscience of the race" represented by the chorus; or the less formulated perceptions of the young and the naïve; or, at the other end of the scale, the hidden councils of the gods. Because the Racinian hero is assumed to intuit the essence of human life from the first, his tragedy is in every sense absolute. He is as responsible as God; is hero and scapegoat at once; his heroic action (like that of Eliot's Thomas of Canterbury) is the same thing as the martyr's suffering for the truth.

Thus the histrionic basis of Baroque tragedy is extremely narrow; a pin-point on the spectrum of action. It determines an art of plotting which is simply the demonstration of an essence; and it defines a dramatic medium natural to reason: that of word and concept. For this reason, the classic French style of acting, capable of great subtlety within its narrow range, tends to identify acting with recitation. The action Racine is conveying generates, as it were automatically, the Alexandrines in which the tragedy is audible and understandable to us; and through his logical and musical verse Racine controls the actor's performance as completely as Wagner does through the musical score.

The art of Racine's Alexandrines is so identified with the genius of the French language that one cannot get at it by way of English, or even, I suppose, enjoy it to the full unless to the manner born. But one can see its main outlines, and one can see that the verse itself realizes in every detail the action of the whole. The play moves between the intensely felt intuition of the tirades, and the more relaxed and discursive dialogue scenes; but it is all put in Alexandrines, and this basically simple, symmetrical form serves equally well in both cases. In the perfect balance of the rhymed couplet, in the perfect balance of the individual line (regularly though not invariably broken in the middle) one feels the logical form of thesis and antithesis, the tragic split between reason and passion, and the irreconcilable contradiction, in the illustrative situation, between Rome and the loves of the three monarchs. But on this very simple formal basis Racine builds logical and musical arabesques of great variety. In the very first line of the play, "Arrêtons un moment, /la pompe de ces lieux," the two halves of the line are equally good illustrations: the awe-struck pause of Antiochus and Arsace (indicated both in the meaning of the words, and by the caesura) and the pomp of Titus's chamber (which the actual stage shows visibly to the actors and to us) mean equally the one essence: the tragic and enlightened moral consciousness. In the beginning of Antiochus' first tirade we get four balanced ways of saying the same thing:

> Eh bien! Antiochus/es-tu toujours le même?
> Pourrai-je, sans trembler/lui dire: Je vous aime?

Antiochus, the question of his continued identity, the tremors of his inner being, and the question of his avowal of love, are felt, and presented in the very structure of the verse, as identical. This is what I mean by the vibrant stillness of the *one* moment of action: in the tirade we are close to the life of the soul itself. Near the end of this tirade the tragic contradiction (which the balanced form conveys even when it is used to present an identity) makes the two balanced halves of a single line:

> Craint autant ce moment/que je l'ai souhaité

The structure of the line, and the equal and opposite forces of fear and desire, all in twelve syllables, make the tragic crux itself. Of Racine's music—his endlessly resourceful rhythms, and his pure and chiming sounds—I do not attempt to speak; but his music is another means of emphasis and variety on the same formal principle. This principle is to be, at every moment, perfect: always at the end. The throb of the tragic split may rise and fall in intensity but essentially it never changes. The balanced illustrations and formulations of the same point may pile up for emphasis but they always *feel* like the balance of thesis and anithesis. From one point of view the tragic split is never transcended: the form of the Alexandrine looks two ways. From another point of view, this split is always transcended: the formal principle is one, the essence envisaged is one. And, in short the form of the Alexandrine itself is the final actualization of the paradoxical life of reason which has been put in so many ways from Racine to Valéry, and yet is one.

If one thinks even in very general terms of two other verse forms wherein action has been imitated, Shakespeare's blank verse and Dante's terza rima, both the perfection and the narrowness of the Alexandrine are evident. Blank verse is so close to daily rhythms of speech, so flexible—one might almost say so formless in itself—that it can take the shape of any action, whether pathetic, or ethical, or realized in the endless variety of individual character. By the same token, it does not offer, like the Alexandrines, one standard view of action; its use depends upon the insight of the artist prior to versifying. Dante's terza rima is a verse form as highly elaborated and consciously developed as the Alexandrine, and in the same way the form itself suggests a conception of action. But this conception is not that of the static completely realized essence, but that of the tragic rhythm; and though the tercet may present a momentary image of great clarity and distinctness, the interlocking rhymes point always ahead, and the movement of the verse, which never ceases, suggests a human essence never finally realized yet always present in its changing actuality.

Thus the language of Bérénice, like its plot, demonstrates the one unchanging essence. But what of the individual characters? How may an individual being demonstrate so univocal a concept? Aristotle's notion is that characters are imitated "with a view to the action," and we have seen how well this formula applies to *Oedipus:* the action of that play is presented in distinct, but analogous, individual forms; in the various characters and in the various modes of being of the one character. In our experience of the completed play, we see the individuals first, and only later divine, by analogy, the unity of the whole. It is evident that in Racine's dramaturgy the reality of the individual is very differently understood: he is interested in individual characters as illustrations of his abstract idea, insofar as they are required for the concrete situation he uses; and he is interested in them insofar as their life is the one life of reason. He imitates character, not "with a view" to revealing action from various angles and in various modes, but either to illustrate an a priori conception of it, or else (as in the Tirades) to present this essence directly.

Thus he makes his kings and queens of Comagene or Palestine according to a recipe for which he formally invokes the authority of Aristotle. Bérénice has nothing to do with Palestine; and it is impossible to care whether she is a queen or not. She does not inhabit that mortal realm in which racial tradition, geography, social status, and the historical context have their fatal importance. Because Racine is interested only in one moment of psychic life, he replaces all the rest with purely illustrative conventional signs.

But it is astonishing how much life, even individual life, Racine is able to show by sticking so consistently to the one angle of vision, and the one mode of action. A visit to the dentist makes the whole world kin: that small buzzing steel sphere has an intimate meaning for all who have heard it approaching the jawbone. It rouses the passions and induces arabesques of rationalizing without regard to race, color, sex, or religion; yet, in the narrow and searching perspective it provides, one might note individual differences. In the same way the rigid perspective of reasoned duty, once accepted as both inescapable and final, transfixes the whole creature and may serve, if one is interested, to bring out individual variations in attitude. Bérénice, though her life is seen only on the abstract stage of reason, nevertheless feels extremely female; and the great duet she has with Titus in the fourth act is full of the most delicate psychological insight. Moreover, Bérénice is felt as a particular woman, very different from Phèdre, for instance. All the encomiums which have been written on Racine's psychology, and the accuracy and resourcefulness of his "knowledge of the heart" have their justification, especially in his portraits of women. If the perspective he adopts is extremely narrow, it is extremely revealing; and his use of it is due to his austere and ambitious conception of form, and to the theater for which he was writing, rather than to lack of direct insight into the individualized diversity of life.

The fact is, of course, that it takes more than pure reason to make a tragedy. And whenever one studies the life of Racine's play, one sees that, for all its efforts toward universality, it is rooted in the actual life of a particular time and place, and fed with his own direct sense of life. And one encounters the fact that the theater of reason, which once seemed in its perfection to be *the* theater itself, preventing any other notion years after all life had left its beautiful forms, now looks as grotesquely French and Baroque as Louis himself; wig, laces, high heels, and all.

The Theater of Reason in Its Time and Place

Rationalistic philosophy bears a relation to Racine's tragedy like that of Aristotle's philosophy to the tragedy of Sophocles, and one may learn from it a good deal about Racine's notion of action, and also about his principles of composition. When Descartes deduces existence from thought, when he demands, for the proper conduct of the mind, clear and distinct ideas only—the clarity of mathematics—he might be describing the principles of Racine's dramaturgy. And Kant's *Metaphysic of Morals,* based upon the intuition of the soul as reasoning, and deducing an infallible guide to conduct from the notion of rationality itself, may be read as an exposition of the action of Bérénice. But the theater of reason, as it actually existed, was an expression of Baroque taste; and it was a public institution, with stage, actors, audience, and general support and comprehension. In short, it was a mirror of human life and action formed at a particular time and place, and enjoying a merely mortal life like that of any other real theater. Its rational principles no longer look self-evident and eternal to us; we see that Racine enjoyed a sanction which we have lost; and we are uncomfortable with the perfection of the mind which he achieved.

Professor Jacques Maritain* offers a perspective upon modern rationalism itself; he enables us to see the difference between the deified reason of the Age of Reason, and the realist intelligence of the Greek and Medieval tradition. Bergson, in *Les Deux Sources de la Morale et de la Religion,* offers another perspective on modern rationalism, derived from his studies of the

---

*For example in *Trois Réformateurs* ("Descartes"), *Réflexions sur l'Intelligence,* and *Distinguer pour Unir.*

role of reason in society. Taking direct issue with Kant, he says that the notion of the absolute constraint of reasonable duty (the basis of Racinian tragedy) is in fact always derived from a concrete and fixed social order. Only after such a social order is (more or less tacitly) accepted as final, can it be rationalized; and only then can one identify duty and reason as Racine and Kant do. The historic moment when ethics is based solely upon reason, would be the moment when society is not too visibly changing, and its order may therefore be regarded as both right and timeless. Such a society Bergson calls "closed": to the possibility of any change except mere destruction; to the sense of analogy between its form and that of different societies, past, present, or imagined; and to the possibility of a different relation between the human community and the surrounding world.

I do not know how accurately Bergson's description would apply to the historic France of Louis XIV; but it certainly describes the idealized society of Racine's theater, the official mirror of the times. The literal detail—the curls, the ruffles, the protocol, the manners—are frozen into immobility and fixed with extraordinary clarity by the eye of the mind; yet they are supposed to illustrate a social order which is univocally the same as that of Rome, Palestine, or Comagene. The people, whether "adorateur" or "volage," is kept off-stage; and upon the narrow platform of the eternal elite the reason focuses, with a passion for both literal and abstract perfection.

If one looks at Racine's theater from this alien point of view—not as truth itself, but as reflecting an image formed at a moment of history—it appears that this theater had its own kind of ceremonial significance: not the religious and natural ritual meaning of the Greek tragic theater, but the more limited and artificial significance of the *game*. M. Denis De Rougemont shows in *Love in the Western World* that during the period of the Enlightenment when society felt righteous and secure in itself, many social functions could be limited and defined, like games, by rules agreed on in advance. Even war, he says, was not our total conflict, but a limited contest for limited stakes, like chess. Strategy was prior to slaughter; form to content. Provinces might change hands, fines be paid, individuals lose their lives—but the basis of civilized life was not at stake. This account throws a good deal of light upon the sacrifice and the ceremonial game of Baroque tragedy. The "sacrifice" was the price of admission to the game: the acceptance of the authority of reason. Only the elite—only monarchs—were eligible; but by convention their ceremonious agony stood for human life itself, as the nuptial combats of queen bees, larger and gaudier than the workers, focus the life of their perfect societies. It is a grave, high, and civilized conception; yet it suffers from its too proud and drastic limitations. And (thinking of the wigs, the glitter, and the stink) one may be reminded of Cocteau's description of the style of his Antigone: "L'ensemble évoquant un carnaval sordide et royale, une famille d'insectes."

M. De Rougemont has very interesting things to say about Racine's *Phèdre*, which interests him as one version of the myth of passion which his book traces. He shows how much passionate life was poured into the reasoned form of the play, and caught in the eye of the mind. He says that Racine is more or less consciously continuing the heretical tradition of *Cortezia*, with its Courts of Love, and its knightly ordeals and game-like tourneys, games of passion. Racine is of course often described as celebrating not reason, but passion; he often thought of himself in this way, but saw no contradiction between *picturing* passion and adhering to his principles of reason and decorum. M. De Rougemont does see this contradiction, and emphasizes it, I think, to the point where the nature of Racine's art is obscured. Nevertheless, it is true that Racine's plays, and indeed Baroque art in general, show signs of strain, as though the rigid forms could not quite contain the life which they were supposed to. The universal terms in which the Neoclassic protagonist puts his plight—Rome frowns or trembles; the universe weeps or applauds—sound a little hysterical to us. The sculptured saints, writhing and weeping in their demand for Grace, seem impotent; the highly evolved dress in which the monarch expresses his reasoned responsibility looks like a sly vengeance of the creature upon his hard strait-jacket.

Bérénice is a convenient instance of this theater precisely because its highly conscious ethical theme is so largely the official theme of the period. But the Baroque dramatists sometimes tried to show moral change in their motionless mirror; and some of these efforts are very interesting, both when they succeed, and when their partial failures show the limitations of the theater of reason itself. Racine's *Phèdre* seems to me to be one of the successes, though it represents only the first step in moral change: dissolution of the rationalized moral being in passion or suffering. The play succeeds because Racine has shown this dissolution strictly from the point of view of the challenged reason. Phèdre appears, she even exists, only in its light; and when she can no longer obey reason she vanishes from the scene:

> Et la mort, à mes yeux dérobant la clarté
> Rend au jour qu'ils souillaient toute sa pureté.

> (And death, taking the light of my eyes away
> Restores to the day they soiled its purity.)

Corneille's *Polyeucte* is more interesting in this connection, because it is designed to show change, of exactly the complete kind upon which the tragic rhythm of Dante and Sophocles is based: from one rational form of human life to another analogous one based upon a wider vision. *Polyeucte, Martyr* is supposed to show the transformation of a pagan gentleman into a Christian saint. But few readers, I think, can believe that a change of heart is really the material of this play. When we first see Polyeucte his Christian friend Néarque is urging him to be baptized, and Polyeucte (taking at this moment a role like that of the *confidents* in *Bérénice*) is presenting all the practical objections—his baptism for instance would alienate his lawful and beloved wife Pauline. When we next see Néarque and Polyeucte, the latter has received the impact of Grace off-stage and been shifted in a twinkling to the level of the martyr: he wants to court death itself by smashing the statues of the pagan gods. Now it is Néarque who plays the *confident*, and presents the practical drawbacks to martyrdom, and Polyeucte who sets forth the logical consistency of his position as saint. In the last part of the play Corneille wishes to contrast the impeccable Christian Polyeucte with the impeccably pagan Roman gentleman Sévère, who is hopelessly in love *à la* Antiochus with

Polyeucte's wife Pauline. But Polyeucte's Christian-tragic renunciation of Pauline seems to be the same action as Sévère's heroic-rational renunciation. Polyeucte's Christian postulate contradicts Sévère's pagan one, but both are based equally upon the integrity of the reasoning soul; and both gentlemen aspire to increase their "gloire" by renouncing the unfortunate Pauline. Polyeucte is proved to be a saint; everything he does, and everything he explains about his feelings, follow with the inevitability of logic from this reasoned position. But the divine irruption of Grace has broken neither the glittering surface of the salon, the politeness of the characters, nor the motionless mirror of reason. In a detailed study of *Polyeucte* one would try to distinguish the piety and the sense of purgatorial change, which Corneille may himself have had, from the picture he presents in the rationalistic terms of his theater. And one would point to moments (like Polyeucte's beautiful lyric, an anomaly in this theater) when Corneille seems to be feeling for a wider stage and a more flexible medium. But the general point would, I think, be substantiated: the change from one level of awareness to another cannot be shown in the rigidly "ideal" theater of the time.

The Baroque notion of "gloire" as we find it throughout *Bérénice, Phèdre,* and *Polyeucte,* indicates both the ideal social hierarchy and the ideal, timeless moment of action of the theater of reason. It would seem on this evidence that when the elite of the age of Louis XIV felt rationality histrionically, whether in the salon or the theater, they called it "gloire." In these three plays the word refers to all the ways in which the individual, in his obedience to reason, could shine forth to his audience. At one extreme, "gloire" is only reputation, as in the scene between Phèdre and Oenone, when they are afraid Thésée will discover what Phèdre has said to Hyppolite. At the other extreme is the "gloire" which Polyeucte seeks in martyrdom. In every instance "gloire" means obedience to reason and duty through the rejection of passion. These uses of the word seem to us to be different; but in the ideal scheme of the theater of reason they were one. The inner light and the glare of publicity, the eye of God and the salon of the Roi Soleil, were all identified, as "gloire," with the unchanging light of reason. So Polyeucte the martyr is as heroic as Sévère the gentleman; and though he stands upon another platform, it is still the platform of reason, bright with the same unchanging "gloire."

If one compares the Baroque theater with the tragic theater of the Greeks, it is evident that the Baroque theater is closed in every way in which Sophocles' theater is open. The scene of *Oedipus* is open to daylight, to common sense, to popular tradition conveyed in myth and ritual; it is sacred, but accessible to all: the old shepherd, with his wilderness taciturnity, has his view of the common mystery of human life, and it is as valid in its way as Creon's or Tiresias'. Behind the human scene we feel the wider scene, dim to us, which only the gods, in the surrounding hills or under the earth, fully understand. That is why the rhythm of human life can be presented here in its shifting forms, and in the varied perspectives of reason and pathos. If the action of Oedipus could be lifted out of the endless rhythm of the play at the moment when he first meets Tiresias' opposition, and repeated again and again without change, he would look like a Baroque hero. If we could see only through his eyes at this timeless moment, we should see a scene like that of the Theater of Reason. Oedipus' rationalization of his moral being, and of his duty as monarch, would be fixed at the brink of his perpetually rejected passion of fear and anger. The order of Oedipus' regime in Thebes would look reasonable, literally perfect, and "closed," both to the potentialities of change represented by the chorus, and to the hidden knowledge of the gods represented by Tiresias. But though Sophocles shows the rational action of the soul, he does not accept it as final, nor close his view of the human situation within the scene which reason reveals.

The *Purgatorio*, as I have pointed out, is the most highly developed presentation of the tragic rhythm of human action which we possess; and in it also the moment of reason and moral responsibility recurs in many figures. In Canto xviii of the *Purgatorio*, Dante the pilgrim, growing up, growing sadder, wiser, and more responsible, is told by Virgil of the rational will which he has experienced and may now hear majestically named:

Coloro che ragionando andaro al fondo
s'accorser d'esta innata libertate,
però moralità lasciaro al mondo.

(Those who in their reasoning went to the foundation,
perceived this innate freedom, wherefore they left
ethics to the world.)

The rational-moral action of the soul, in its opposition to sensation and emotion, is material of the daylight scenes in the central cantos of the *Purgatorio*. The pilgrim, in his climb, is under the sign of "reason," and must endeavor to reduce the world he sees to its facts and univocal concepts. Sometimes he sees things with photographic but meaningless clarity, like the black, the white, and the red stair in the brilliant morning light. Sometimes his rationalization makes him reject the world *in toto*, as all black, for which he is scolded: *Lo mondo è cieco, e tu vien ben da lui* ("the world is blind, and you come from the world indeed"). If he attempts to conceive God, it is in the abstractions of rationalistic Deism. But this action of reason, which is presented in so many ways, is taken as part of a wider and longer action, and placed in a scene or "theater" which, like the real world, is wider than reason itself. Thus the pilgrim's reasoned concepts never quite fit, and he is troubled, even in his rationalizing, by sensuous images of undecipherable significance; by sympathetic awareness of other persons, by a vague desire for light and freedom of another order, and by memories of his unregenerate state when his soul, in the innocence of childhood and with an animal-like unity of thought and feeling, moved simply "toward what delights it." Dante shows the Baroque split between passion and reason in a thousand forms; but because he has his eye always upon "the whole psyche in its total situation" he never senses this split as final, and never makes a fetish and a static scene out of purely rational modes of understanding.

The action of reason which makes Baroque drama, corresponds to these moments in the tragic rhythm of Sophocles and Dante; and the Theater of Reason represents the human condition as it appears at that abstracted, timeless moment: clear, known, and unchanging. It is a much more limited view of the human than that of Sophocles or Dante; but, with its precision and integrity, it is both deep and inescapable. Moreover the very limitation of this view permits a kind of artistic perfection or absoluteness, which Sophocles did not even seek. The Baroque drama itself, as we look back on it, betrays its mortality: it obviously depends upon the sanctions and the fetishes of its time and place, like other forms which make less absolute pretensions. But it offers one of the few great images of human life and action, and its principles and habits of mind are still with us in a thousand forms.

The Diminished Scene of Modern Rationalism

It has been necessary to study the notion of the Baroque theater from several points of view (perhaps at the cost of repetitiousness) because of its crucial importance in our tradition. In the age of Racine, many enduring foundations were laid down, which still determine our efforts to understand both our own times and the more remote past. We still have a habitual tendency to look at the Greeks rationalistically, and to lump Racine and Sophocles together as simply "classic." And though Baroque drama makes a first impression of old-fashioned stiffness, many of its principles still govern the writing of plays, especially those which are supposed to be the most up-to-date and enlightened.

If we have lost the tradition represented by Sophocles, Dante, and Shakespeare beyond all recovery, it is hard to see how we can escape the heroic principles of the Age of Reason. It is natural and courageous to try (as Racine did) to face the human scene as we see it literally before us; fix it in the light of reason, and present a logically coherent picture of it. It is natural to demand that the past measure up (or down) to our reasoned views, and to reject all other modes of understanding as primitive, vague, and childish. There is a close and self-conscious kinship between Valéry's version of the plight of reason, and Racine's, as I indicated at the beginning of this chapter. Joyce's one play, *Exiles,* presents a reasoned moral effort of an almost Racinian strictness—which seems all the more strict because it is incongruously placed in a contemporary naturalistic setting. Eliot's *Murder in the Cathedral* and Cocteau's *The Infernal Machine* both employ versions of Neoclassic dramaturgy. I propose to return to these plays below apropos, of the modern poetic theater.

These writers provide a bridge to Racine; but they show also how far we are from the Baroque theater as a living institution at the center of society, and of society's awareness of itself. In spite of the intellectual and artistic triumphs of the modern writers, we cannot say what relation they have to the modern world. What relation is possible to a society with no actual focus of understanding, responsible power, common values?

The full life of the Baroque theater lasted only about two generations. It is true that the Comédie Française still preserves it as a precious heirloom. But by the early nineteenth century (certainly by the time Sardon wrote *The Black Pearl*) another, far cruder but more generally useful, notion of dramatic form had developed, which came to be known as that of the "well-made play." This recipe for play-making has enabled countless dramatists to present the uncentered busyness of our times in entertaining forms. It is taught in innumerable courses in playwriting, and it is the machinery both of the erotic intrigues of the entertainment industry, and of the thesis-plays of Marxians and other social reformers. It is essentially a rationalized art of plot-making, with a very narrow purpose; and it is derived from one aspect of the Baroque plot. In it one may see how a reduced version of drama as rational survives into our day.

In studying the form of Racinian tragedy, I showed that the plot (or formal cause) was best understood as "the demonstration of an essence": i.e., the tragic life of the soul as reasoning. In this view, Racine's plot answers to Aristotle's definition: it is the soul of tragedy, as the soul is said to be the form of the body—it realizes that mode of action which is the matter of the play. But since Racine assumed this mode of action, he never talked about it, and when he says *plot* he usually means simply the intrigue—plot in Aristotle's second sense—the facts of the situation and their logical concatenation. By means of the intrigue he could hold the interest of the audience, and build it to a point of high excitement, whether that audience was interested in the life of reason or not. In *Bérénice* these two aspects of the Rational plot are easy to distinguish. At every moment the tragic plight of reason is made clear, if we care to look at it; hence the crystalline intellectual consistency and the beauty of form. But the incidents are also so arranged as to pique our curiosity about the literal facts of the story. Will Bérénice relent, and accept Antiochus? Will the Roman Senate change its mind? Which of the men will Bérénice marry? Every act ends with such a question, and by this means "suspense" is built up, and we are held by the machinery of the intrigue until the denouement. This aspect of the art of plot-making follows quite naturally from the rational basis of Racine's art; and he and Corneille were very proud of it. They rightly saw that the whole notion of suspense, to be gained through alternately piquing and thwarting our curiosity about the literal facts of the situation, was a discovery of theirs: Sophocles, with his ritual basis, does not primarily seek suspense of this kind.

The art of the well-made play is plot-making in the second sense (of arranging the intrigue to pique the curiosity) but not in the first: blind to the formal cause of tragedy, it does not envisage the art of the drama as the imitation of action at all, but as a means of gripping the audience in abstraction from all content whatever. Its purpose is solely to catch the mind of the audience, and to hold it by alternately satisfying and thwarting the needs of the discursive reason. That is why, like engineering, it is so generally useful. The great Sarcey said that the art of drama can only be understood as that of holding an audience in a theater; beyond that it is merely a subjective matter of taste. The art of the well-made plot is based on this rational-empirical notion, and it is a device which works infallibly. It is pernicious only because it does work so well. In the nineteenth century its "objective facts" and its logical machinery seemed to define the scene and the shape of human life itself. Even an Ibsen could hardly see that his direct and subtle vision of life would demand a different version of dramatic form for its complete realization on the stage, and some of his best plays are marred by the meretricious effectiveness of the well-made plot, which he understood and handled so well.

The well-made plot has in common with Racinian tragedy the "scene" of the discursive reason. In *Bérénice*, the intrigue is logically analyzed by Antiochus and Arsace; in *Phèdre*, by Phèdre and her *confidente* Oenone. The *confidents* (looking as it were outward, at the situation) are very alert to the facts, and very logical, and they ask all the questions which a shrewd audience, that wanted to know how the story turned out, would ask. But they are free from all sense of the peril, the responsibility, and the limitations of reason itself, which makes the tragic life of the protagonist—and fixes, as "facts," the situation and the scene in which they are so agile. As the life gradually left the Baroque theater—when the society of Louis XIV ceased to seem eternal, and the strictness of reason itself no longer could be accepted as the one infallible guide to conduct—the protagonist (Phèdre, or Bérénice, or the life of reason which they illustrate) disappeared, and the cynical Oenones and practical Arsaces took the stage. After the "categorical imperative," the "felicific calculus": reason itself no longer appears, but the stage is still the static "scene" which reason has fixed, the movement of the intrigue is still the mechanical one of the rationalized plot.

If one could understand the properties of the well-made plot, one could understand a great deal about the whole modern theater. Because it is so abstract, and so limited in purpose, it can use the facts of any situation and confer upon their presentation the same cachet of professional competence. But because it assumes so narrow and static a scene, so impoverished a human life and action, the ostensible variety it presents—from the ancient Rome of Robert Sherwood to the Alabama of Lillian Hellman—is illusory: its agile little life is actually unchanging and meaningless. I shall return to this point below, when I study the attempts of Ibsen and of Shaw to work out forms which would be truer to their real sense of life.

But the stultifying limitations of the rationalized scene were felt as soon as it took over the public theater of Europe; and the romanticists sought in many ways to break or to escape its shackles. By the time of Wagner a form of drama which rejects not only the static scene of rationalism, but reason itself, was fully developed. Wagnerian music drama, as we see it in *Tristan und Isolde*, is the diametric opposite of Racine's tragedy of reason, though in its artistic absoluteness it is the same.

CHAPTER III

TRISTAN UND ISOLDE: THE ACTION AND THEATER OF PASSION

Affection! thy intention stabs the centre:
Thou dost make possible things not so held,
Communicat'st with dreams;—how can this be?—
With what's unreal thou coactive art,
And fellow'st nothing. —*The Winter's Tale*

From Racine to Wagner

THE conception of the theater and of the dramatic art which is realized in Wagner's *Tristan und Isolde* is as complete and self-conscious as Racine's. Wagner also went back to the foundations; and *Tristan*, like Neoclassic tragedy, is supposed to be the very spirit of Greek tragedy reborn in the modern world. The image of human life and action, the art of drama, and the underlying idea of a theater which we find in *Tristan* are as "ideal"—as absolute and final—as Racine's, but opposed in almost every respect to the tragedy and the theater of reason.

Between the time when the theater of reason was alive and the time of Wagner, fundamental changes had occurred in the life of Europe and in the theaters which reflected it. In the foreground, throughout the nineteenth century, the newly rich bourgeoisie (Matthew Arnold's Philistines) is in secure possession, held together by rigid political and social forms, and complacently viewing itself in the commercial theater. The commercial theater, or as we now call it, the Entertainment Industry, presents the literal facts of contemporary life and the endless intrigues of the well-made play: in short, that static and impoverished "scene of rationalism" (as I described it in the last chapter). But in the background, the masses, having lost their moorings in tradition, are on that march of which we do not yet see the end; while the gloomy artist-prophets proclaim in a thousand ways that the public life of the times—the marketable product, the acceptable human image—is stultifying and illusory.

One can see in a general way that Wagner belongs among the artist-prophets (as I have called them); that he is akin to Beethoven, to Delacroix, to Ibsen, to Dostoevsky. At the beginning of his career he tried to make common cause with the political revolutionaries also. But we do not yet know what to make of the romantic and revolutionary movements of the period; I suppose we are still in them. We can see that *Tristan* represents the end, the classic statement, of *one* impulse inherent in the romantic tradition. We can see that in it the conception of human life, and of the art of imitating it, has come full circle since Racine. Reason itself is rejected, along with the diminished rationalizations of the commercial theater, and the whole action and meaning is placed in a realm which Racine thought of as outer darkness. But we cannot say that *Tristan* epitomizes the whole romantic impulse, or even that it realizes all the potentialities in Wagner's inspiration. Both he and Nietzsche at last rejected *Tristan:* they tried to recover and move on.

Tristan is important for my purposes, a crucial instance of the art of drama, because it is comparable in depth and artistic integrity with the Neoclassic theater and with the Greeks; but to understand it one must form some idea of its *raison d'être*, its life in its own time and place. I do not wish to try to trace the genesis of Wagner's theater historically. But in order to compare it with Racine's, one must propose some notion of the problems and purposes of the great romantics. And for this purpose the general scheme which Bergson sets forth in *Les Deux Sources de la Religion et de la Morale* is again very useful.

I have explained how his description of the "closed" and completely rationalized society helps one to understand the actual social focus of the Baroque theater. Similarly his description of society and the individual soul at the historic moment of transition out of a closed society applies in a general way to the historic moment of *Tristan*, gives one a clue to its actual life in romantic Europe. The prophetic artists and the revolutionaries of the nineteenth century have at least this in common, that they proclaim the deathliness of the static, closed bourgeois society, and attempt to take their stand in a wider and truer scene than the reduced, rationalized scene which was publicly accepted.

But how can we determine whether the prophets of doom, or of a better life—in heaven or in the future—are telling the truth about the wider stage of human life which they have experienced and we have not? They try to make us share their emotion and see their visions, but they do not accept either the literal facts or the clear little rationalizations of our habitual life. How can we distinguish between the visions of the artist or mystic and the hallucinations of the psychopath? Bergson's answer to such questions as these (which are very properly asked about romantic art) is that the psychopath suffers his hallucinations for themselves, to no further end, while the great artist or the mystic suffers his emotion and his visions in view of a new stable condition, a new order which he demands, and foresees as it were by faith:

"The truth," he writes, "that these abnormal states (of the artist or mystic) have their resemblance to and sometimes also no doubt their participation in morbid states, will easily be understood if one considers the disturbance which is the passage from the static to the dynamic, from the closed to the open, from habitual life to the mystic life. When the obscure depths of the soul are agitated, what rises to the surface and reaches consciousness, there takes on, if the intensity is sufficient, the form of an image or of an emotion. The image is most often only a hallucination, just as the emotion is only futile agitation. But both indicate that the disturbance is a systematic rearrangement looking toward a higher equilibrium: the image is then symbolic of what is being prepared, and the emotion is a concentration of the soul in the expectation of a transformation."*

Bergson here describes with great exactness the recurrent moment of pathos in the tragic rhythm: the choruses in *Oedipus*, and the nights on the Mount of Purgatory, when the surge of emotion with its sensuous images is suffered *in the expectation of a transformation*. It is this "concentration in expectation" (the

Les Deux Sources de la Morale et de la Religion, p. 220. Editions Albert Skira, Geneva, 1945. My translation.

piety of Sophocles' chorus, the obedience under the sign of Faith, Hope, and Charity, of Dante the pilgrim) which gives form to the passion itself; places it in a wider rhythm of life and action, and in due time brings it to an end. It is evident that this passion of purgation is quite unlike the luxury of merely yielding to feeling, the gloomy satisfaction which does not look beyond the dissolution of the moral being; and the questions to ask about romantic art are whether dissolution or a new equilibrium is envisaged; and in the latter case, what the "new equilibrium" seems to be.

I suppose that much romantic art does not look beyond the feeling itself; that it does not, therefore, have much meaning except in relation to the psychology of the artist; and that it may in good conscience be abandoned to the psychopathologists. But when it succeeds as art, the artist has envisaged or expected a transformation, and this expectation gives a *generally* significant form to his emotion and his sensuous images. One must understand this element of natural faith in order to grasp the *raison d'être* of the romantic movement in its time and place. One may then see that it represents a movement of the psyche at least as natural, healthy, and true to experience as the snug positivism which it so totally rejects. Baudelaire makes this clear in his *L'Art Romantique,* especially in the essays devoted to the defense of Delacroix and Wagner from the nimble Philistines of Paris. For he is concerned with the order and intelligibility of the works of these masters as much as he is with their passion; and he opposes to the little scene of rationalism, not formless emotion, but the expectation of life transformed upon a wider stage.

After paying his respects to that vulgar journalism, with its *gamineries professionelles,* which surrounded the theater in Paris —the rationalized stage which had rejected Wagner, as Wagner rejected it—Baudelaire proceeds to describe the sources and principles of Wagner's art-of-passion. "The man who wrote that 'he who was not endowed by the fairies, from his cradle, with the spirit of dissatisfaction with all that exists, will never come to the discovery of the new,' must certainly find more suffering than anyone else in the conflicts of life. It is from this

proneness to suffer, common to all artists, and greater in proportion as the instinct for the just [*le juste*] and the beautiful is
stronger, that I derive the explanation of Wagner's revolutionary opinions." The source of Wagner's revolutionary opinions
(political, artistic, or religious) is passion or suffering; but this
is of a piece with the instinct for "le juste et le beau"; and Baudelaire shows the rightness and beauty of those passionate dramas,
Tannhäuser and *The Flying Dutchman*. They are plotted dramatically with the utmost clarity, consistency, and concious
technical control; and in both the music presents and discriminates the movements of feeling with extraordinary accuracy.
Moreover, both works are based upon legends, or myths, and
the myth also represents a certain principle of order and intelligibility. Baudelaire quotes Wagner himself on this subject: "In
the myth, human relations almost completely lose their conventional form, which is intelligible only to the abstract reason;
they show what is eternally human and eternally comprehensible in life, and show it in that concrete form, exclusive of all
imitation, which gives all true myths their individual character."
The passages from Wagner which Baudelaire quotes at this
point, together with his comments and elaborations, constitute a
classic statement of what artists in every generation seek in
myths: an ordering of human experience at a level (or in a
"scene") wider, deeper, and more permanent than the rationalized scene and the literal facts of the moment.

In order to learn how to realize his myths on the stage, Wagner took the road which Corneille and Racine had followed
before him: he sought in Greek tragedy the fundamental principles of his art. Here again he seems to expect a transformation
and a new equilibrium, as Baudelaire shows in his quotations
from the *Letter on Music* and the preface to *Opera and Drama*,
where Wagner himself explains his recourse to the Greeks. But—
again like Corneille and Racine—Wagner found what he was
looking for rather than the Greeks themselves as they now
appear to us. He sought and found, as Baudelaire put it, "the
absolute and despotic esthetic of a dramatic ideal in which
everything—from a declamation so carefully notated and under-
lined by the music that it is impossible for a singer to deviate

by a syllable, a veritable arabesque of sounds designed by passion, down to the most minute care for the setting and staging—where *all* the details must incessantly concur in the one effect."

Baudelaire was fully aware that Wagner's despotic art was very different from that of a Sophocles, and the whole passage is important for understanding the relations between romantic and Sophoclean tragedy. Baudelaire relishes the Black Mass aspect of Wagner's drama without supposing that it is Greek. If the spirit of Greek tragedy is alive again in Wagner's opera, he says, it is no longer in the real world, but "at the bottom of a cave, magnificent it is true, but lit by fires which are not those of the benevolent Phoebus." In short, Baudelaire sees Wagner very clearly. But the special value of his study, an apologia for the whole Romantic movement as he saw it, is that it makes clear the objective basis, the historic necessity for this movement; and he shows how it sought the esthetically satisfying order and the wider and more timeless meanings which artists of all kinds and periods seek. Society was suffering the long transition from the closed and static order of rationalism; but the artist-prophets of the period suffered the passions of dissolution "in concentration and expectation," and their sensuous and dreamlike images are "symbolic of what is being prepared."

The crucial question with regard to any particular work of the period is what the artist saw "as being prepared." *Tristan und Isolde* (the subject of this chapter) interprets the dissolution in passion of the closed scene of reason in a uniquely seductive way. Passion itself is taken as the paradoxical clue to human life transformed; to the true nocturnal scene of our existence; and to the "absolute and despotic" form of the work itself. It is evident that we are here again on the edge of Freudian psychopathology, and many have tried to interpret *Tristan* as only a symptom of the disturbances in Wagner's own psyche following his thwarted affair with Frau Wesendonck. But the power of the work itself, demonstrated again and again in every capital of Europe and in America, and resting upon its own perfect order, shows that it has very wide meanings, and its own esthetic validity. Passion is the clue, but this gloomy clue is followed by an all-out effort of the will and the intelligence. Like other great dramas, *Tristan* is the imitation of a certain action: it shows with finality one direction which the lost spirit may take.

Nietzsche's *The Birth of Tragedy from the Spirit of Music* is chiefly concerned with the "spirit" which he takes to be the root of Greek tragedy. But he wrote the book under the direct inspiration of *Tristan;* the "Music" in his title is Wagner's music, and the spirit in question is that which he felt so powerfully alive in the opera. Looking at Greek tragedy in this light, he decided that the spiritual root of that form was most directly expressed in the unindividualized passion of the Aeschylean and Sophoclean chorus—especially those choruses (like the next to the last in Sophocles' *Antigone*) where Dionysos is directly invoked, and the feeling most violent. The great value of Nietzsche's book is that it enables one to see where the action of *Tristan* is related to that of the Sophoclean tragic rhythm: namely, at the moment when passion breaks through the conflicts of the protagonists, with their individual beings and their reasoned platforms, and before this surge of feeling and imagery has assumed the form which the pious expectation of the Sophoclean chorus will give it. This "moment" is just after that of reason and individual responsibility which, as we saw, Racine took as the clue to life and action.

But when one tries to see what Nietzsche means by this formless passion, one is left literally in the dark. He describes this *Wille*, as he calls it (so like Freud's libido) in a thousand ways. But when he wrote *The Birth of Tragedy* he was a believer in the *Tristan* revelation, and so accepted its passion as ultimate: being in nothingness, light in darkness, and the like. Even to. say (as I wish to do) that the Wagnerian passion stems from a moment in the tragic rhythm is to do violence to the faith. Thus Nietzsche says nothing about the intelligible elements in the opera. The characters, the story, the events themselves, are regarded merely as expressions of the underlying passion. Even the myth of *Tristan*, on this basis, would be regarded as superficial, a necessary concession to our mortal darkness, but essentially illusory.

Fortunately it is precisely the *myth* of *Tristan*—its probable sources in an ancient heretical cult of passion, its realization in Wagner's opera, and its all-pervasive influence in modern life—which is the subject of De Rougemont's *Love in the Western World*. I have referred to it already in connection with Racine. M. De Rougemont points out that it was the ancient tale of *Tristan und Isolde*, victims and adepts of the fatality of passion, which enabled Wagner to realize his gloomy vision dramatically, and it is this myth which enables M. De Rougemont in turn to place the Wagnerian inspiration with reference to the real world, to other faiths, and to other versions of human action. An all-devouring passion which, as Leontes says in *The Winter's Tale*, intends to "stab the center," to make possible the impossible, and invert the real and the unreal, had been pictured before; but only Wagner endeavors to accept such a passion on its own terms. The myth of Tristan is the bridge, for him and for us, between the real world and that worldless world which absolute passion demands.

Tristan as Myth and as Ritual

The story of Tristan and Isolde has been retold, like all myths, many times, with endless variations and elaborations. For his opera Wagner selected what he thought the essential elements: such circumstances, characters and events as would convey most powerfully and simply the gloomy fatality of passion which he took to be the life and meaning of the legend, and (at that time, at least) of human existence in general. The story he tells is the following:

The knight Tristan was adopted by his uncle, King Mark of Cornwall, and lived at the Cornish Court. In the wars between Cornwall and Ireland, Tristan killed the Irish knight Morold, who was the fiancé of Isolde, Princess of Ireland. Isolde found Tristan wounded after his battle with Morold, and though he called himself Tantris, she recognized him. She was about to stab him, when a glance from his eyes filled her with pity. At this moment passion marks Tristan and Isolde for its own, but both impiously refuse to recognize it. Isolde, who is a sorceress, cures Tristan with her magic arts and sends him back to Cornwall. In Cornwall Tristan rather disingenuously persuades King.

Mark to marry the incomparable Isolde; and Mark sends him back to Ireland to fetch her. On the ship returning to Cornwall and King Mark, the lovers at last recognize the passion which ties them together, and to escape it they agree to seek release in death. They drink a cup which they think is poison. But Brangaene, Isolde's nurse, has substituted the love potion for the death potion; and now Tristan and Isolde feel their subjection to passion in all its scope and irresistible force. They seal their fate with a single kiss, just before their ship docks. But later, in Cornwall, after Isolde's marriage to Mark, they deceive the King. Melot, Tristan's friend, betrays them. He interrupts the lovers' night with King Mark and many followers; fights with Tristan, and wounds him. Tristan's faithful Kurwenal takes him home, to his own ruined castle on the edge of the sea. There Tristan dies—but not before Isolde has found him again. She dies too, and in their death they find the fulfillment of their passion.

This story has much in common with other tales of fatal love —that of Romeo and Juliet, for instance, or of Paolo and Francesca—which lead to love-in-death, death-in-love, the death of love, and the love of death. But Dante and Shakespeare (though they convey the experience with incomparable poignancy) do not identify themselves with the fatality of passion, nor ask us to. This is precisely what Wagner does do: he takes the inner, nocturnal world of passion as real, and the common outer world as illusory, rejecting not only the little scene of bourgeois respectability, but the objective scene of common sense altogether. *Tristan und Isolde* is not so much a love-story as it is the celebration of a mystical motive; not the story of a passion, as we observe it realistically, attached to some object—the passion for golf, or Beethoven, or Lana Turner—but the mystic obedience to passion itself. This, according to M. De Rougemont, is the real meaning of the Tristan myth: Wagner, he thinks, felt it truly, and conveyed it with unique force.

The great value of M. De Rougemont's book for the purposes of this study, is that he enables one to understand the "magical" power which all feel in a good performance of the opera: a magic which uses the most searchingly intimate erotic incitements to enthrall, but not to satisfy, the hearer, i.e., in the service of an essentially insatiable and undefinable longing. The myth, he tells us, is rooted in an ancient and half-forgotten pessimistic and ascetic cult of passion; in the Cathars' heretical Church of Love, and in the pagan sources of Gaelic literature. "Taking these convergences in the aggregate," he writes (*op. cit.*, p. 111) "it becomes possible to say that the passionate love which the myth celebrates actually became in the twelfth century—the moment when first it began to be cultivated—a religion in the full sense of the word, and in particular a Christian heresy historically determined."

It is easy for me to believe that Wagner's opera does reawaken to life such ancient forms buried in our culture, just as it taps obscure sources in the individual psyche; but I, of course, leave the historic questions to those competent to deal with them. Certainly the action of Wagner's music drama, as we come to know it in the work itself, is such a mystic and absolute obedience to passion as M. De Rougemont describes. And the actual form of the opera may be understood as both the myth and the ritual of a religion of passion.

Thus the myth of Tristan serves, in the opera, the purpose which Wagner describes in the passage quoted by Baudelaire: it shows concretely what is "eternally human and eternally comprehensible in life"—i.e., passion as the one reality in our experience. (This is a very different sense of human life and destiny from the one conveyed by Sophocles by means of the myth, and the ritual tragedy, of *Oedipus;* and from this circumstance one may derive a certain skepticism about the notion of myth-in-general, as well as a more timid respect for the anomalous power which great myths manifest from time to time.)

M. De Rougemont also shows how Wagner's opera is based upon the chief moments in the Cathars' ritual of passion. As in the case of *Oedipus,* the connection between the ritual and the drama is in the action which the author feels they share: the Cathars' ritual, and Wagner's opera, both imitate and celebrate the mystic obedience to passion. The first act of *Tristan* corresponds to the Cathars' Initiation: the lovers, on the ship bound for Cornwall, drink the potion which reveals to them the "real" world of passion. They exchange one kiss, corresponding to the

Cathars' *consolamentum;* the one physical satisfaction permitted to adepts of the ascetic cult. Act II is "the passion song of souls imprisoned in material form." It is the lovers' night; the triumph and the failure of lust—from the point of view of the cult, a sin and a mistake. Act III is "fatal fulfillment"; the end of the Cathars' heretical via purgativa; light in darkness, love in death, realization in nothingness, and the like.

With these clues in mind one can,. I think, account for the contradictory impressions which *Tristan* makes at different times, and upon different auditors. It certainly has, as many have pointed out, a desperate and gloomy eroticism, close to suicidal longings, and on the brink of some sort of psychopathic dissolution. But these images and emotions, these exorbitant and solitary glooms, are (in M. Bergson's phrase once more) suffered "in the expectation of a transformation" and "as symbolic of what is being prepared." *Tristan* is akin to other great romantic works, which arose out of the disturbing rejection of bourgeois conventions. It has the religious import which the young Nietzsche felt in it: the obedience to passion which underlies it is a mystic obedience.

This action—"to obey Passion as the one reality"—is the basis of Wagner's very original dramaturgy. The opera in its every detail "imitates" this action; or, as Wagner himself might have put it, "expresses" the absolute passion which possessed him.

The Dramaturgy of *Tristan*

If one thinks of *Tristan und Isolde* as simply another love-story, one can see that it is plotted on the serviceable principles of the well-made play. The first act is an exposition of the basic conflict, that between the love of Tristan and Isolde and their moral obligations, especially to King Mark. It ends with an incident which raises the suspense: they kiss just as the ship docks, and the curtain falls with a burst of musical excitement. The second act is built on top of the first, and shows the overt deed which the first act promised. This act also ends with an exciting event, the betrayal and the stabbing; and the second act curtain marks the "climax" of the conflict. The third act is the denouement: all is resolved, or dissolved, in death.

The single purpose of this scheme, thus abstractly understood, is to hold and excite the audience by means of the *facts* of the story. It would have been equally useful as the framework for a drama of ethical motivation, like Racinian tragedy; the same facts, in the same order, might have been used to present the life of the reasoning soul in its struggle with inclination, instead of the invisible life of passion transcending rationalizable reality altogether. Thus the plot of the opera as "intrigue" shows something about Wagner's relation to the audience, and something about the well-made play, but very little about his real principles of composition.

In order to investigate these, one must, as usual, consider the plot as the first form which the action (in this case the "action of passion") takes; i.e., as the "soul of the tragedy." It is then clear how the first act may be regarded (on the ritual analogy) as initiation; the second as the struggle of passion in its worldly prison, and the third as fated fulfillment, or the passionate transcendance of the world altogether. Wagner has so arranged the incidents of the story as always to show on stage passionate moments. These successive moments constitute a sequence, or rhythm of feeling, or (if one thinks of them together, instead of in the temporal succession in which we get them) a spectrum of emotions generated by absolute passion in its struggle out of the illusory world. We are led from the remote nostalgic aspiration of the beginnings of Act I, to the close violence of the lovers' night in Act II, and thence to the physically spent, but paradoxically comforted, release of the love-death.

What Wagner is "imitating" by means of these events is a passion which knows no bounds, in spite of its physical involvements. But the plot is only the "first actualization," and Wagner also imitates or expresses the life of passion by means of his personages, the ideas they express, and the imagery of the poetry and of the stage-setting.

When the curtain rises after the overture, we see Isolde and her faithful Brangaene moping in a curtained part of the ship, and we hear a young sailor, aloft in the rigging, sing the following words:

Westwarts	Westward
Schweift der Blick;	your eyes stray;
ostwarts	eastward
streicht das Schiff.	the ship flies.
Frisch weht der Wind	Fresh blows the wind
der Heimat zu;	toward home;
mein irisch Kind,	my Irish child,
wo weilest du?	where are you lingering?

The words define the beginnings of the objectless movement, and the insubstantial scene, of passion. Isolde is looking one way, and going another. She is leaving home, on a ship going home; and on the other hand she is not moving at all, but "lingering." These willful paradoxes do not cohere logically; but the sensations of getting nowhere with the utmost speed; of leaving and coming at once, all in a languor of gloom, do compose to define a moment of feeling with great accuracy. It is the beginning of that course of passion which is the life of the drama.

Isolde, in despair and anger, tells Brangaene the story of her relations with Tristan: his present black aloofness, staring at the sea; the savagery and self-pity of their first meeting, with Tristan wounded and Isolde bent on murder; and finally the sinister fatality which brings them together on the ship. Wagner continues to develop this relation as though passion created both the characters and the circumstances. To follow this development, with its "logic of feeling," one must feel the passion directly—excluding the perspectives of reason on pain of having it all break up in absurdity. Would Isolde's and Tristan's passion be satisfied by lust, murder, or suicide? Suicide seems to the lovers the most promising means of release, and they drink the cup which they think will be their death. When it turns out to be in fact a love-potion, their kiss seems equally right and equally obedient to the other-worldly fate which commands them. So Wagner contrives to bring the passion, which first appeared far off, like an airplane on the horizon, roaring over us with all its power.

Mr. Kenneth Burke, in an essay entitled "Psychology and Form," distinguishes two kinds of literary composition, "syllogistic progression," in which the reader is led from one part of the composition to another by means of logical relationships, and "qualitative progression" (characteristic of modern lyric poetry), in which the reader is led, according to a "logic of feeling," by means of association and contrast. Syllogistic progression well describes the principles of composition of Baroque tragedy; and qualitative progression the principles on which Wagner's music-drama is composed: he composes, not with real and substantial persons and things, but with qualities. Thus the ship which carries Isolde is not a ship in its own right, but only those aqueous and unfixed qualities which it shares with the lost beginnings of passion. As for the wind, it would ruin everything to know its velocity in knots; it is (like Isolde's sighs) merely one of the dreamlike emanations of passion. Even the characters are not to be thought of as real, but only as shifting moral qualities which express passion—or, from the point of view of the audience, induce passion. By thus composing with qualities only (sensuously and emotionally charged appearances) passion becomes the one reality in the drama. If you think realistically of Wagner's act of composition, you might say that he selected only such qualities of persons and things as would convey the passion he intended. But if you think of his creative art as German idealism would describe it—as Nietzsche, following Schopenhauer, describes it, and as Wagner himself often thought of it—you would say that Wagner's passion created, or "dreamed up" out of itself, all of the visible and intelligible elements of the drama. And this is the feeling one should ideally have at a performance: the shifting pictures on stage seem to come directly and solely from the emotion which the music has induced in the audience.

Tristan owes its significance partly to the fact that it is the most perfect instance of drama as "the expression of emotion": the doctrine which identifies action with passion. M. De Rougemont has pointed out the all-pervasive, though half-unconscious influence of the cult of passion in the modern world. It underlies, for example, the deathly pilgrimage of Proust's hero, as he wraps himself in the cocoon of remembered feeling, and of Thomas Mann's Aschenbach (in *Death in Venice*) who makes

out of selected aspects of Venice a scene as despotic and halluci-
natory as that of *Tristan*.

In Act II, after the initiation of Act I, Wagner comes closest
to presenting passion itself—no mean feat in the case of an emotion to which nothing is adequate. The basic symbolism, both in
the setting and in the poetry, is that of Night versus Day. The
Night is the lovers', and it feels to them and to us secret, true,
unitive, and holy, in direct contrast to public, illusory, divisive,
and evil Day. All physical light, even that of the torch, is violently rejected, along with all that it stands for—the light of
reason, the actual circumstances of the lovers, and their moral
obligation to King Mark. And Night is sought as eagerly as the
death, love and primordial oneness for which it stands. Wagner
has these words for their first culmination of utter obedience:

BOTH.	bricht mein Blick sich	My sight broken
	wonn'-erblindet,	blinded in bliss
	erbleicht die Welt	the world goes pale
	mit ihrem Blenden:	in all its dazzling:
ISOLDE.	die uns der Tag	which deceitful Day
	trügend erhellt,	lighted for us,
TRISTAN.	zu täuschenden Wahn	Raising against us
	entgegengestellt,	its lying illusion—
BOTH.	selbst dann	only now
	bin ich die Welt:	am I the world:
	Wonne-hehrstes-Weben,	Majestic web of joy,
	Liebe-heiligstes Leben	Most holy life of love,
	Nie-wieder-erwachens	The never-more-waking
	wahnlos	undeluded
	hold bewusster Wunsch.	longing benign and known.

To reason, these ecstatic cries seem even more nonsensical than
the words of the sailor's song at the beginning of Act I; but,
given the passion Wagner intends and induces with his music,
they are exact, and every word is meant. Tristan, Isolde, the
performers on stage and in the orchestra, and the audience, are

all identified with the one passion, and all could say, if they had the strength, "I am the world."

M. De Rougemont has a great deal to say about Wagner's Night symbolism (pervading the whole work, and elaborately developed in Act II) which is so similar in many respects to the symbolism of light and darkness which mystics often use. He compares Wagner's darkness, for instance, with the Dark Night of the Soul of St. John of the Cross. This inquiry is right and suggestive; but it leads M. De Rougemont into questions of interpretation and of theology which I propose to avoid. In order to get some perspective on the possible meanings, especially the dramatic use, of Wagner's mystical Night, one may think of the very different use which Dante makes of night, and nocturnal imagery, not at the inaccessible summit of the *Paradiso*, but in the *Purgatorio*. Dante's pilgrim has three nights in the course of his ascent of the mountain, which mark the moments of pathos leading to a new perception in the tragic rhythm of his progress. His nocturnal pathos is unquestionably analogous to the passion of *Tristan*. He too finds the values and the truths of daylight, reason and the moral will, no longer relevant at night; and he too depends upon the anomalous power of love when daylight vanishes. But he finds that "love," no longer fixed by the real objects of the daylight world, suggests the undefined potentiality of the psyche for evil as well as for good. The nocturnal world which may be "colored as love wills," is no more necessarily or absolutely true than the world of day and reason, and may even be poisonously false, as it turns out to be in Canto XIX under the influence of the Siren. If he finds new insights in these nocturnal moments, it is partly because he does not take them as final: they refer, however obscurely, to his actual situation, and will be tested and clarified, when he wakes, under the scrutiny of reason and the light of day. But Tristan and Isolde wish never to wake; they do not want to see the daylight world in a truer way, but to get rid of it altogether. And in the opera the symbol of Night stands, not for a transitional moment of human experience, and for one among many modes of knowledge, but for the threshold of the void of truth itself.

It has often been pointed out that the music of Act II unmistakably mounts the lovers "for the hot encounter." Passion is here manifested in desperate sensuality, and the mystic annihilation-in-oneness of the climax which I quoted is figured by implication in the sexual act—which is said to provide a little death of the spirit. But these meanings are (for the pessimistic other-worldly faith in passion) erroneous, because sensual and physical. We are not yet at the end of the act, the end of the action, the end of the story, or the more terrible loss of self which passion demands. What, then, is the dramatic content of the third act? How does Wagner convey the anomalous triumph of the void?

He conveys it of course by the music; and for his mystical intention in this act one may apply to Nietzsche, who speaks as a complete believer both in the Wagnerian revelation and in the magical power of the music itself. He says in part: "I ask the question of genuine musicians: whether they can imagine a man capable of hearing the third act of *Tristan* without expiring by a spasmodic distension of all the wings of the soul? A man who has thus, so to speak, put his ear to the heart-chamber of the cosmic will . . . would he not collapse at once? Could he endure, in the wretched fragile tenement of the human individual, to hear the re-echo of countless cries of joy and sorrow from 'the vast void of cosmic night,' without flying irresistably to his primitive home?"* The direct answer to Nietzsche's rhetorical question would be that, when the curtain falls on Act III, one does in fact catch the subway towards one's unprimitive home, such as it is—unutterably feeble and discouraged perhaps, but a wretched human individual still. Nevertheless Nietzsche's words do describe the action which informs the passion of the end: the absolute and mystical aim which Wagner intended. And this culmination is dramatically and poetically prepared in the first part of the act.

The motive of the third act is still ostensibly that "love" which has possessed Tristan and Isolde all along, and thus the

*The Birth of Tragedy, p. 161. Translated by William A. Haussmann, in the Complete works of Friedrich Nietzsche, ed. by Dr. Oscar Levy, T. N. Foulis, Edinburgh, 1910-1927.

last act in a sense continues the movement of the first two. But "love" is to be sought, this time, not by way of sensuality but by way of death, and for this ultimate effort of passion new beginnings are required. The opening sequences of the last act show the approaching triumph of death as equivalent to the triumph of love, which the erotic violence of Act II just failed to reach. This approach is the more painful for being pleasurable, and the more pleasurable for being painful; and now, at last, we understand that the fated and true end is near. But the beginning of this movement is nostalgic and far-off, like the beginning of Act I, and Isolde's vigil at the beginning of Act II. The empty sea, Tristan's fatal wound, his dark and ruinous "home," and the inexpressibly dreary and seductive sound of the shepherd's pipe, combine to produce the most disquieting version of the paradox of getting nowhere with the utmost speed—for now "nowhere" is reality itself.

Tristan's fatal wound is necessary for the "intrigue." It serves to account for his death rationally, in case there should be a mind in the audience still capable of demanding facts and logic. But what Wagner is presenting here is Tristan's pleasurable-painful, willing-unwilling death-seeking action, and this he conveys dramatically by means of the symbols he has assembled. Tristan has come home—to the shadowy tree, tall walls, and empty ocean of his childhood. These elements have their immediate effect and they also serve, with the sound of the pipe, to induce a Proustian *intermittence du coeur:* Tristan feels again the most devastating moments of his early experience, the death of father and mother. And behind these we are to divine that "vast void of cosmic night" full of joy and sorrow which Nietzsche calls our "primitive home." This backward rush of Tristan is still further speeded and intensified by Kurwenal, who spoils and caresses him with uncomprehending and helpless maternal solicitude, like that which Isolde, with her woman's hands and voice, will presently lavish upon him, expressing the painful pleasure of dissolution: of leaving everything for good, and of judging the whole course of life since the cradle as a mistake and an illusion.

It is in the analysis of the third act that one is most tempted to substitute a Freudian mythology for the one which Wagner offers, in the effort to understand the meaning of the opera. One might say that Tristan's progress in this act is a fine example of pathological regression, from a thwarted love affair back through the morose introversions of childhood to the thrillingly irrational demand for the impermeable gloom of the womb itself. But the Freudian vocabulary merely begs the ultimate questions which few in our time venture to answer. It does not tell us (for all its play with the death wish and the pleasure principle) in what direction the reality of the human situation is to be sought; and when applied to the opera it leaves out the power of the faith which informs it. For *Tristan* fulfills Bergson's requirements for a true mystic experience: its emotions are suffered "in the expectation of a transformation," and its images "as symbolic of what is being prepared," sinister though this preparation feels to us here below. Wagner provides a dramatic form and psychological documentation for his gloomy act of faith; but its true power and scope can only be felt in the work as a whole, and especially and most directly in the music.

I do not attempt to raise the technical question of the nature and merits of Wagner's music as music. But if one is to understand Wagner's dramaturgy, it is essential to consider the crucial role which Wagner and his closest disciples thought that music played, or should play, in the art of drama.

Nietzsche describes the creative act of the "Dionysian" or musical dramatist (by which he meant Wagner) as follows: "He is in the first place become altogether one with the primordial unity, its pain and contradiction, and he produces the copy of this primordial unity as music."[*] This is the orthodox account of the relation between music and the religion of passion: music is direct obedience to passion (or the primordial unity) itself, and only subsequently, out of the music, do the stageable, visible, and intelligible elements of the opera emerge: "Under the Apollonian dream-impulse the music again becomes visible to him as in a *symbolic dream-picture*." (The italics are Nietzsche's.)

Nietzsche's account sounds hysterical to us, as it did to him

[*]*Op. cit.*, p. 45.

later in his career, but the relation he indicates between the music and the drama is correct. Baudelaire described it more soberly in the passage I have already quoted. The music defines with the greatest exactitude an "arabesque of passion," determining not only the performers' tiniest movements of feeling, but also the last detail of the setting and staging. Baudelaire saw very clearly what a "despotic ideal" this is. The music conveys directly the "action of passion," and from it the story, the characters, and everything on-stage is to be deduced, by an inexorable esthetic logic, in complete obedience to the artist's will.

The great Swiss stage designer, Adolphe Appia, attempted in his youth to work out the principles of a theatrical art which would really satisfy the despotic Wagnerian ideal. In *Die Musik und die Inschenïerung* he shows what it would take to make the stage really obedient to the master's will. The settings, the lighting, and the performers would simply have to be as flexible (and therefore as abstracted from mortal and physical limitations) as musical sound. Only by means of such an infinitely responsive theatrical medium could one realize the dreamlike consistency that Wagner intended, and realized in his music. Appia goes further than Wagner himself, pointing out that in spite of his demoniac energy Wagner could not quite conquer the realism of the bourgeois stage. But the developments which Appia demands are in the strict Wagnerian line, and they help one to understand Wagner's whole conception of the dramatic art and of the theater.

Like Racine, Wagner demanded perfection, and to get it he proposed to deduce the entire form and content of the art from one mode of action, that of passion. With his music he induces this passion in the audience. And as long as one stays within the realm of passion, everything coheres with magical perfection. In analyzing Wagner's composition I have endeavored to keep as far as possible this "perspective of passion." But it is necessary to point out that if one abandons it for even a moment, the coherence and formal beauty of the work is gone. One may notice, at a performance, that Isolde is not the "finest parts of pure passion" but a breathless blonde trying to negotiate a flight of steps in the papier-mâché cliff. One may remark that the cyclorama shakes, and so be reminded that the stage is the stage, and not one's dream—whereupon the whole illusion is gone, as if sunlight, or the worklight, had suddenly reduced the setting to a disorderly pile of frames and muslin. This extreme vulnerability of the opera, always poised on the edge of the saddest absurdity, shows the over-ambitious postulate upon which all is based. Wagner demands absolute obedience not only from the performers and the physical stage, but from the audience, which is supposed to live solely the life of his music, forgetting all else, and abandoning every scruple: adhering, at least for the time, to the mystic faith of passion which is the life, and the clue to the form, of the whole.

The Theater of the German People, or "The Birth of Tragedy from the Spirit of Music"

When Nietzsche reconsidered *The Birth of Tragedy* late in life, he tried to dissociate his theory of the Greek tragic theater from his theory of the Wagnerian theater. He wished to disown Wagner who, he thought, had proved to be Schopenhauerian, pessimistic, and (in *Parsifal*) even Christian; but he wanted to retain what he called his own "Hellenism."

Jane Ellen Harrison says that her studies of the Greeks, as well as Murray's, Cornford's, and others of this school, owed a great deal to Nietzsche's insights. Thanks partly to Nietzsche, we are rid of the static, marbleized Neoclassic picture of the Greeks, and aware of the chthonic and Dionysian elements in their religion and their tragedy. The choruses of Aeschylus and Sophocles are revealed as profoundly significant, and the whole tragic form looks more living, if less perfect and timeless, to us than it did to Corneille and Racine. But Nietzsche's own view of Greek tragedy has now been superseded, and in the light of subsequent investigations, looks nightmarishly partial and distorted.

On the other hand, his philosophy of the Wagnerian theater, as we see this theater exemplified in *Tristan* still looks extremely accurate—all the more so because he presents it as the tragic theater itself, and a rebirth of the very theater of the Festival of Dionysos. This enables one to understand the scope of Wagner's ambitions, and to see, behind the particular work, Wagner's original and powerful conception of the theater. If one thinks of a performance of *Tristan* with Nietzsche's explanation in mind, one can see the grandiose outlines of the "theater of the German people" take shape.

A performance of *Tristan* at Bayreuth, the mecca of the cult, is supposed to occupy as central a place in the life of the German people as the tragic theater did in the life of the city state—and more central than the Baroque theater in its society. But Sophocles and Racine both assumed a society, which their theaters mirrored but did not actually create. Wagner assumes that the bourgeois society of his day is totally false, and also that no one really believes in it. He does not address the awareness of society, but the "true" life and spirit of the German *Volk*, which he takes to be without any social, moral, or intellectual form whatever—passion itself, or sheer potentiality. He proposes to awaken this formless *Wille*, and in his theater to create a tragic form for it.

The most conspicuous people at a performance of *Tristan* are of course those who can afford to go to the opera—bankers, stockbrokers, advertising executives, idle wives—the pillars of such society as we have. This Wagner knew; but he did not take them seriously as individuals or as powerful elements in the community. The lights go down, the orchestra begins; and the hypnotic will of the artist induces that "musical mood" in which all actual or intelligible distinctions vanish. The distinction between audience and stage vanishes too, and performers and auditors alike live the one life of the music. By means of the music Wagner as it were by-passes not only the shrewd discriminations of daily life, but all the values of the common world. He manipulates directly the morose *Innerlichkeit* of the faithless population. This is the process which psychologists describe as the formation of a mob: all the individuals identify themselves, in intense emotion, with the will and the feeling of the leader. But Wagner and Nietzsche understood the process as the awakening of the German spirit, where it is in touch with the inchoate sources of all being, that it may be "freed" to dream a tragic life for itself.

Both Nietzsche and Wagner were acutely aware that this appeal to the audience as passionate and faithless, and the prophetic or revivalistic conception of the theater which it implies, was in direct conflict with the whole rationalist tradition, and therefore anti-Latin. Their theater was to be not only passionate as opposed to rational, musical as opposed to plastic, free as opposed to hidebound, true as opposed to false, unitive as opposed to divisive, but also German as opposed to French. Nietzsche, in his most enthusiastic moments, thought this theater was the culmination of a long struggle of the German spirit (which he traces back through the German musicians and philosophers to Luther) to free itself from rationalism and Christianity. In this nationalistic diagnosis M. Jean Cocteau was to agree with them. Between the first and second world wars, meditating upon his efforts and those of the young French composers to rebuild a *French* theatrical art, he finds himself impeded by the all-pervasive Wagnerian influence, "One must have the courage to go back to Beethoven," he says in *The Call to Order*. "[Since Mozart's death] a theatrical funeral procession has been going by, which prevents me from crossing the street to get home." By that time the circle had come round again, and it was the French who were trying to "free" themselves from German ways of seeing human life and action, in order to "get home."

Nietzsche and Wagner rejected the theater of reason completely, but with equal absoluteness they wished to identify their theater of passion with the tragic theater of the Greeks—and in this they were far less accurate. It is easy to see why Nietzsche found what he was looking for in the Greek chorus. I suppose that when Sophocles' actors departed after an agon, and the chorus began to dance and chant to the accompaniment of musical instruments, some sort of appeal to the common feeling of the audience was intended, analogous to that made by the Wagnerian overture. But Sophocle's chorus did not enter until after the prologue had presented a realistic and intelligible basis for the action which was to follow. Its music, its dance-rhythms, and its imagery then produce the wider and vaguer modes of awareness associated with passion, removing us, as it were, to a distance from the concrete and intelligible issues of the agons. But the choral passion in Sophocles' drama is not Nietzsche's "cosmic void," formless reality itself, but a passion informed by faith in a ritual order in the real world. This order may be momentarily lost to sight; it may appear differently at different moments and to different individuals; but the end of the chorus reaffirms it, and returns us to the disputes of the actual protagonists. In order to derive the whole tragic form from the passion of the chorus, Nietzsche is compelled to say that the individual characters, their conflicts, and the myth they represent, are its dreamy *product*, like the images in the choral odes. And he is compelled to picture the chorus as a mob: i.e., unified in feeling, but informed by no objective perceptions or beliefs whatever. Thus he roots it in the metaphysical void of *Wille* itself; and so he sees the Greek tragic theater, like Wagner's, as the creation of the artist's will upon the formless passion of a mob.

Hamlet's definition of the theater as the mirror of nature sounds ambitious enough to us, who suffer such divided counsels about human nature. Hamlet could still think of drama as imitation, and of the human reality as somehow perceptible apart from the closed world of our own feeling. But Wagner builds upon the most radical modern subjectivism, and accepts the full implications of art as the expression of emotion. The musical dramatist, with his passion and the crowd's, like the legendary Moses with his divine thunder, will create—not perceive or reflect—the dynamic ethos of the tribe. The distinction between art and life (or between opera and revolution) disappears; and the neglected artist totally replaces the Philistines and their little world.

It is very difficult to take this notion as seriously as it deserves without becoming involved in dubious profundities, like those of the early Wagnerians. Nietzsche and Wagner themselves seem to have felt this qualm; both changed their minds about the meaning of *Tristan*, and both qualified their notions of the theater of the German people. But their first prophetic and revolutionary conception has lived on after them, not only in the theater itself, but in politics. Its importance has thereby been confirmed, and its nature has become clearer. I suppose that Nietzsche and Wagner would have been dismayed to see the Nazi propaganda film, *Triumph des Willens.* Yet it exactly fulfills their prescription for a theater of the German people, and, in spite of its cynical vulgarizations, it makes very knowing use of the dramaturgy which is based upon the sense of action as passion only.

It would be possible to demonstrate the Wagnerian genealogy of *Triumph des Willens,* both through Hitler, its real begetter, and through Leni Riefensthal, who directed it; but it is sufficient for my purposes to consider only certain features of the film itself. It was made at Nuremberg during the party rallies of 1934, and so is ostensibly a "documentary" record of a historic moment in German politics. But the same despotic imagination which assembled the faithful hordes, and devised their rituals of dedication, also made the film; and the effect of this is to destroy the distinction between art and life, between the theater and politics, and between the monolithic passion of Fuehrer and Volk and the events and "appearances" it dreams into being. Here, if anywhere, one may see the theater actually make the passionate action of the tribe, and the crowd-passion make the theater.

The story of the film is that of the yearning of the Fuehrer and the Volk for each other; of their orgasmic junction, and of their unification in and with the one mystic German *Wille.* But we are given very few of the facts of Hitler's rise to power, and not much about the actual situation in Germany—just enough to provide a few slogans, and a very simplified creed, to quiet the mind of the faithful. The film is not so much a narrative (the love-story of Hitler and Germany) as it is a ritual of passion, like *Tristan.* It starts nostalgically, with shots of Rhine castles silhouetted against the dawn to the accompaniment of some of Wagner's music. Then we see clouds which open to reveal an airplane bringing Hitler. We look down at the German landscape and we see that all the roads are black with converging throngs. We are in the sky again, with the sense of the urgency, power, and speed of the airplane; and then we get a closer view of picturesque towers of Nuremberg. The climax of this sequence is the frantic roaring of the crowd when Hitler lands.

This rhythm of feeling, so like that of an act of *Tristan*, is repeated again and again throughout the film. This rhythm always starts with that "musical mood" which Nietzsche accepted from Schiller: i.e., with nostalgic music and nostalgic images. The pictures on the screen, at these beginning moments, are always full of childhood associations, suggesting the Germany of fairy tales—pretty cottages, toy-like landscapes, bulbous church-towers, romantic castles. As the emotion grows nearer and stronger we quickly approach the modern world, with its crowds, its machinery, and its non-human power: we see Hitler, for instance, in a big car, riding past an endless sea of rapt faces. The climax of the growing emotion is always in the desperate excitement of one of the formal Party meetings—in the gigantic stadium by daylight or torchlight, or indoors, where the cries of the leaders—"Hitler ist die Partei! Die Partei ist Deutschland! Deutschland ist Eins!"—remind one of Tristan and Isolde in ecstasy affirming their mystic identity with the world. After such explosions, all becomes vague and faraway again, and we start rebuilding with a new "musical mood." The film ends with a long sequence of marching: labor battalions, Storm Troopers, the army, women, children, and motorized cavalcades. The hebetude produced by many feet tramping together is not quite a Liebestodt, but it serves to convey the mystic unity of the national passion. And it points to the real death which so many in the film, and in the rest of the world, were to find before the end of the march.

I am not, of course, trying to say that this film is a great work of art like *Tristan*. Yet in its structure, and in the use of the camera, and of sounds and music, there is a degree of self-conscious and consistent art usually associated with less venal ends: "associated and contrasted images" serve, as in *Tristan*, to define and produce an irresistible rhythm of feeling. If one compares these images with those in *Tristan*, the film may look like a mere pastiche; yet one must recognize that it is informed by a passionate faith, a faith in the oneness of passion, which makes it very different from propaganda in the usual sense. There are, for example, some unforgettable shots of German boys in the early dawn, pledging themselves to work in the fields for the Fatherland, and shouldering their picks and shovels. In their solemn faces and awe-struck young voices one must recognize the "purity of faith"—which is equally impressive whether one considers the nightmare which was its object, the death and destruction to which it was to lead, or the fallibility of human faith itself.

When I say that *Triumph des Willens* fulfills the prescription for a theater of the German people, I do not mean that Wagner's prophetic idea of the theater alone generated Nazism. Nor do I mean to imply that the Nazis were alone in finding a clue in the Wagnerian cult and in passionate modes of understanding. M. De Rougemont has shown that Wagner's gloomy song re-echoes in a thousand ways in all the modern media of communication.

Moreover, *Triumph des Willens*, though at once Wagnerian and the plan of the moral atom bomb of Nazism, does not represent the real seriousness of Wagner's vision as we get it in *Tristan*. The feeling that our intellectual life, our loyalties, and our relationships are all deluded—that we are really moved by undefinable and insatiable passion—is never far away. Wagner made the most consistent and profound use of a lingua franca of feeling which all, in our times, can easily understand. I shall return to this point in connection with Eliot's *Murder in the Cathedral* and Cocteau's *Infernal Machine*, both of them works after Wagner in the sense that they try to go beyond his revelation.

The art of *Tristan* is as serious as the vision it embodies; and Wagner's despotic esthetic ideal has also not yet been digested. It continues to appeal to poets and to artists of the theater who seek some sort of integrity to replace a living tradition.

Tristan and *Bérénice*: The "Perfect" Unity of Action and the Univocal Sense of Form

> Come in lo specchio il sol, non altrimenti
> la doppia fiera dentro vi raggiava
> or con uni, or con altri reggimenti.

Pensa, lettor, s'io mi maravigliava
quando vedea la cosa in sè star queta,
e nell' idolo suo si trasmutava.*

If one accepts the presuppositions of Racine's theater, keeping the single angle of vision which he demands, *Bérénice* is revealed as having a crystalline perfection of form. Because the vision of the human being which it presents is so consistent, it seems "truer" than any image we can derive directly from our experience. In the same way, if one accepts the nocturnal world of passion which Wagner demands, *Tristan* coheres with a magical and dreamlike consistency; and it feels to us like the very truth of the human condition. But if one attempts to do justice to both, one has an experience like that which Dante describes in the above quotation. The pilgrim, at the top of the mount of Purgatory, has just experienced some of the deepest contradictions in human experience; and he meets Christ as a griffon, or double beast—double because at once divine and human. Looking into Beatrice's eyes, he can see first one nature, then the other, but not both at once; yet the anomalous beast Himself is there before him. Listening to Racine, one may sense the human psyche as basically reasoning, and all the rest of experience as outer darkness. Listening to Wagner, one may sense it as "really" only passion, and all the rest as meaningless illusion. Thinking of them thus, in alternation, one may conclude, I think, that the human animal, like Dante's griffon, is in some way present to us before either the Racinian or the Wagnerian image thereof.

The images of life in *Tristan* and *Bérénice* are opposite, and mutually exclusive, and so are their dramatic principles. But they have in common a certain absoluteness. Both reduce the life of the psyche to one moment of action, or one mode of being, and both demand of the art of drama an Idealist perfection of form, a literal and "univocal" kind of unity. In this absoluteness they are similar to each other, and very unlike Dante, Sophocles, and Shakespeare, who are realists in the Greek or Medieval sense,

*As the sun in a mirror, not otherwise, the twofold beast was beaming within them, now with the attributes of one, now of the other nature. Think, reader, if I marveled within me, when I saw the thing itself remain motionless, and in its image it was changing.—*Purgatorio,* CANTO XXXI.

and who, in their art, seek not univocity but "oneness by analogy." When Dante meets the griffon, he makes a distinction between that beast and either "idolo" or image which he can make of it—though neither image is simply wrong. This distinction Racine and Wagner do not make: in them the image is taken to be single, perfect, and final, replacing or transcending the more primitive awareness we have of the beast itself.

The distinction between the idealist conception of the theater and its univocal sense of form (which Wagner and Racine share) and the realist theater, and analogical sense of form, represented by Dante, Sophocles, and Shakespeare, is of fundamental importance. If one is to understand Sophocles, one must see that the perspectives of Racine and Wagner, though they reveal a great deal, distort Sophocles, each in its own way. If one is to understand both Racine and Wagner—following their profound insights and enjoying their miraculous artistic perfections —one must seek a point of view different from that of either one. Such a point of view is offered by the realist idea of the theater, with its skepticism, its faith in a real world, and its direct appeal to the primitive histrionic sensibility of the audience.

The idealist and univocal principles of Racine and Wagner (in various forms and combinations) govern the writing of a great deal of modern drama, often the best modern drama. It has proved extraordinarily difficult since the eighteenth century for artists, or anyone else, to make any sense out of the human life they could actually see around them. We have lacked anything corresponding to that naturally formed and centrally placed mirror of man and society which the Greek tragic theater provided. Therefore it is natural for the dramatic poet in our times to seek a priori intellectual, moral, and esthetic principles, and so to understand the basis of drama, in Eliot's words, as "any form or rhythm *imposed* upon the world of action." Such a conception is not only the natural answer to the centerless confusion of the times, it also promises to satisfy the artist's need for strictness in his art, for a complete and intelligible discipline, and for esthetic perfection.

But there are important elements in the modern theater, notably modern realism, which cannot be grasped at all on these idealist principles. The art of Ibsen and the art of Chekov rediscover some of the ancient sense of drama as the *imitation* of action. This question is considered at length in the chapter on modern realism.

And at the threshold of the modern world, with its many shifting perspectives and its many incommensurable "theaters," there is the theater of Shakespeare. Our understanding of Shakespeare has suffered greatly from the tendency to demand of him a univocal perfection of form which he never sought. In the next chapter I wish to show that one cannot understand *Hamlet* on modern idealist principles and to propose the view that Shakespeare's theater, though on the very brink of the modern world, is the direct heir of the realist tradition of Sophocles and Dante, appealing to the histrionic sensibility, and presenting the familiar mystery of the human animal in diverse, shifting, and analogous images.

CHAPTER IV

HAMLET, PRINCE OF DENMARK:
THE ANALOGY OF ACTION

THOUGH *Hamlet* was written long before *Bérénice*, or *Tristan*, modern readers are more at ease with it than with either of the others. We may admire the masterpiece of Racine, or be genuinely "sunk" by *Tristan*, but compared with *Hamlet* they are artificial, limited, and arbitrary. Shakespeare's mysterious play has, even in our day, a directness and an intimacy which the others lack.

That is because *Hamlet* was formed in a Theater which was close to the root of drama itself—that art which is both more primitive and more subtle than Philosophy. Since the destruction of the great "mirror" of the Elizabethan theater, it has been necessary to restore or invent the theater; and modern drama has been a succession of more limited *genres*, based upon more limited postulates about human life, like Racine's "action as rational," or Wagner's "action as passion." These sharp perspectives may seem to their own times to reveal the essence of life but to the next generation they may appear partial or even depraved. But *Hamlet*, like *Oedipus* and the *Purgatorio*, can take myth and ritual as still alive. Its imitation of human action "undercuts" or precedes all theory. If it is "the" modern play, it is also very ancient, the heir of the great tradition in its completeness. Thus it is necessary to examine *Hamlet* (mysterious though it is) in order to complete the study of the idea of a theater in our tradition.

This view of *Hamlet* has been emerging slowly since the end of the eighteenth century. Every generation has regarded it in the light of its own taste which was formed by the then regnant form of drama. The critics have been fascinated with it, but they have made it over in their own image: as Hamlet himself tells Ophelia, "the power of beauty will sooner transform honesty from what it is to a bawd than the force of honesty can translate beauty into his likeness: this was sometime a paradox, but now the time gives it proof." The beauty of *Hamlet*, its endless suggestiveness, the iridescent play of the analogical relationships within it, will no doubt continue to seduce, and then show up its well-intentioned lovers. But this process, as I say, has been going on for a hundred and fifty years at least; the efforts of Hamlet's critics to some extent correct each other; and in our time, with modern drama almost dead, it may be possible to get a little closer to the play itself.

For this purpose, the first step is to become aware of certain preconceptions, certain instinctive demands which the modern theater has taught us to make of all drama. The most common complaint made of *Hamlet* is that in spite of its vitality it is not intelligible; it is fascinating but an artistic failure. Is this criticism based upon an understanding of Shakespeare's dramaturgy or does it judge him on the basis of alien standards?

Hamlet as an Artistic Failure

Robertson's essay on *Hamlet** together with Mr. Eliot's essay,† which was apparently inspired by a reading of Robertson, may be taken as typical of the objections which many critics make to the play: they cannot find that it has any unity, or intellectual consistency, as a whole. Thus Robertson, while he admits that it makes superb entertainment and that it is full of brilliant characterization and passages of wonderful poetry, reports that it leaves the critical intellect unsatisfied. He suggests that Shakespeare may have intended nothing more than an entertainment and never bothered about the deeper unity or wider meaning of the whole: "If Shakespeare could be recreated and asked why he managed here and there so oddly, he might with an unanswerable effect open eyes of wonder and ask what should make us thus put his mechanism to the rack. 'Do you want an absolute,' he might ask, 'as a stage entertainment?' . . . But the critical intellect too has its right: its concern is simply conceptual truth."

---

*"Hamlet," by J. M. Robertson.
†"Hamlet and His Problems," by T. S. Eliot.

Robertson, and after him Mr. Eliot, seek in *Hamlet* conceptual truth, and do not find it. They wish to be able to reduce *Hamlet* to terms which the reason can accept; and, in the attempt to satisfy this demand, they make an interpretation of the play which certainly makes it appear confused, formless, and, in short, a failure. "Mr. Robertson is undoubtedly correct." Mr. Eliot writes, "in concluding that the essential emotion of the play is the feeling of a son toward a guilty mother." He then shows that there are many elements and several entire scenes in the play which have nothing to do with the feeling of a son toward a guilty mother. He shows that on this interpretation, Hamlet himself is incomprehensible; and he concludes that Shakespeare failed to find "objective equivalents" for Hamlet's feeling: "Hamlet (the man) is dominated by an emotion which is inexpressible, because it is in excess of the facts as they appear. And the supposed identity of Hamlet with his author is genuine to this point: that Hamlet's bafflement at the absence of objective equivalent to his feelings is a prolongation of the bafflement of his creator in the face of his artistic problem."

I am not sure that I understand Mr. Eliot's famous formula of the objective equivalent of a feeling, at least in its application to this play. Does Mr. Eliot mean that the many objects, facts, and chains of events which Shakespeare presents to make us share and understand Hamlet's feeling, do not work for us? In other words, that as we read or see the play we cannot sympathize with Hamlet's feeling? Or does he mean that we cannot understand Hamlet's psychology? Hamlet is full of feeling— much more so than Polonius, for example; but is this feeling "in excess"? One may hazard the guess that what troubles Mr. Eliot here is not that the character fails to live dramatically—his stage vitality, his fascination for many and varied audiences proves the contrary—but rather that neither he nor his author explains his situation in the clear and univocal terms of reason. Hamlet is presented directly, in his concrete and many-sided setting, in his complex situation as prince, son, and lover. If we are to understand him, we must take him thus directly, and not try to simplify and reduce the picture Shakespeare offers.

The view that "the essential emotion of the play is the feeling of a son toward a guilty mother" is a drastic reduction of the play as Shakespeare wrote it. Hamlet's feeling toward his guilty mother is certainly essential, but not more essential than his dismay at the loss of a father. Stephen Daedalus in *Ulysses* builds up an interpretation of the play on this basis, which reveals at least as much as the Eliot-Robertson interpretation. And Mr. Dover Wilson offers an explanation of Hamlet's feeling which is perhaps still more fruitful: Hamlet has lost a throne, and he has lost thereby a social, publicly acceptable *persona:* a local habitation and a name. It is for this reason that he haunts the stage like the dispossessed of classical drama: like an Electra, who has lost the traditional life which was her due as daughter, wife, and mother—or even like the ghost of Polyneikes, who cannot rest because the ritual order of society which might have provided such a place has been destroyed. And Mr. Wilson assures us that an Elizabethan audience (more or less aware of such implications as these) would have accepted the loss of the throne as sufficient explanation for Hamlet's dismay.

It is not necessary to rule out the Eliot-Robertson, or the Joycean interpretation, merely because one accepts Mr. Dover Wilson's: on the contrary, the various critics should be taken as Jamesian "reflectors," each lighting a facet of the whole from his own peculiar angle. Mr. Dover Wilson's "angle," however, has a special value, for it enables one to see beyond the plight of Hamlet as an individual to certain traditional values of society which underlie the play as a whole. And one of the chief objections to the type of criticism which Mr. Eliot brings to bear, is that it does not distinguish clearly between the story of Hamlet the individual and the story of the play as a whole. He objects to the criticism of Hamlet abstracted from the work in which he appears; but his own essay deals with "Hamlet without the Prince of Denmark"—i.e., the character without reference to the society in which he endeavors to realize himself. Hence he cannot understand the relevance of the minor characters, nor the significance of certain scenes which do not bear directly upon Hamlet's individual fate.

"There are unexplained scenes," he writes, "the Polonius-Laertes and the Polonius-Reynaldo scene—for which there is little excuse." There is no explanation and no excuse for them if Shakespeare was merely trying to convey the feeling of a son toward a guilty mother. If he was also picturing the relation of a son to his father, then the whole Polonius-Laertes-Reynaldo sequence makes sense as a comic-pathetic sub-plot, with many ironic parallels to the story of Hamlet and his father's Ghost. If to this we add Mr. Dover Wilson's suggestions, we see that the welfare of Denmark—the traditional order of society, with its father-king upon whom depend "the lives of many"—is the matter of the play as a whole, rather than Hamlet's individual plight. In the welfare of Denmark, Polonius, Laertes and Reynaldo have a stake also. The postulate upon which the entire action is based (from the first scene on the parapet, with the soldiers peering through the darkness to discern what danger may threaten the body politic) is that "the times are out of joint." It is Hamlet's misfortune that, as Prince, and as a man of profound insight, he especially should have been "born to set them right."

The Eliot-Robertson reading of *Hamlet* makes it clear that none of the characters, and none of the plots or narrative sequences, is intended to convey the meaning of the play as a whole. Nor does the play offer, even in the meditations of Hamlet, the finality of conceptual truth wherein the reason could find its satisfaction and its rest. This reading has the value of showing what *Hamlet* is not, rather than throwing light upon its actual complexity. It has also the value of summing up a sense of the theater and of drama which has largely prevailed since the Elizabethan theater ceased to exist. The demands and the criticism which Robertson and Eliot make would have been approved by the critics of the age of reason from Corneille to Voltaire. They are, in principle, very much like those that William Archer made in his book on Elizabethan drama, *The Old Drama and the New.* Archer demanded naturalistic psychology like that of Ibsen and his structural principles were the rationalistic ones of the well-made play. Therefore he too found the drama of Shakespeare's theater unsatisfying. It is our habit to insist on literal unity and conceptual truth; the value of the Eliot-Robertson reading is that it does so with such clarity as to show what we are doing. Once we understand that, the way is clear, and we may inquire whether Shakespeare was not composing on a different principle altogether.

For such an inquiry there is plenty of material available. There are studies of that characteristic device of the Elizabethans, the double plot. And there are the many recent works which show the Elizabethan theater not from our contemporary standpoint but as the heir of the Middle Ages and, behind that, even of classical antiquity. In their light one can see, if not the unity of *Hamlet,* at least the kind of "oneness by analogy" which Shakespeare's dramaturgy aimed at.

Hamlet as Multiple Plot

It has been well established by now that the Elizabethan "double plot," at its best, is more than a device for resting the audience. The comic sequences which are woven through the tragedies are not to be dismissed as mere "comic relief," or as punctuation for the main story, like the music that Corneille used between the acts. In Shakespeare, and in the best of his contemporaries, the minor plots are essential parts of the whole composition. This much is, I think, generally recognized. But there is little agreement about the nature of these relationships: we lack a generally accepted critical vocabulary for describing them.

Thus Moulton, in his *Shakespeare the Dramatic Artist,* studied the plots themselves as intelligible chains of events, and showed (for *Lear* and *The Merchant of Venice,* for example) that the various narrative strands depend causally upon each other; that their climaxes, coming together, reinforce each other; and that their denouements are interdependent. Moulton was thinking of the objections of rationalistic critics like Robertson, and answering them in their own terms. But Mr. William Empson, in his extremely illuminating study, *Some Versions of Pastoral,* is interested, not in the logical concatenation of the stories, but in the ironic parallels between them: the tragi-comic parallel between the motivations of love and war, as in *Troilus and Cressida;* between the lives of "clowns" and the lives of "heroes" in the whole tradition of British drama to the middle of the eighteenth century.

Henry James's technical concept of the "reflector" is akin to the notion of the double plot as Mr. Empson explains it. The "occasions," or the more or less peripheral intelligences which James used to mirror his action, serve to reveal it from various (ironically different) angles. Neither the author nor the protagonist is to be allowed to break down and "tell all": that would not be truly dramatic; it would not be "objective" in the realist sense. The situation, the moral and metaphysical "scene" of the drama, is presented only as one character after another sees and reflects it; and the action of the drama as a whole is presented only as each character in turn actualizes it in his story and according to his lights. This is as much as to say that the various stories with their diverse casts of characters are analogous, and that the drama as a whole is therefore "one by analogy" only. It does not have the literal and rational unity of the single logically and causally connected chain of events or story. And if we are to grasp a novel of Henry James or a play by Shakespeare, we must be prepared to follow these shifting perspectives, as we move from character to character and from story to story, trying, as we go, to divine the supreme analogue, the underlying theme, to which they all point in their various ways.

This "supreme analogue" or "underlying theme" is the main action of the play, as Aristotle explains in a neglected passage of the *Poetics*. Aristotle knew plays with a double plot-thread, one of which issues "happily," the other tragically; and he did not like them—they are "less perfect," he says, than pure tragedy; a concession to popular taste. But in his few remarks on the *Odyssey* he comes closer to describing a multiple plot as Shakespeare employed it. The *Odyssey* has neither the literal unity of the one cast of characters, nor the rational unity of the single plot-line. There is the story of Telemachus's search for his father, the *Telemacheia*. There is the intrigue between Penelope and the suitors. There are the many smaller stories of Odysseus' adventures on the islands and the sea; and at last his conflict with the suitors. The stories are many but they are analogous: they are all "actualizations" of the one general action, which is the attempt "to return home." The Odyssey (*hoi nostoi*) sets forth, in many figures, this basic action, this quest for home.

In considering the structure of *Hamlet*, all of these studies of the properties of the double plot are useful. The stories of the play—the struggle between Hamlet and Claudius; between Hamlet, Polonius and Laertes; between Fortinbras and Claudius' regime—are tightly woven together, causally and logically interdependent, in the manner Moulton demonstrates for *The Merchant of Venice*. At the same time the various stories are presented as ironically parallel in the ways Mr. Empson describes. Polonius, for instance, plays the "clown" to Hamlet's "hero," to use Mr. Empson's words; at the same time Hamlet frequently feels himself in the role of clown in relation to Fortinbras and even Laertes. Or, taking Henry James's phrase, you may put it that we are continually shifting from reflector to reflector throughout the play: from the simple soldiers of Scene 1 to the smoothly hypocritical Claudius of Scene 2; from the myopic shrewdness of Polonius, to the troubled but profound intuitions of Ophelia. The action is illumined from so many angles that we have an embarrassment of riches; the problem is not to demonstrate that the play moves in ironic parallels but rather to show that they add up to something—are intended to convey (with however rich a profusion) an underlying unity of theme. For this purpose Aristotle's notion of analogous actions is the most useful.

The main action of Hamlet may be described as the attempt to find and destroy the hidden "imposthume" which is poisoning the life of Claudius' Denmark. All of the characters—from Polonius with his "windlasses" and "assays of bias," to Hamlet with his parables and symbolic shows—realize this action, in comic, or evil, or inspired ways. And the organic parts of the plot the movement of the play as a whole—show forth the beginning, middle, and end of this action according to the traditional scheme.

The Prologue includes approximately the first three scenes of Act I. Scene 1, Act I (the parapet) makes the simplest and most general statement of the main theme or action of the play. The soldiers, in the cold and darkness of the night, are watching for the hidden danger (the physical or metaphysical malady) which may threaten the present Danish regime. Is it war—and thus connected with young Fortinbras in neighboring Norway? Or something less natural, and thus connected with Hamlet's father's ghost, who appears but will not speak? The soldiers' peering-through-the-dark constitutes a sort of overture, in sensuous terms, to their speculations about the Ghost and his meanings.

Act I, scene 2 (Claudius's Court) restates the main theme, this time from the point of view of Claudius and his regime. What possible ill is threatening his rule? His marriage to Gertrude on the heels of the death of Hamlet's father has been accepted by all, so that cannot be the danger. But three young men, unaccountable quantities, all with the restlessness of youth, are potential sources of trouble. Fortinbras, who wishes to avenge his father for the loss of lands to Denmark, is threatening war in nearby Norway. Laertes is asking his father, Polonius, for permission to travel; and Hamlet, in black, moody, seems not to have accepted Claudius' regime with good grace—perhaps because of the loss of *his* father. Claudius deals with Fortinbras through his uncle, the present king of Norway; satisfies Laertes by giving permission for the traditional fling in Paris; but fails to appease Hamlet, who thus begins to appear to him as the most dangerous center of infection. When Claudius departs, with his glittering court, and Hamlet, in his solemn black, is left alone on-stage, we get his sharply different version of Denmark's trouble: "Things rank and gross in nature possess it merely." And then, when Horatio and the soldiers come to report the Ghost, we are led to connect this apparition with Hamlet's sense that the body politic is sick.

Act I, scene 3 (Polonius' house) is a comic variation on the main theme. Laertes is warning his sister Ophelia about the dangers of youth, particularly *Hamlet's* youth—for Laertes, with his simple-minded conventionality, instinctively thinks of Hamlet as the source of infection, much as Claudius does, though for less specific reasons. When Polonius appears, he gives Laertes the same advice that Laertes had given Ophelia. We see that Laertes is a chip off the old block; and that for this family there is no hidden malady which ordinary prudence and the experience of the aged cannot find and cure. But Ophelia, with her love for Hamlet, throws doubt on Polonius' simple diagnosis. (Ophelia, like Gertrude, has great symbolic value in the economy of the play as a whole. Both women base their very beings upon their men; and both of them are attached at once to Hamlet and to Claudius' regime. Thus they are at once touching reminders of what might have been—the unity and health of the whole state—and victims of its actual illness and disunity.)

The Agons, or conflicts of the play, are developed in scenes 4 and 5 of Act I, in Act II, and in the first scene of Act III. It is established that all of the characters are seeking to identify and to destroy the actual or potential malady of Claudius' Denmark; but they interpret it differently, and hence conflicts and contrasts develop between their various lines of action. Because the "malady" is so mysterious, and because it would be perilous to trouble the smooth surface of Claudius' regime, the characters all act secretly, indirectly, and in mutual mistrust. Hamlet does not even trust the Ghost; he cannot tell whether it is a "spirit of health or goblin damned"; and thus there is contrast and conflict even in this relationship. Polonius is endeavoring to serve Claudius' regime; But Claudius does not trust Polonius' diagnosis of the trouble; he summons Rosencrantz and Guildenstern as a check. Thus the struggles which develop in this part of the play are all struggles in the dark, as though the antagonists, waiting and listening, could not find each other, and fought only briefly and desperately when they happened to bump together.

But by the first scenes of Act III the main lines of the many-sided conflict which the Prologue prepared, are visible. Claudius, having satisfied Laertes with his trip to Paris, and having diverted the dutiful Fortinbras from Denmark to Poland, has decided that Hamlet is the source of his dis-ease, and must be rendered harmless. Polonius agrees with him, and is now beginning to feel a little out of his depth: he is no longer sure that Hamlet's malady is merely thwarted love for Ophelia. As for Hamlet, he sees Claudius as the chief plague-spot, and his main antagonist though, at the same time, the spreading disease has vitiated his every relationship.

I have said that the agon shows conflicts *and contrasts*. The contrasts between the visions and the lines of action of the various characters are more important than their overt struggles, and reveal far more about the real malady of Denmark and the attempt to find and destroy it. These *contrasts* are brought out by the order of the scenes, as we shift from comic to tragic versions of the main action. This may be illustrated by considering the alternation of the Polonius story and the Hamlet story in Acts I and II—the scenes for which Mr. Eliot says there is no explanation or excuse.

The last scene of the Prologue, Polonius' house (Act I, scene 3) is at once a comic version of the opening statement of the main action, and the prologue to the story of Polonius and Laertes which is closely analogous in many respects to the story of Hamlet's "father" (the Ghost *and* Claudius) and Hamlet. The clownish and comic father-son relationship of Polonius and Laertes throws ironic lights upon the tragic relationship of Hamlet to his anomalous parent. Thus as soon as we have seen Polonius attempting to guide and advise Laertes in preparation for his trip to Paris, we are shifted to the dark parapet with Hamlet awaiting word from his Ghost-father and hearing, below, the roaring and the booming which Claudius, his other "father," is making at his drunken celebration. The Ghost appears, and speaks to Hamlet; but, from the other side of the grave, he can convey little to his son—and that only in hints and metaphors. He is definite enough about the fact that Claudius killed him; but Hamlet does not know what to make even of that:

> O all you host of heaven! O earth! What else?
> And shall I couple hell? O fie!

After this we return to Polonius who is sending Reynaldo to Paris to watch over Laertes. It is another father trying to reach and guide his son—who is not on the other side of the grave, this time, but on the other side of the sea; yet as absurdly remote as Hamlet from the Ghost. We can be sure that when

Reynaldo gets to Paris, and tries to apply to Laertes the "bait of falsehood," the "indirections" and "windlasses and assays of bias" which father Polonius devised to reach him, Laertes will also reply "O fie!"

Thus these three scenes are closely parallel, yet sharply contrasted: the divided world of Polonius-Laertes is incommensurable with the divided world of the Ghost-Hamlet; and this incommensurability is deeper than any overt conflict, and shows more about Hamlet's problem and the true malady of Denmark than any fact, or any explicit issue, could do. And when Ophelia appears on Reynaldo's exit, torn and frightened by her sight of Hamlet, we have before us the most pathetic victim of this division within the sick society; and with this vision, the Hamlet-Ghost, Laertes-Polonius sequence ends.

The Climax, Peripety and Recognition are presented in Act III, scenes 2, 3, and 4—the players' scene, and the two scenes following. In the first of these scenes which follow the players' scene (scene 3) Claudius, convicted of the crime, attempts to pray, and Hamlet rejects his chance to kill him. In the next (scene 4) Hamlet faces his mother with her guilt, and inadvertently kills Polonius.

Hamlet's presentation of his play to the Danish Court is both a direct attack on Claudius, as his chief antagonist, and an attempt to resolve the deeper "contrasts," the divided counsels, the incommensurable visions, which constitute the malady of Denmark—or at least its chief symptom. By hinting broadly at Claudius' crime Hamlet, of course, shakes Claudius' whole position, for that depends upon concealment. At the same time he convicts all of the supporters of the regime, even including Ophelia and Gertrude, of a share in the guilt.

The further meanings of Hamlet's play are considered at more length below. At this point I merely wish to point out that the presentation of the play is the peripety: it puts the King and his regime on the defensive, and justifies the most hidden intuitions of Hamlet and the most secret messages of the Ghost. The two scenes following the players' scene merely drive home its effects: Claudius becomes in his own eyes an outlaw; Gertrude's heart is "cleft in twain" and, as a sort of absurd and pathetic parenthesis, Polonius is destroyed. The "hidden imposthume," in all its ramifications, is opened; and from this point the action, beyond anyone's control, runs down to its fated end.

The Pathos and/or Sparagmos coincides with Act iv. Both the state and the individuals that compose it "suffer" the results of Hamlet's opening the "hidden imposthume." Laertes, hearing of his father's death, comes back to avenge him, and starts a rebellion; and the scenes which show this overt social disorder alternate with Ophelia's mad scenes: "Schism in the State and Schism in the soul," in Toynbee's phrase. Meanwhile Hamlet, on his trip to England and his return, and Fortinbras, at the head of his troops, approach for the kill. The King (who conceals Hamlet's murder of Polonius, minimizes Ophelia's tragedy, and corrupts Laertes' demand for justice) is trying to "skin and film the ulcerous place." But his efforts do not re-establish his regime; they make at most a horrible simulacrum of a healthy state; smooth on the surface but dead within.

The Epiphany or Collective Revelation is shown in Act v. It is Shakespeare's habit to wind up his complicated plots at the very end; and the big killings do not occur until the last scene. But these sensational events tell us little that is new; they seem to be only minor corollaries of the great peripety in Act iii. The substance of Act v is chiefly what Hamlet, the "chief reflector," sees, when he returns, spent, nervously exhausted, but clear-eyed, from England. He sees the fatal illness of Denmark: the literal bones in the graveyard; the many details of social disorder (the Prince, for instance, on a level with the grave-digging clowns); the "maimèd rite" of Ophelia's funeral, and the death-trap of Claudius' last court assembled for his duel with Laertes. The widespread malady of Denmark is clear at last; and with the end of Claudius and his regime it is gone like a bad dream. Fortinbras appears at last in Denmark: a new hope for a new, purged state.

The purpose of this sketch, of course, is not to exhaust the analogical relationships among the narrative strands in *Hamlet*, but only to suggest, by means of a few illustrations, that they are there, and that they are an all-important element in the structure of the play. They point, I think, to the main action, and to the concern for the welfare of Denmark which all the characters share.

Ernest Jones* has an interpretation of the play also based upon analogies between its stories and characters, but reducing them all to the machinery of the Oedipus complex: "The main theme of this story," Dr. Jones writes, "is a highly elaborated and disguised account of a boy's love for his mother, and consequent jealousy of and hatred toward his father." Dr. Jones's study is very suggestive and, while confirming what might be called the analogical texture of the play, it raises important questions about the essential nature of these analogical relationships and the underlying theme to which they all point. I have no doubt that the father-son relationships are there: I have suggested it in my remarks on the Polonius-Laertes, Ghost-Hamlet sequence. Shakespeare seems to have missed none of the tensions, none of the ambivalence, in this crucial relationship. But can it be regarded as the fundamental theme of the play?

My objection to Jones's interpretation is that it reduces the motivation of the play to the emotional drives of the Oedipus complex. This overworks that complex, and takes us too far from the play itself. Thus part of the point of the Polonius-Laertes, Ghost-Hamlet analogy is the comic similarity and the tragic difference between the insights of Hamlet and Polonius; and this tension cannot be reduced to the Oedipus complex. The Oedipus complex does not account for the fact that Hamlet, besides being a son, is also a dispossessed prince; nor that Claudius, besides being a father symbol, is also the actual ruler of the state. But the actual movement of the play—to say nothing of its ultimate meaning—depends upon such objective facts and values as these.

Jones has studied the changes and elaborations which Shakespeare made in the Hamlet story, with its very ancient mythic roots, transforming it from what was perhaps a simple revenge motif into something much deeper. Jones thinks that the "deeper" theme which Shakespeare unconsciously felt was the son's desire to kill his father and possess his mother; and that the elabora-

Hamlet. By William Shakespeare. With a psycho-analytical study by Ernest Jones M.D. New York: Funk and Wagnalls, 1948.

tions and variations he made were disguises of the theme which really held him. But the elaborations Shakespeare made could equally well be understood as due to his extremely critical and skeptical bent; his need to criticize one version of his theme by means of another analogous one.

In short, the analogous stories, situations, and relationships in *Hamlet* point, not to the Oedipus complex, but to the main action or underlying theme of the play. And in that the emotional tensions of the Oedipus complex are only one element. The disease which is killing Denmark does not have a purely psychological explanation and cure, and the attempt to understand and destroy it has a moral as well as an emotional content. The religious, cultural, moral values of the tradition are at stake in this action; and the play as a whole has dimensions which cannot be completely understood if one thinks of it in these psychological terms, in abstraction from the theater in which it was formed.

A study of the interwoven plots of *Hamlet* points to the underlying theme, the main action of the play as a whole. But it does not quite enable us to understand Hamlet's shifting motives; and it does not throw much light upon the rhythms, the spectacular effects, and the rise and fall of tension, in the play considered as a performance before an audience. If we are to come a little closer to the play as play, it is necessary to consider the whole idea of the theater which Shakespeare used and assumed in his audience; for this theater offered means of "imitating the action" which cannot be subsumed under the art of plot-making as it is generally understood.

Hamlet as Ritual and Improvisation

If one could see a performance of *Hamlet*, uncut, unbroken by intermissions, and employing the kind of simple make-believe which Shakespeare, with his bare stage, must have intended, we should find much to enthrall us besides the stories themselves. The stories, of course, start at once, and are felt continuously as working themselves out: fate, behind the scenes, makes, from time to time, its sudden pronouncements. But on-stage, the music and the drums and the marching of royal and military pageantry, are directly absorbing, and they assure us that something of great and general significance is going on. From time to time the stage is emptied; the pageantry is gone; the stories seem to be marking time—and Hamlet emerges, alone, or with one or two interlocutors. Sometimes he suffers his visions before us; sometimes he makes jokes and topical allusions; sometimes he spars with his interlocutors like the gag-man in a minstrel show, or the master of ceremonies in a modern musical.

The scenes of pageantry are all civic or military or religious rituals; the changing of the guard, the formal assembling of the court of Denmark; the funeral of Ophelia. Though they all have their relevance to the interwoven stories of the play and to the discordant purposes of the various characters, their chief function is to show forth the main action or underlying theme, at various stages in its development. At these ritual moments the plot-lines are, as it were, gathered together; the issues are held in suspension, and we are reminded of the traditional social values in which all have some sort of stake.

Hamlet's monologues, and his nimble exchanges with Polonius or Rosencrantz and Guildenstern, his "topical allusions" to drunkenness or to the state of the theater, make a very different kind of theatrical appeal. He steps out of the narrative course of the play, out of the "world of Denmark" which is the basic postulate of the make-believe, refers directly to the parallels between "Denmark" and the England of his audience. From one point of view Shakespeare seems to be counting on the inherent dramatic and theatrical interest which this character has apart from the story—permitting him, like the first violin in a concerto, a cadenza on his own, after which we are returned to the matter in hand. From another point of view, Hamlet's "improvized" moments are carried by our confidence in him as "chief reflector": we look to him, as to the ritual scenes, to show us the underlying theme of the whole.

Both the ritual and the improvisational elements in *Hamlet* are essential—as essential as the stories—in the structure of the whole. The Elizabethan theater, at once as frankly "theatrical" as vaudeville, and as central to the life of its time as an ancient rite, offered Shakespeare two resources, two theatrical "dimensions" which the modern naturalistic tradition of serious drama must try, or pretend, to do without. In the table on the following page I have shown the chief ritual and the chief improvisational scenes in relation to the main parts of the plot.

If one thinks over the succession of ritual scenes as they appear in the play, it is clear that they serve to focus attention on the Danish body politic and its hidden malady: they are ceremonious invocations of the well-being of society, and secular or religious devices for securing it. As the play progresses, the rituals change in character, from the dim but honest changing of the guard, through Ophelia's mock rites, to the black mass of Claudius' last court. And it appears that the improvisational scenes bear a significant and developing relationship to the rituals. In general, they throw doubt upon the efficacy of the official magic, as when Hamlet refuses to take Claudius' first court at its face value; yet even the most cutting ironies of Hamlet do not disavow the mystery which the rituals celebrate, or reject the purposes that inform them.

The rituals, the stories, and the improvisations together make the peculiar rhythm of *Hamlet* as a performance. Denmark is shown as waiting, as it were, in the darkness of its ineffective ceremonies and hollow communal prayers while the infection, "mining all within," divides every man in secret from every other and bursts forth, from time to time, in savage but brief and ineffective fights.

But before examining the sequence of rituals, with its center in the players scene, it is necessary to endeavor to support the view that the Elizabethan theater had, in fact, this ritual aspect: that Shakespeare's audience, like that of Sophocles, was prepared to accept his play not only as an exciting story but as the "celebration of the mystery" of human life.

The Globe Theater and the Festival of Dionysos

The main evidence (apart from the play itself) for taking *Hamlet* as a species of ritual drama, is provided by recent studies which show that a great deal of the religious culture of the Middle Ages was still alive in Shakespeare's time. Tillyard's *The Elizabethan World Picture*, for example, makes this clear. Mr.

THE PARTS OF THE PLOT	RITUAL SCENES	IMPROVISATIONAL ENTERTAINMENT
he Prologue	Act I, sc. 1 The changing of the Guard Act I, sc. 2 Claudius' First Court	
he Agons — development of conflicting purposes of various characters; contrasts of their ories; "purposes misok"; indecision and ghting in the dark		Act I, sc. 4 Hamlet's sermon on drunkenness (in Denmark and / or England) Act II, sc. 2 Hamlet exchanges wisecracks with Polonius, Rosencrantz, Guildenstern, and the players. Act III, sc. 2 Hamlet's charge to the players—his opinions on the art of acting.

RITUAL AND ENTERTAINMENT
Act III, sc. 2
The performance of Hamlet's play is both rite and entertainment, and shows the Prince as at once clown and ritual head of the state.

THE PARTS OF THE PLOT	RITUAL SCENES	IMPROVISATIONAL ENTERTAINMENT
he Climax, Peripety, d Recognitions; all rrative strands brought gether		
he Pathos or "sparagos," both of the state d the individuals, leadg to the epiphany or ollective revelation" of e general disease. (Cf. oynbee's "schism in the ate and schism in the ul")	Act IV, sc. 5 Ophelia's Madness is a mock ritual, a mixture of false and lewd marriage, and false and savage funeral; refers also to the funeral of Hamlet's father and Gertrude's false marriage. Alternates with rebellion in the state.	
he Epiphany, or Final ision of the underlying uth of the action	Act V, sc. 1 Ophelia's funeral. A "maimed rite" but a real death. Act V, sc. 2 The duel between Hamlet and Laertes. This duel is surrounded with all the ceremonies of Claudius' Court, like the players' scene, and Claudius' other loud and drunken celebrations; but every element in it is false or mistaken: a mockery of invocation; and it eventuates in death, and "resurrection" in the shape of Fortinbras, who, now that Claudius' regime is gone, can appear with his new faith and hope.	Act V Hamlet jokes and moralizes with the Gravedigger and Horatio. He feels like the gag-man and the royal victim in one. Gravedigger corresponds to Polonius.

Tillyard quotes Hamlet's famous speech on man: "What a piece of work is a man: how noble in reason; how infinite in faculty; in form and moving how express and admirable; in action how like an angel; in apprehension how like a god; the beauty of the world, the paragon of animals."—"This has been taken," Mr. Tillyard explains, "as one of the great English versions of Renaissance humanism, an assertion of the dignity of man against the asceticisms of medieval misanthropy. Actually it is in the purest medieval tradition: Shakespeare's version of the orthodox encomia of what man, created in God's image, was like in his prelapsarian state and of what ideally he is still capable of being. It also shows Shakespeare placing man in the traditional cosmic setting between the angels and the beasts. It is what the theologians had been saying for centuries." And Mr. Tilyard proceeds to show that most of the "world picture which the Middle Ages inherited" was still tacitly assumed by the Elizabethans: "an ordered universe arranged in a fixed system of hierarchies but modified by man's sin and the hope of his redemption."

The Elizabethan stage itself, that central mirror of the life of its times, was a symbolic representation of this traditional cosmos: it was thus taken both as the physical and as the metaphysical "scene" of man's life. Mr. Kernodle has shown this in detail in his illuminating study, *From Art to Theater*. He traces the genealogy of the symbolic façade of the Elizabethan stage house back through street pageantry to painting and to the architecture of tombs and altars; and thence to the arcade screen of the Greek tragic theater itself. "More than an arrangement of side doors and inner and upper stages, that façade was itself a symbol of castle, throne, triumphal arch, altar, tomb"—in short, an all-purpose, eminently practicable setting, implying the constant elements in the Elizabethan world picture, yet flexible enough to serve the shifting make-believe of the actors. Over the whole was a permanent canopy, painted to represent the heavens, a vault literally "fretted with golden fire."

The symbolic character of this stage seems to imply a conception of the theater akin to that of ritual: the celebration of the mystery of human life. This stage and its drama did not, it is true, develop directly from the Mass; it developed from the secular theater of the Middle Ages and, as Mr. Kernodle shows, from royal and civic pageantry. But in the Renaissance the monarchy and its rites was taking over some of the religious significance of the church and its rites. The pope tended to be superseded by the prince as vicar, or "type" of Christ, the pageantry and ceremony of the church by the pageantry and ceremony of the national state. The Tudor monarch was the symbol, and the visible center of the traditional world order, so that Donne could write, on the death of Prince Henry:

> Of Weight one Centre, one of Greatness is,
> And Both my Centres feel this Period.

The role of the monarch in Shakespeare's time (and in his plays) was thus very close to that of Sophocles' Oedipus or Creon: he was at once ruler, high priest, and father of the community. And the ceremonies which Shakespeare and Hamlet's Danes engaged in—whether obviously religious, like the funeral, or more secular, like the Court—were taken as celebrating and securing the welfare of the whole, of the monarchy, and of the "lives of many" that depended on it.

The Elizabethan theater may thus be regarded as the heir of the Greek tragic theater with its ritual basis. The Elizabethan cosmos is still that of the great tradition*, which the Middle Ages inherited from the city state. The physical stage itself is symbolic in the same way as the tragic stage of the Greeks; and the ritual component in its drama has similar deep and general meanings.

This does not mean, of course, that Shakespeare's audience, or even Shakespeare himself, could have expounded this genealogy and these parallels. If the tradition was alive in Shakespeare's time, it was as a "habit of thought and feeling" rather than as an explicit and integrated philosophy. But Shakespeare seems to have felt the essential elements of this great "theater" as alive still; to have assumed that his audience would respond to them, and to have based his dramaturgy upon them.

If Shakespeare's theater is thus akin to the theater of Sopho-

*The Great Chain of Being, by Arthur Lovejoy, is a chief source of this view of what the Renaissance inherited.

cles, their drama should be composed on similar principles: appealing in both cases to ancient and publicly accepted values and modes of understanding, rather than preaching, inventing, and arguing in the manner of modern drama. And the comparison should throw some light on both.

The themes of *Oedipus* are, from many points of view, strikingly similar to those of *Hamlet*. Oedipus gave his name to that "complex" to which, as we saw, Ernest Jones reduces *Hamlet*. Whatever one may think of this reduction, it is clear that in both plays a royal sufferer is associated with pollution, in its very sources, of an entire social order. Both plays open with an invocation of the well-being of the endangered body politic. In both, the destiny of the individual and of society are closely intertwined; and in both the suffering of the royal victim seems to be necessary before purgation and renewal can be achieved.

But my purpose here is not to attempt an extended comparison of the two plays; it is, rather, to contrast the structural principles of these two ritual dramas, one from the beginnings of the tradition, the other from the end, at the very brink of the modern world.

The extraordinary unity and clarity of *Oedipus*, in comparison with *Hamlet*, is perhaps due to the fact that it is closer to the form, purpose, and occasion (the Festival of Dionysos) of its ritual source than *Hamlet*, in the Globe Theater, is to its ritual sources. Oedipus is the one and obvious protagonist, his story the literal subject of the play. He is the diagrammatic royal scapegoat, a marked man, from the first. And the parts of the play, which show the stages of his destruction, correspond very closely to the stages of the ancient ritual sacrifice.

In *Hamlet* it is as though every one of these elements had been elaborated by a process of critical analysis. Hamlet himself, though a prince, is without a throne; though a sufferer for the truth, he can appear in public as a mere infatuated or whimsical youth. We have seen how many ironic parallels Shakespeare provides to his story—and to this I may add that it takes both Hamlet and Claudius to represent the royal victim of the tradition. Though the play has the general shape of the tragic rhythm, and the traditional parts of the plot, each part is presented in several ironically analogous versions. The prologue is in three scenes of contrasting moods. The agon is so complicated that the very purposes of the antagonists are critically seen as false, hidden, or "mistook." It takes all of Act v to represent the epiphany, the final vision of death, from all the angles that Shakespeare knows.

Even the ritual process itself is, in *Hamlet*, directly dramatized: i.e., presented in a tragic, ironic light. There are no rituals in *Oedipus*: Oedipus is a ritual. But Hamlet has an extremely modern and skeptical, a Pirandellesque, theatricality as well; Shakespeare plays with the basis of his own make-believe. Sophocles uses the tragic theater with its ritual basis to mirror human life directly. Shakespeare uses the Elizabethan theater in the same way; but at the same time he has another mirror—his own and Hamlet's supermodern awareness—in which the making of the ritual is itself ironically reflected.

Oedipus moves, as it were, straight to its end, in clear figures of the tragic rhythm. But in *Hamlet* there is also a movement of ironic analysis, represented by the analogous versions of the main theme which the interwoven plots embody, and by Hamlet's monologues and wry jokes: improvisations which are beside the story of the play, in closer relationship to the audience. But though Shakespeare thus sees the ritual order of Claudius' Denmark as it were from without, he does not, like Euripides, simply satirize the values and the order of the traditional religion: the movement of analysis is corrected from time to time by a synthesis (a funeral or a Court scene) in which the main theme of the play, and the interdependence of all the dramatis personae, is reaffirmed. These rituals in Hamlet are not simply absurd, as a Euripidean *deus ex machina* is absurd; they are rather tragic failures, like Claudius' private attempt to pray: "Words without thoughts never to heaven go." In spite of the ironic device of the double plot, and the deeper irony of the Pirandellesque improvisation (Is all the world a stage or the stage life itself?) Shakespeare also clings to the conception of the theater as ritual.

Ritual and Improvisation: Hamlet's Play as the Center

Shakespeare's theater, because of its ancient roots and its central place in society, permitted the development of ritual drama—or at least a drama which had this dimension as well as others. In the structure of *Hamlet* the rituals, as distinguished from the plots, serve to present the main action at various points in its development. Shakespeare uses them in much the same way in which Henry James used his "social occasions" to present the main theme of *The Awkward Age*. The structure of *Hamlet* could be described in Henry James's words: "A circle consisting of a number of small rounds disposed at equal distance about a central object. The central object was my situation, my subject in itself, to which the thing would owe its title, and the small rounds represented so many distinct lamps, as I liked to call them, the function of each of which would be to light up with all due intensity one of its aspects. . . . I revelled in this notion of the Occasion as a thing by itself." That is the important point: the social rite or occasion is taken as a thing by itself; it enables the author to assemble his dramatis personae in a wider light than any of their individual intelligences could provide. If my analysis of *Hamlet* is correct, the rituals (though they have deeper meanings than James's social gatherings) are also "occasions" of this kind: lamps lighting the rottenness of Denmark (the basic situation of the play) and the many-sided action which results, at various points in its course, and in various aspects.

In the table showing the relation of the plot to the ritual scenes and the improvisations, the players' scene is at the center. It has a ritual aspect, it is Hamlet's most ambitious improvisation, and it is the climax and peripety of the whole complex plot-scheme. If one can understand this scene, one will be close to grasping Shakespeare's sense of the theater, and his direct, profoundly histrionic dramaturgy.

The prologue contains two rituals, the changing of the guard and Claudius' first court. The changing of the guard is conducted by the honest and simple-minded soldiers, in perfect good faith: the welfare of the state is conceived in the most obvious and acceptable terms, and with the solemnity and authority of the military function. The motives of the soldiers are not impugned; and the only ironic angle we get on this scene is due to the arrival of the Ghost, which clearly suggests that the military rite is not an appropriate means for dealing with the actual danger. Claudius' court, on the other hand, is conducted by the new King; and here we feel (both in the light of Hamlet's disabused view of Claudius, and in the light of the visit of the Ghost) that there is something false about Claudius' discharge of the royal function. Together the two scenes establish the fact of danger and the common concern with the threatened welfare of the state. But they throw ironic lights upon each other. The point of view of the regime is in conflict with that of the simple soldiers. Neither the soldiers nor the regime have the magic for dealing with the Ghost; and it appears that the rituals of the state in general are false or mistaken.

The many conflicts, which the prologue presents as it were in suspension, are further developed (though without coming to direct issue) during the rest of the first act, the second act, and the first scene of Act III. Then (bringing the climax, peripety, and recognition) comes Hamlet's improvised ritual, the players' scene. Hamlet, as the "chief reflector," the widest consciousness in literature, as Henry James called him, is aware of what the soldiers see, of what Claudius sees, and of what the Ghost sees, and he is torn by all the conflicts implicit in these partial values and myopic vested interests. His "ritual occasion" is thus an answer to both rituals in the prologue; and at the same time (because he has also seen what the ghost sees) it is an answer to, and a substitute for, the inadequate or false ritual order of Denmark. It is itself a "ritual" in that it assembles the whole tribe for an act symbolic of their deepest welfare; it is false and ineffective, like the other public occasions, in that the Danes do not really understand or intend the enactment which they witness. It is, on the other hand, not a true ritual, but an improvisation—for here the role of Hamlet, as showman, as master of ceremonies, as clown, as night-club entertainer who lewdly jokes with the embarrassed patrons—Hamlet the ironist, in sharpest contact with the audience on-stage and the audience off-stage, yet a bit outside the literal belief in the story: it is here that this aspect of Hamlet's role is clearest. But notice that, if Hamlet is the joking clown, he is also like those improvising Old Testament prophets who, gathering a handful of dust or of little bones, or a damaged pot from the potter's wheel, present to a blind generation a sudden image of their state. It is in the players' scene that the peculiar theatricality of *Hamlet*—ritual as theater and theater as ritual; at once the lightest inprovisation and the solemnest occasion—is most clearly visible.

What then is the image, the parable, the "fear in a handful of dust," which Hamlet thus places—with all the pomp of court and all the impudence of the night-club entertainer—in the very center of the public consciousness of Denmark?

The most detailed analysis I know of the players' scene is Mr. Dover Wilson's, in his excellent book, *What Happens in Hamlet*. The reader is referred to that study, and to its companion-piece, Granville-Barker's book on *Hamlet*, for a discussion of the theatrical problems which the scene presents and for an understanding of the complexity of the scene as a whole, wherein the focus of the audience's attention is shifted from Hamlet (the "central reflector") to Horatio, to the Queen, to Ophelia, to the King—as though the play-within-a-play were being lighted from many angles by reflection from many mirrors. My purpose here is only to describe Hamlet's play itself, in order to show how it reveals the malady of the regime in all its ambiguity, mystery, and spreading ramifications. For this little play is indeed an all-purpose mousetrap—and it catches more than the conscience of the King.

First of all the play presents the hidden crime (the murder of a king and the more or less incestuous theft of his queen and his throne) upon which, as in *Oedipus*, all the threads of the interwoven plots depend. It is the presentation of this literal fact which has the immediate effect upon the innocent bystanders of the court and upon the innocent groundlings in the audience, though in Hamlet's violent view none are innocent. Because the security of the regime and the purposes of its supporters depend either upon ignorance or concealment, the public representation of the crime is itself an act of aggression, Hamlet's attack, the

turning point in the story. This attack reaches the guilty Claudius first, Gertrude second, Polonius third; then Laertes and
Ophelia. And at length it clears the way for Fortinbras, the new
faith and the new regime.

But though the fact of murder, incest, and usurpation is clearly presented, the time of the murder—is it still to come?—is vague;
and the dramatis personae in the playlet are shifted about in such
a way as to leave the identity of the criminal in question, and so
to spread the guilt. The actual crime was that of Claudius; but
in the play the guilty one is nephew to the King. This could
mean (as Polonius and Gertrude seem to think) a direct threat
by Hamlet to Claudius; it also means that Hamlet (who had admitted to himself a "weakness and melancholy" which makes
him subject to devilish solicitations, and who had assured Ophelia, that "I am myself indifferent honest, yet I could accuse me
of such things it were better my mother had not borne me")
had granted Claudius, in advance, that he too is at least potentially guilty. Neither Hamlet nor Shakespeare seem to rule out
a Freudian interpretation of the tangle; Hamlet comes close to
representing himself as the diagrammatic son of the Oedipus
complex, killing the father and possessing the mother. Yet his
awareness of such motivations lifts the problems from the level of
pathology to that of drama; he sees himself, Claudius, Denmark,
the race itself, as subject to greeds and lusts which the hypocritical façade of the regime guiltily conceals.

Thus the literal meaning of the playlet is the fact of the crime;
but the trope and the anagoge convey a picture of the human in
general as weak, guilty, and foolish: the deepest and most sinister version of the malady of Claudius' regime in Denmark. This
picture should emerge directly from the staging of the playlet
before the corrupt and hypocritical court, under the inspired
and triumphant irony of the regisseur-prince. The whining of
pipes, the parade of mummers, the wooden gestures of the
dumb-show, the tinkle of the rhymes, should have the magical
solemnity of a play-party or children's singing-game ("London
bridge is falling down"). Yet because of the crimes represented,
this atmosphere is felt as unbearably weak and frivolous, a parody of all solemn rites. If this playlet invokes the magic potency

of the theater ("the play's the thing") it does so with as much despairing irony as love. The staging is crude and childish: Hamlet's actors vainly take things into their own hands, and the court audience is as condescendingly unperceptive (until the scandal dawns on them) as any cynical crowd at a Broadway opening.

Hamlet's audience on-stage (and perhaps off-stage as well) misses the deeper meanings of his play. Yet he and his author have put it as simply as possible in the weary couplets of the Player-King. The Player-King seems to stand for Hamlet's father, and thus for the Ghost; and he speaks in fact with the clarity but helplessness (in this world) of the dead—addressing the frivolous Player-Queen without much hope of understanding. Since he is Hamlet's puppet, he speaks also for Hamlet, and since he is the King, he stands also for Claudius. Claudius, in the course of the play, will gradually acquire a helplessness like that of the Ghost; a faithlessness and an indecision like that of Hamlet. It is the function of the Player-King to state as directly as possible that gloomy and fatalistic sense of human action which is the subject of the play, and which all the various characters have by analogy.

The way to show this in detail would be to study the action of each character and to show what frivolity and gloomy faithlessness they have in common, but this would take too long. The point may be briefly illustrated by juxtaposing a few utterances of Hamlet and Claudius with analogous couplets of the Player-King:

HAMLET:	There's a divinity that shapes our ends,
Act v	Rough-hew them how we will.
scene 2	
	Was't Hamlet wronged Laertes? Never Hamlet:
	. . . .
	. . . . Hamlet denies it.
	Who does it then? His madness.
CLAUDIUS:	My stronger guilt defeats my strong
Act iii	intent:
scene 3	And, like a man to double business bound,

I stand in pause where I shall first begin,
And both neglect.

Not that I think you did not love your
    father,
But that I know love is begun by time,
And that I see, in passages of proof,
Time qualifies the spark and fire of it.
There lives within the very flame of love
A kind of wick or snuff that will abate it,
And nothing is at a like goodness still,
For goodness, growing to a plurisy,
Dies in his own too much. That we
    would do,
We should do when we would, for this
    "would" changes
And hath abatements and delays as many
As there are tongues, are hands, are ac-
    cidents;
And then this "should" is like a spend-
    thrift sigh,
That hurts by easing.

PLAYER KING: Our wills and fates do so contrary run
That our devices still are overthrown,
Our thoughts are ours, their ends none
    of our own.

What to ourselves in passion we propose,
The passion ending, doth the purpose
    lose.

Purpose is but the slave to memory
Of violent birth, but poor validity.

The speeches of Hamlet and Claudius which I have quoted
come late in the play, when both of them gain a deathly insight
into their destinies—the hidden and uncontrolled springs of
their own and others' actions. Even Claudius sees so deeply at
this moment that he gets the sense of human action which all
the characters have by analogy. His speech to Laertes (Act IV,

scene 7) is, moreover, both made more ironic and more general by being addressed to Laertes in order to deceive him into a course which is contrary to his deepest purposes and best interests. As for Hamlet, his sense of pathos, of the suffering of motivations beyond our understanding or control, does not save him from violent outbursts any more than that of Claudius does. Shakespeare usually grants his victims a moment of great clarity when it is too late—and then shows them returning, like automatons, to "ravin down their proper bane" and die.

But the chief point I wish to make here is that the Player-King presents very pithily the basic vision of human action in the play, at a level so deep that it applies to all the characters: the guilty, the free, the principals, the bystanders, those in power and the dispossessed. This vision of course comes directly from the crime of Claudius and the other "accidental judgements, casual slaughters, purposes mistook" (as Horatio describes them when summing up for Fortinbras) upon which the complicated plot depends; yet this generalized vision is more terrible than any of the particular crimes, and much more important for understanding Hamlet's motivation. To this point I shall return later.

The immediate effect of Hamlet's play comes by way of the concrete scandal which brings the climax and peripety of the narratives. The presentation of the play is Hamlet's attack; it succeeds; it convicts Claudius' regime, and "the lives of many" that depend upon it, of impotence and corruption. After that revelation all is lost (just as Macbeth is lost after the banquet scene)—and the desperate devices of the King and Laertes, the brief folly of Polonius, and the unimpeded progress of Fortinbras, in the healthy rhythm of the march, are seen as clearly fated or doomed.

For this reason also the "rituals" which follow the players' scene have a different quality from those which precede it. Since the regime has lost its manna—been "shown up"—the rituals in Acts IV and V, marking the stages of the collective pathos and epiphany, are clearly presented as mad or evil. Ophelia's mad ritual presents the "sparagmos" or tearing asunder of the individual and society at once ("schism in the state and schism in the soul"); mingling marriage and funeral, lewdness and prettiness, love and destruction to the accompaniment of plotting and rebellion. Ophelia's funeral is a real death but a "maimèd rite"; the duel between Hamlet and Laertes is ostensibly a ritual and actually a murder. With the assembling of the court and the royal family for the duel, the picture of Claudius' regime (the collective revelation of his black masses) is complete.

In the succession of "ritual scenes" with its center and climax in Hamlet's little play, it is obvious that Hamlet himself plays a central role. In the two rituals of the prologue he is, like the audience, a mere puzzled and troubled bystander. After the hidden struggles of Act I, II, and III, he presents, with his play, his own black mass, his own parody of a rite. He does not appear for the "tearing asunder" of Ophelia's madness, for this marks the pathos of the regime, and of the lives that depend directly on it; and his life (wherever it may be) has already withdrawn from all loyalty to Claudius' Denmark. But he returns to record Ophelia's truncated funeral in his cold, spent, but clear awareness; and to take his fated role in the duel at the end. I have endeavored to study the rituals as marking the progress of the "play as a whole"; but it is evident that in the play, and in the order of the rituals, Hamlet himself is both chief "agonist" and central "reflector." With this in mind it is possible to offer an interpretation of the role of Hamlet in relation to Shakespeare's idea of the theater, and the traditional social values which the play assumes.

An Interpretation of the Role of Hamlet

> "For, by the image of my cause, I see
> The portraiture of his."

Oedipus, as I have pointed out, starts out as the hero, the triumphant human adequate to rule, and ends, like Tiresias, a scapegoat, a witness and a sufferer for the hidden truth of the human condition. The play starts with the conflict and contrast between Oedipus and Tiresias, shows the steps of Oedipus' dismemberment, and ends when he is blind and all-seeing and helpless, as Tiresias was in the beginning. Hamlet is apparently thought of as undergoing a similar transformation, from hero to scapegoat, from "the expectancy and rose of the fair state" to the distracted, suffering witness and victim of Act v. But this development is not neatly laid out for him according to a publicly understood series of struggles: he feels his way toward it, not with public sanction but against the faithless worldliness of the Danes. It is not until Act v that his martyr-like destiny "feels right" to him.

We see him in the first three acts of the play as a puzzled and, as it were, unconvinced hero and prince. He knows that "the times are out of joint" and that he is born to set them right; he knows that the Prince should be moved by honor and ambition: but he cannot reconcile this worldly code with his sense of evil in Denmark nor with the otherworldly solicitations of his Ghost-father. From Corneille to Dryden the ethical values of "honor" will be taken as sufficient basis for the drama of human life; but Hamlet's sense of his own and Denmark's condition contradicts this simplified philosophy. When he looks at Laertes, that "noble youth," he envies him—envies, at least, his simple and honorable motivations. When he looks at Fortinbras, he envies him the ability to risk his own and other lives for honor—"even for an eggshell." If he could accept this code, he would feel that the murder of Claudius would heal the schism in his own soul and in society; but just as his sense of evil preceded his knowledge of Claudius' literal guilt, so he cannot believe that the literal punishment of Claudius (an eye for an eye) will cure the damage he has done. And so his drama becomes far deeper than a simple revenge play.

If Hamlet is not content with the simple soldierly code of honor, it is because he sees too deeply and skeptically into that cosmic setting of human life which Shakespeare's theater symbolically represented. He sees beyond the tiny human involvements of the foreground to the social order indicated by the stage house façade and, above that, to the order in the stars implied by the canopy over his head. This is especially clear in his first scene with Rosencrantz and Guildenstern (Act ii, scene 2). It is in this scene that he makes the great speech on Man which Tillyard quotes as an exposition of the traditional ordered universe. But the speech ends bitterly: "And yet, to me, what is this quintessence of dust?"

Though Hamlet accepts this order, he does not know where he belongs in it; he is not even sure which way is up. He would have felt the force of that remark of Heracleitus which Eliot uses as epigraph to *Burnt Norton*: "The way up and the way down are one and the same." His intellect plays over the world of the religious tradition with an all-dissolving irony like that of Montaigne in the *Apologie de Raimond Sebonde*: a truly double-edged irony, for he can neither do with nor do without the ancient moral and cosmic order.

That is why he has a despairing fellow-feeling for Rosencrantz and Guildenstern. He knows them for little trimmers, neither for God nor for the Devil, but "for themselves," like the dim figures in Dante's Limbo: "indifferent children of the earth," "Fortune's privates," as they call themselves. He is himself anything but indifferent, yet he does not at that moment know how to care, and so he feels himself, like them, lost between "greatness" and the chill of mere bodily "weight" and utter faithlessness at the bottom of the universe. Thus he is troubled with "bad dreams":

> GUIL. Which dreams, indeed, are ambition, for the very substance of the ambitious is but the shadow of a dream.
> HAM. A dream itself is but a shadow.
> Ros. Truly, and I hold ambition of so airy and light a quality that it is but a shadow's shadow.
> HAM. Then are our beggars bodies, and our monarchs and outstretched heroes the beggars' shadows. Shall we to the court? for, by my fay, I cannot reason.

Hamlet draws the deduction which troubles *him*, but not Rosencrantz and Guildenstern: if ambition like Fortinbras' is illusory, what, in Denmark, is to show us the way, and prevent us from taking the "shadow as a solid thing"?

It would be an exaggeration to say that Hamlet envies these two as he envies Fortinbras and Laertes. But his fellow-feeling for them—call it sympathy, or a sense of the analogy between them, or seeing their cause as mirroring his—comes, like his envy, from the fact that he himself is lost. Until the success of his play, Hamlet feels his over-quick sympathy as a weakness, and covers it up with murderous sarcasm. On his return from England, he has accepted it, and in Act v his abnormally quick sympathy has acquired some of the quiet of the vision integrated and lived-up-to, some of the breadth of charity.

What has intervened is chiefly the presentation of his play. When the players come, and do a speech for Hamlet, he envies *them*; but at this time it turns out that he has found a real clue to his own action. He cannot act like a simple soldier but he can employ the theater in an equally dangerous, and far more significant, project. He can use it as a trap for the conscience of the King, and at the same time as a test of his own and the Ghost's vision. Thus empirically, or improvisationally, feeling his way through the concrete elements of his situation, he finds his own proper line of action, and a use of the theater very much like that which two other autobiographical characters of Shakespeare make of it.

The two other characters who use the theater in this way are the Duke in *Measure for Measure* and Prospero in *The Tempest*. These two plays are, of course, very different from each other and from Hamlet. But the analogies between the three dispossessed rulers, and their attempts to purify the spiritual atmosphere of their societies by means of significant shows, are close enough to throw a good deal of light on the nature of the role of Hamlet.

The "Duke of dark corners" is dispossessed and anonymous much as Hamlet is, even though he himself had rejected the official role of ruler. His theatricality consists in casting Angelo and Claudio and Isabella for tragic roles, and then moving about behind the scenes like a nervous regisseur, to make sure that the moral of the drama is clear, and yet that the real tragedy does not go too far. The play he arranges is almost a practical joke; yet, like Hamlet's play, it both tests and reveals a wider and healthier vision of human society than Vienna publicly accepts. And by this means he proposes to substitute the rule of charity for Angelo's blind and univocal conception of Mosaic justice.

Measure for Measure has been called a problem comedy, and it has, in fact, a discursive clarity, a kind of modern intellectuality, quite unlike *Hamlet*. But with this reservation, the Duke as regisseur-prince is very closely akin to Hamlet in that role.

The Tempest has neither the analytic naturalism of *Hamlet* nor the "thesis" quality of *Measure for Measure*. It partakes of the qualities of myth, of Medieval allegory, and of dream; as though Shakespeare's mind, at the end of his career, were in that state which Dante knew, in the early morning, at the threshold of the Mount of Purgatory:

Canto IX: e che la mente nostra, peregrina / più dalla carne e men da' pensier presa, / alle sue vision quasi è divina.	When our mind, wandering farther from the flesh and less caught by thought, is in its visions almost prophetic.

The basic donné of the play is the magic of Prospero. And hence the shows with which he purges the worldly exiles from Milan can be close to the very idea of such shows. Mr. Colin Still (in *The Timeless Theme*) has traced in them many ancient ritual themes. It is in this play that Shakespeare comes to terms with his own imaginative power as a wielder of the theater—indicating its use in the service of truth, and its limitations as a means of salvation. For at the end, when Prospero has demonstrated both the magic power of the theater and its use, he buries his book and staff and prays for grace. He has a ripeness and a clarity and a power which Hamlet lacks, but for that very reason he helps one to see what Hamlet, with his play, was trying to do.

Hamlet, more than either the Duke or Prospero, is defenseless and uninstructed in the midst of life; and if he stumbles on the theater as a means of realizing his vision and his anonymous being, he does not clearly understand what he has accomplished. When the King rises after the play, Hamlet takes his success with almost childish pleasure: "Would not this, sir, and a forest of feathers, if the rest of my fortunes turn Turk with me, with two Provincial roses on my razed shoes, get me a fellowship in a cry of players, sir?" The delight is, of course, partly ironic; moreover he has still to confirm his success with his mother and the King. Even after those two interviews he is puzzled and tormented; he does not really feel that he has done his part, borne his witness, taken his stand, until he returns from England. By that time his testimony has had its effect: the regime is wounded beyond repair, and he himself is doomed.

In Act v, while he records in the graveyard the vision of death —literal death and the death of society, to the accompaniment of the clowns' heartless equivocations—and finally suffers the truncated funeral of Ophelia—he feels that his role, all but the very last episode, has been played. He is still uncertain what this will be, still feels that it must include the killing of Claudius: "Is't not perfect conscience to quit him with this arm?" His personal hatred for the King is sharp as ever; but he is content, now, to let the fated end come as it will. "It will be short: the interim is mine; and a man's life's no more than to say 'one'." He feels, I think, whether he or his author would put it so or not, that he is ready to take the consequences of his revelation, to suffer for that truth: "Thou wouldst not think how ill's all here about my heart; but it is no matter. . . . It is such a kind of gain-giving as would perhaps trouble a woman. . . . The readiness is all." One could say that he feels the poetic rightness of his own death. One could say, with Ernest Jones, that because of his Oedipus complex he had a death-wish all along. Or one could say that his death was the only adequate expiation for the evil of Denmark, according to the ancient emotional logic of the scapegoat; or one could say that only by accepting death to prove it could the truth of his vision be properly affirmed.

However one may interpret it, when his death comes it "feels right," the only possible end for the play. Horatio makes music for his going-off like that which accompanies Oedipus' death at Colonnus: "Good night, sweet prince, and flights of angels sing thee to thy rest." And Fortinbras treats him like one of those honor-seekers that had puzzled him all along, as though in his career the hero had somehow been subsumed in the martyr: "Let four captains bear Hamlet, like a soldier, to the stage." We are certainly intended to feel that Hamlet, however darkly and uncertainly he worked, had discerned the way to be obedient to his deepest values, and accomplished some sort of purgatorial progress for himself and Denmark.

I am aware that this interpretation of the role of Hamlet is open to the same sort of objections as all other interpretations; there is no substitute for the direct knowledge which a good performance of the play would give. But I think that Shakespeare, in writing the play, was counting on such a performance, and upon the willing make-believe of his audience and his performers. The elements of the Tudor monarchy, of the emblematic stage of the Globe, and of the traditional cosmos they stood for, were accepted for the purposes of the play as real; and within the concrete elements of this scene the role of Hamlet has its own logic.

Analogous Action: An Interpretation of the Play

> "For goodness, growing to a plurisy,
> Dies in his own too much."

The remark of the King, which he uses as a warning to Laertes, and which I have used to describe Hamlet's over-quick and over-subtle sympathy, applies also to Shakespeare's principles of composition in the play as a whole. Shakespeare's sense of analogy is perhaps too productive, burgeoning too richly in all directions, as though the dramatic life he had got hold of gave him more instances than he needed. Yet it is my belief that the life itself, the germ, the "unity" is there, however overlaid with elaborations and confusingly illumined from many directions.

Miss Caroline Spurgeon discerned this underlying life, quite accurately, as a result of her studies of the metaphors in the play: "To Shakespeare's pictorial imagination," she writes, "the problem in *Hamlet* is not predominantly that of the will and reason, of a mind too philosophic or a nature temperamentally unfitted to act quickly: he sees it pictorially *not as the problem of an individual at all,* but as something greater and even more mysterious, as a *condition* for which the individual himself is apparently not responsible, any more than the sick man is to blame for the infection which strikes and devours him, but which, nevertheless, in its course and development, impartially and relentlessly annihilates him and others, innocent and guilty alike.

That is the tragedy of *Hamlet*, and it is perhaps the chief tragic mystery of life."

Miss Spurgeon offers a kind of scientific proof of her view of the play by showing that the predominant metaphors are those of disease. An analysis of the play as the imitation of action gives the same result. The action of the play as a whole is "to identify and destroy the hidden imposthume which is endangering the life of Denmark." But because the source of infection is hidden, and there is no general agreement about its nature or location, the action of the play is predominantly in the passive mode—the suffering of forces not controlled or understood, rather than the consistent drive of an intelligible purpose. *Hamlet* is, like *The Cherry Orchard*, in its essential structure an "ensemble pathos," broken from time to time by the spasmodic moves of one or two of the characters.

This action is realized in many analogous ways in the contrasted characters. Claudius, who identifies the health of Denmark with the safety of his own corrupt regime, and therefore merely wishes to hold what he has, gradually comes to feel that the imposthume which poisons the communal life and his own is Hamlet: "for like the hectic in my blood he rages." Polonius, the chief figure in the comic sub-plot, also identifies the health of the body politic with the status quo; and for him the dis-ease is only the normal but troublesome fires of youth: Laertes' appetite for drabbing and gambling, Hamlet's infatuation for Ophelia—both to be cured by a judicious mixture of discipline and indulgence, which his age and experience can easily concoct.

Gertrude and Ophelia (like other women pictured by Shakespeare) define their actions and their beings only with reference to their men; and since they both have a stake in the regime, and at the same time in the rebellious Hamlet, they suffer the worst of the disease itself. In the economy of the play, they are symbols and measures of the health of the body politic—glamorous signs of what might have been, and torn and dishonored images of what is.

Hamlet himself, as we saw, comes the closest to seeing the whole range of the disease, as it spreads from the immediate guilt of Claudius to ruin all dependent lives. And we have seen that the adequate response to the rottenness of Denmark, as he sees it, is not a simple, purposive course of action, but a bearing-witness and a suffering-for-the-truth.

The characters have not only analogous objects of their actions, they all act in a similar way, indirectly. Polonius has his "windlasses" and his "essays of bias." Claudius acts only through intermediaries: Polonius, Rosencrantz and Guildenstern, Laertes. Ophelia acts as the puppet of her father, and Hamlet by means of his symbolic play. The Gravedigger speaks in equivocations, and Osric in such a "yesty collection" of ornamental clichés that he is barely comprehensible.

In defining the action of the play as a whole, the one underlying "essence" which the actions of the various characters "adumbrate" in their different ways, the character of Claudius is all important—not because he sees more, or realizes a deeper life, but because as head of the state he is, *de facto*, the one center of "weight" and of "greatness." As Tudor monarch, father, king, and high-priest—the massy wheel upon which the lives of the many depend—he makes, so to speak, the spiritual weather in Denmark. It is his particular kind of spiritual night—his motionless worldly presence, like a wall; his gratified lust ("fat weed on Lethe wharf," "things rank and gross in nature") —which defines the action in *Hamlet*. In such a nonconducting atmosphere, all purposes are short, hidden, and mistook, and they soon sink into frightened or oblivious stagnation. As long as he rules, "Denmark is a prison," "one of the worst" of the world's many confines, closed away from Dante's "dolce mondo."

From this point of view, Claudius' place in the economy of the play is like that of Macbeth in his play: Shakespeare thinks of the usurper in both cases as defining the "scene" and thereby the action of the play. Macbeth is in his moral being quite unlike Claudius; and he produces a different action and a different rhythm in the play as a whole. Macbeth is like a man running down-hill to escape himself: however fast he goes, "the pauser, reason," is still with him. In his depraved career he lays an irrational and obsessive basis for all human thought and intercourse; hence every action is paradoxical and unnatural. Even the peripety, when Macduff, Malcolm, and Ross are forced to take action against Macbeth, is realized as a tissue of denials and paradoxes. The final assault upon the castle is (in spite of its healthy marching rhythm) unreasonable and unnatural too. The wood moves, the leader is unborn of woman, and the soldiers are sustained by the super-rational, the miraculous blessings and graces that hang about King Edward's throne.

Mr. Kenneth Burke has pointed out that "action" may be defined in terms of "scene." This is one of the principles of composition in the *Divine Comedy:* human actions are presented in an orderly succession of scenes which concretely realize and define them. But Dante's tremendous subject was human life and action in general, while the subject of a Shakespearean tragedy is, more immediately, human action under a particular regime, or at a particular historic moment. His dramatis personae are seldom seeking salvation directly, but rather trying to realize a human life in a concrete society. That is why an analysis like Miss Spurgeon's is so suggestive, and takes one so far toward an understanding of the play as a whole—much further, for example, than the attempt to rationalize Hamlet's character, as though Shakespeare had been writing a drama of the individual will and reason only.

Yet there are dangers in an analysis based on metaphor. Such an analysis leaves *Hamlet* at the level of the romantic lyric, as though its "logic" were a logic of feeling only, and its principles of composition those of "association and contrast," as Mr. Burke calls them. Such an analysis works better for *Tristan* than for *Hamlet*, for it leaves out the substantial elements (the beings of the individual characters, the stable elements in the traditional cosmos) which underlie the associated or contrasted *qualities* of their lives, the "atmosphere" or feeling tone of the play. Miss Spurgeon's lyrical or subjective or qualitative analysis needs to be supported and extended by a more realist analysis, one based for instance on the four levels of Medieval symbolism.

According to this system, the analogous actions of the characters in their attempts to destroy the hidden disease of Denmark would constitute the "trope" or moral meaning of the play. The rottenness of the regime itself, from which they all suffer, could be called the "allegory," for it refers to a particular moment in history when a corrupt regime falsifies the life of the community. We have seen that in *Hamlet*, as in *Macbeth*, Shakespeare takes this historic moment as defining his subject. But Shakespeare is no Spenglerian determinist; in spite of his worldly focus, his preoccupation with social order, and his feeling for the "divine sanction" of kingship, he places Claudius' Denmark in a wider setting; and this "placing" of Claudius' regime is the anagoge, the meaning of the play in relation to ultimate values.

Miss Spurgeon records the fact that there is in *Hamlet* a series of images contrasting with those of disease and darkness; and, indeed, from the first we are made to feel that the condition of the Danes is not the human condition *überhaupt* but only a particular version of it. Ophelia's description of Hamlet, "What a noble mind is here o'erthrown," contrasts his present plight with what she feels to be his natural role: "the expectancy and rose of the fair state." Hamlet's description of his father, in his terrible interview with his mother, has a similar effect—to make us feel that a natural and divinely sanctioned order has been betrayed and lost. And in his famous speech on "man, the paragon of animals," though the context gives it depths of irony, Hamlet unrolls the traditional moral order as both good and true though he has somehow lost a vital relation to it. But it is chiefly in Act v that Claudius' regime is seen for what it is, brought to its temporal end, and placed in a wider and therefore truer scene.

Act v unrolls for us, first of all, a picture of Denmark after it has been torn asunder, its deathliness or its nonentity laid as it were flat and open to the eye of the audience and the eyes of Hamlet. The vision, as usual in Shakespeare, is firmly based upon the most concrete sensory impact (like the darkness of Act i, scene i) and proceeds then to elaborate ever wider and more complex perspectives. The basic sensual impression is the brutal digging up of skulls; then comes the solemn-joyful equivocating of the clowns—a denial of all meaning, the end result of Claudius' falsity. With this goes a series of hints of social disorder: the dead receive no respect; the professions, especially law, are laughably helpless; "the age is grown so picked that the toe of the peasant comes so near the heel of the courtier, he galls his kibe." As for the courtiers, we shall presently have Osric: "He did comply with his dug before he sucked it." Osric corresponds to Rosencrantz and Guildenstern, a more shameless hypocrite and time-server, much as the clowns correspond to Polonius in their complacent irrelevancy but speak in equivocations where Polonius, less deathly, merely rationalizes upon false premises.

From this opening impression of literal death and meaninglessness in many forms comes the funeral of Ophelia, the "maimèd rite." I have already pointed out its place in the succession of rituals. It is full of cross-references: to the funerals of Hamlet the first and Polonius; to Gertrude's corrupt marriage; to the marriage of Ophelia and Hamlet, which never occurred; and to Ophelia's mad mixture of funeral and marriage.

The second scene of Act v, with the duel between Hamlet and Laertes, shows the denouements of all the intrigues in the play: Polonius is avenged by Laertes; Laertes, like Hamlet, falls victim to Claudius' deceits; Gertrude follows Ophelia; Hamlet kills the King at last, and Fortinbras finally appears upon the Danish scene, the new faith and hope which Claudius no longer prevents. But these events, which literally end the narratives in the play, and bring Claudius' regime to its temporal end, tell us nothing new but the fact: that the sentence, which fate or providence pronounced long since, has now been executed. It is the pageantry, the ceremonial mummery, in short the ritual character of this last scene which makes us feel it as the final epiphany, the showing-forth of the true nature of Claudius' regime.

The staging of this scene is parallel to that of Claudius' first court (Act i, scene 2) and to that of the players' scene. It is the last time we see all the dramatis personae gathered to celebrate the social order upon which they all depend. But whereas we saw Claudius' first court as smooth, plausible, almost majestic, and ostensibly devoted to guarding the welfare of all the subjects, we see this last court, all in mourning, for the death-trap it is. The vision of Claudius' Denmark which Hamlet's play presented as a parable, is now brilliantly and literally visible. As soon as we glimpse it with this literal clarity, it is gone like a bad dream, and we are returned, with the healthy rhythms of young Fortinbras, to the wider world of the order of nature, with the possibility at least of divine sanction.

Thus the "placing" of the play follows immediately upon the completion of its action. Fortinbras is the agent; and in the scheme of the whole the role of Fortinbras, though it is very economically developed, is of major importance.

I have already pointed out that Fortinbras' story is one of the variations on the son-father theme. When we first hear of Fortinbras he, like Hamlet (and later, Laertes) is trying to avenge a dead and dishonored father. Like Hamlet, he has an uncle who stands *in loco parentis*. Like Laertes, he is a simple and noble youth, expending his high spirits upon the worldly code of "honor," yet at the same time he is a "good child," obedient to age—so that when his uncle tells him to, he is quite willing to turn his martial ambitions from the Danes to the Poles. But unlike both Hamlet and Laertes he does not live under Claudius' shadow: his obedience is not (like Laertes' obedience to Claudius) misplaced—and his life works itself out (as we hear) in a region free of the Danish infection.

Thus the role of Fortinbras, in *Hamlet*, corresponds to those of Malcolm, Macduff, and King Edward in *Macbeth*. Like them, he is felt as a constant, though off-stage, threat to the corrupt regime. Like them, he does not appear in the flesh until after the peripety and, though we feel his approach, does not enter Denmark until Claudius is gone. Like Malcolm and Macduff, he has his own version of the main action of the play. He moves and fights in the dark as much as his contemporaries, Hamlet and Laertes; but his darkness is not the artificial shadow of Claudius but the natural darkness of inexperience. He confronts it with a kind of sanguine natural faith, "exposing all that's mortal and unsure even for an eggshell"—as he could not (Laertes' example is there to prove it) in Denmark. That is why he cannot enter Denmark until the end. In the same way, in *Macbeth*, we are not ready for Macduff's and Malcolm's reception of Grace until Macbeth and his Queen have reached the nightmarish stalemate of the banquet scene. When the avengers appear before Macbeth's castle, they show him that there is another way to "outrun reason"; and when Fortinbras comes in at the end, he places the action we have seen in Denmark, both with reference to the wider world from which he comes, and with reference to his healthier version of "the fight in the dark," the "quest for the unseen danger." Fortinbras' darkness of natural faith is the last variation, this time in a major key, which Shakespeare plays upon his great theme.

This does not mean that Fortinbras, either in his character or in his vision, provides an answer to Hamlet's "problem"—nor does it mean that his example is intended to show that the experience of the play was simply illusory. This experience was "real," just as Dante's experience of Hell was real—though this is the region of low ceilings, and of those who have lost the good of the intellect. Hamlet sees a great deal that Fortinbras will never see; but Hamlet, who has his own limited being, is defined by it, and by the spiritual realm in which he moves; and this is not all of life. Fortinbras does not destroy, he "places" the action of the play by suddenly revealing a new analogue of this action. The effect, once more, is not to provide us with an intellectual key, an explicit philosophy, but to release us from the contemplation of the limited mystery of Denmark by returning us to the wider mystery of life in the world at large.

Thus it seems to me that the elements of Shakespeare's composition (like those of Sophocles and Dante before him) are not qualities, like those of the romantics with their logic of feeling, not abstract concepts, like those of the dramatists of the Age of Reason, with their clear and distinct moral ideas, but beings, real people in a real world, related to each other in a vast and intricate web of analogies.

I know that analogy is a very difficult concept to use with accuracy. I have endeavored to raise some of the questions connected with it in the Appendix. At this point I merely wish to point out that the anagoge, or ultimate meaning of the play, can only be sought through a study of the analogical relationships within the play and between the world of Denmark and the traditional cosmos. There are the analogous actions of all the characters, pointing to the action which is the underlying substance of the play. There are the analogous father-son relationships, and the analogous man-woman relationships. There are the analogous stories, or chains of events, the fated results of the characters' actions. And stretching beyond the play in all directions are the analogies between Denmark and England; Denmark and Rome under "the mightiest Julius"; Hamlet's stage and Shakespeare's stage; the theater and life. Because Shakespeare takes all these elements as "real," he can respect their essential mystery, not replacing them with abstractions, nor merely exploiting their qualities as mood-makers, nor confining us in an artificial world with no exit. He asks us to sense the unity of his play through the direct perception of these analogies; he does not ask us to replace our sense of a real and mysterious world with a consistent artifact, "the world of the play."

If Shakespeare's Hamlet is realist in the tradition represented by Sophocles and Dante, if he composes by analogy rather than by "qualitative progression" or "syllogistic progression," then the question of *Hamlet* as an artistic success appears in a different light. Because it is rooted in an ancient tradition, and in a theater central to its culture, it is not only a work of art, but a kind of more-than-individual natural growth, like the culture itself, and Shakespeare is not so much its inventor as its god-like recorder: "Cuando amor spira, vo significando." The question is not whether the subject Shakespeare intends is there, but whether it is there in too bewildering a richness and complexity. The besetting sin of the Renaissance, as Pico foresaw, was an overindulgence in the imagination as it discerns analogies of every kind. M. Gilson has explained how even Bonaventura could abuse his gift for analogizing, losing at times the distinction between real analogy and the superficial correspondences which his faith led him to see. And Mr. Scott Buchanan in *Poetry and Mathematics* asks the suggestive question, at what point in history, and by what process, was the clue to the vast system of Medieval analogies lost, the thread broken, and the way cleared for the centerless proliferations of modern culture?

Of this question too Shakespeare seems to have been prophetically aware. Like Hamlet, he felt, perhaps, too wide a sympathy, too precise a scruple. His endless sense of analogical relationships, though a good, *could* "grow to a plurisy." And *Hamlet* can be regarded as a dramatization of the process which led, in the Renaissance, to the modern world and its fragmentary theaters.

Hamlet and the Modern Theater

Mr. Eliot remarked that the age of Shakespeare "moved toward chaos"; and he noted that Shakespeare's theater (compared, say, with Racine's) had no consistent and clear conventions which might have prevented it from degenerating into naturalism, sensationalism, or editoralizing. If Shakespeare had an "idea of the theater" it was a very comprehensive and many-sided one which, to be realized at all, was obliged to comprehend many discordant elements in precarious and hidden harmony. Or you may say, if you take the view that he "succeeded," that his notion of the theater was so deep that it foresaw, as it were in significant relationship, the more limited dramatic genres which were to develop later.

Mr. Mark Van Doren noted, about *The Tempest*, that "any set of symbols, moved close to this play, lights up as in an electric field." *Hamlet* has the same mysterious property. Most dramas that were written since Shakespeare, when moved close to *Hamlet*, are themselves illumined, and seem to offer the clue to the interpretation of Shakespeare's great work.

If there is an exception to this observation, it is the drama of rationalism. Racine's masterpieces have a kind of consistency and explicit unity which is utterly foreign to Shakespeare. If the rationalism of the next age is foreseen at all in *Hamlet*, it is in the role of Polonius, with his faith in logic, his feeling for the neat antithesis and the triumphant demonstration, and his rhythms of speech—for, though he speaks in blank verse, his sense of language suggests the heroic couplet.

But the romantics took *Hamlet* for their own; and a generation later most critics thought that the greatness of the play lay in its naturalistic truth to nature—and when they criticized it, they objected that Shakespeare was less photographic than Ibsen. In our own time, Pirandello's desperate theatricality is seen as having been anticipated by Hamlet the *improvisateur*.

The age of Shakespeare "moved toward chaos," and the great mirror of his theater was broken into fragments. But it lasted long enough to give us the last image of western man in the light of his great tradition.

PART II

THE PARTIAL PERSPECTIVES OF
THE MODERN THEATER

INTRODUCTION

THE PARTIAL PERSPECTIVES OF THE MODERN THEATER

It would be possible to support the view (which I suggested in the last chapter) that the modern theater, in its vitality and diversity, its richness or anarchy, was in fact historically derived from the break-up of that traditional theater of human action which Shakespeare could still assume. One might accept this notion of the actual historic sequence and still leave room for various interpretations of it, depending on one's judgment of Shakespeare's drama. Mr. Eliot writes, in *Four Elizabethan Dramatists, A Preface to an Unwritten Book,* "The Elizabethans are in fact a part of the movement of progress or deterioration which has culminated in Sir Arthur Pinero and in the present regimen of Europe." This recognizes the sequence, but it assumes that the anarchy was present already in Shakespeare. Perhaps Mr. Eliot would go back to Dante to discover the traditional theater of human life in all its order, consistency, and complexity. But with regard to the theater itself and the contemporary problems of the dramatic art, he proposes to get his bearings in relation to the idea, not of a theater, but of a convention. "The great vice of English drama from Kyd to Galsworthy has been that its aim of realism was unlimited," he writes. "In one play, *Everyman,* and perhaps in that one play only, we have a drama within the limitations of art; since Kyd, since *Arden of Feversham,* since *The Yorkshire Tragedy,* there has been no form to arrest, so to speak, the flow of spirit at any particular point before it expands and ends its course in the desert of exact likeness to the reality which is perceived by the most commonplace mind." And he explains that "when I say convention, I do not necessarily mean any particular convention of subject matter, of treatment, of verse or of dramatic form, of general philosophy of life or any other convention which has already been used. It may be some quite new selection or structure or distortion in subject matter or technique; any form or rhythm imposed upon the world of action."

The essay from which I have taken these quotations adumbrates a profound and consistent view of the dramatic art; it is one of the indispensable sources for an understanding of the modern theater. It is supported by Eliot's own accomplishments both as poet and dramatist, and I shall return to it in Chapter III apropos of *Murder in The Cathedral*. But the notion of a convention, even as defined in the very general terms which Mr. Eliot uses, seems to me to be too narrow. "A form or rhythm *imposed* upon the world of action" accurately describes the ideal dramas of Racine and of Wagner, as well as many lesser genres, Restoration comedy, ballet, Gilbert and Sullivan, perhaps even Brieux's thesis play, which has a certain conventional consistency. But it does not suggest any way of conceiving a relation between these forms, or between convention and the reality of the human situation. It does not account satisfactorily for the Realism of Shakespeare and Sophocles, nor more particularly the modern Realism represented by Ibsen and Chekhov, which, in many developments and modifications, is the basis for so much, and so much of the best as well as the worst, of the modern theater. The realists of all kinds do not so much impose as discern a form of action; they do not so much demonstrate or express, as they imitate their vision. That is why I propose to substitute the traditional idea of a theater for the notion of a convention; to consider a few samples of modern drama with reference to Shakespeare rather than Racine or *Everyman*.

Mr. Eliot may well be right about the kind of drama which is possible in our time. And, if one thinks of the French theater, of Cocteau and Obey as well as Racine and Molière, the extraordinary fertility of conventionality itself (oddly enough, its flexibility and adaptability) is very evident: it produces, in Paris, successes generation after generation. But, as for us in this country, having so little in the way of a theater, we are free to want everything: Ibsen as well as Yeats, Chekhov along with Cocteau. Since we are only window-shopping, we may try to select the best, the most all-inclusive way of understanding drama. That is the use I propose to make of the traditional idea of the theater: as a way to recognize the complementary values in various dramatic forms which have appeared in the modern world rather than as a clue to historic development; and as a way of establishing, in reference to modern practice, the notion of the dramatic art at its best and most inclusive. We do not know whether such a drama can ever reappear; we can see that in the past its appearances have been brief and dependent upon many factors beyond individual conscious control; but its masterpieces are landmarks which permit some sort of map of the diversity of drama since Shakespeare.

In the next three chapters are brief studies of half a dozen plays, as examples of modern dramatic form. So meager a sampling of so vast a field is necessarily arbitrary: at best suggestive, at worst misleading. But each of the plays I have selected shows something essential about the dramatic art as it may be practiced in our time, an attitude or a perspective with some viability in the modern theater. This general significance is suggested in the titles of the chapters, "Modern Realism," "Theatricality," "Poetry." Each play has, more or less consciously and consistently, some form of limitation which, as Mr. Eliot points out, is essential for art; but none of them aspires to the absoluteness and finality of the ideal theaters of Racine or Wagner, each of which is implicitly *the* theater. And with reference to the theater of Shakespeare, the perspectives upon which they are based (however beautiful, or brilliant, or true, or touching) are partial—highly developed fragments of his great mirror, which can only be considered together by keeping it in mind.

CHAPTER V

GHOSTS AND *THE CHERRY ORCHARD*: THE THEATER OF MODERN REALISM

ՊՊՊՊՊՊՊՊՊՊՊՊՊՊՊՊՊՊՊՊՊՊՊՊ

"Then are our beggars bodies, and our outstretched monarchs and heroes the beggars' shadows."

—Hamlet to Rosencrantz and Guildenstern

ՊՊՊՊՊՊՊՊՊՊՊՊՊՊՊՊՊՊՊՊՊՊՊՊ

WHEN I say *modern realism* I am taking the term in the broad sense of the strictly photographic imitation of the human scene. In this sense modern realism is a lingua franca, a pidgin-English of the imagination which everyone in our time can understand. The camera and the radio, continuing a process which began at least a hundred years ago, reproduce more and more accurately the surfaces, the sounds and sights of contemporary life: vastly distended on the screen, or murmured in the ears of a million housewives. If we have lost our bearings, if we automatically reject any stable picture of the human condition, we can still gossip about the neighbors and eavesdrop on other lives. It would seem that this medium, and the narrow scene of human life it implies, are too meager for drama at all. Yet Ibsen and Chekhov accepted its limitations, and made superb plays.

The theater of modern realism is greatly shrunken compared with the theaters I studied in Part I. It came out of that "diminished scene of rationalism" which I described as the degeneration of Racine's theater of reason: the heroes are gone, the struggle of reason itself is lost to sight; the literal-minded Oenones and Arsaces take the stage, with their myopic shrewdness. It is the little scene which Wagner totally rejected, in favor of his nocturnal world of passion. If one thinks of the theater of Shakespeare, one may place the little scene of modern realism at the point where Hamlet meets Rosencrantz and Guildenstern: the non-commital "center" of human awareness, the "middle" of Fortune's favors, where the beggarly body looks sure and solid, and all the motivations which might lead to wider awarenesses look shadowy and deluded. Thus the theater of modern realism does not offer a strictly defined medium, a limited but deeply based convention for revealing human action, like the ideal Wagnerian or Racinian theater. It rejects the traditional order of myth and ritual which Shakespeare could assume. And the question is how, and to what extent, it may be used for the purposes of drama at all.

It is easy to see why Mr. Eliot should think of it as essentially anti-poetic, leading inevitably to the "desert of exact likeness to the reality which is perceived by the most commonplace mind." We have seen this desert in a thousand forms, meaningless reports of life in Paris and Pernambuco, Hoboken and Helsingfors. It is certainly true that the theater of modern realism does not offer the dramatist a defined art medium; it even imposes upon him the necessity of pretending that he has no poetic purpose at all, but truth in some pseudo-scientific sense. Yet Ibsen and Chekhov (to say nothing of other writers of less scope) were able to place in this narrow theater a certain kind of theatrical poetry. It is a hidden poetry, masquerading as reporting; it is a "poetry of the theater" (in M. Cocteau's phrase) and not a poetry of words; and it is based upon the histrionic sensibility and the art of acting: it can only be seen in performance or by imagining a performance. This property of modern realism—its close dependance upon acting—Henry James regarded as a sure sign of its vitality, and Eliot regards as a great weakness. It seems to me that James was right; it is in their direct histrionic awareness that the masters of modern realism are most closely akin to the intentions and the modes of awareness of Shakespeare and Sophocles.

Modern realism does not define an art medium, nor does it, in itself, offer the dramatist any clue to form. Ibsen and Chekhov do not enjoy the perspectives of myth or of ritual whereby action is both placed and defined in the traditional theater. But they are able to define the action they wish to imitate by means of their plots; and the actions of their plays, having a shape and rhythm of their own, a beginning, middle and end, dictate a dramatic form. At their best Ibsen and Chekhov are imitating action according to the Aristotelian prescription: not a concatenation of events but a movement of the psyche, and not the action of an individual but a more general action which all share by analogy, and which we see adumbrated by way of the individual characters and their relationships. Thus they both accept the literal and transcend it; their intention is poetic—as Aristotle says, "more philosophical than history."

This achievement represents a triumph over the limitations of the modern realistic theater, and not a development of any resources which were publicly available. The basic problem which they encountered was the same as that of Wagner: the publicly accepted scene of human life was that of the Philistine bourgeoisie with its rigid moral and social forms, its sharp blank positivism, the parlor of the carriage-trade—and all the rest of human experience illusion. But their strategy was the opposite of Wagner's: to accept this little public area as their battlefield and endeavor to place their wider vision in it. If they succeeded, it was only after many false starts, and only to a degree.

Ibsen's *Ghosts* and Chekhov's *The Cherry Orchard* have little in common except the theater of modern realism itself. By considering them one may get some notion of the potentialities and the limitations of this paradoxical theater, which pretends to be not art but life itself.

The Plot of *Ghosts*: Thesis, Thriller, and Tragedy

Ghosts is not Ibsen's best play, but it serves my purpose, which is to study the foundations of modern realism, just because of its imperfections. Its power, and the poetry of some of its effects, are evident; yet a contemporary audience may be bored with its old-fashioned iconoclasm and offended by the clatter of its too-obviously well-made plot. On the surface it is a *drame à thèse*, of the kind Brieux was to develop to its logical conclusion twenty years later: it proves the hollowness of the conventional bourgeois marriage. At the same time it is a thriller with all the tricks of the Boulevard entertainment: Ibsen was a student of Scribe in his middle period. But underneath this superficial form of thesis-thriller—the play which Ibsen started to write, the angry diatribe as he first conceived it—there is another form, the shape of the underlying action, which Ibsen gradually made out in the course of his two-years' labor upon the play, in obedience to his scruple of truthfulness, his profound attention to the reality of his fictive characters' lives. The form of the play is understood according to two conceptions of plot, which Ibsen himself did not at this point clearly distinguish: the rationalized concatenation of events with a univocal moral, and the plot as the "soul" or first actualization of the directly perceived action.

Halvdahn Khot, in his excellent study *Henrik Ibsen*, has explained the circumstances under which *Ghosts* was written. It was first planned as an attack upon marriage, in answer to the critics of *A Doll's House*. The story of the play is perfectly coherent as the demonstration and illustration of this thesis. When the play opens, Captain Alving has just died, his son Oswald is back from Paris where he had been studying painting, and his wife is straightening out the estate. The Captain had been accepted locally as a pillar of society but was in secret a drunkard and debauchee. He had seduced his wife's maid, and had a child by her; and this child, Regina, is now in her turn Mrs. Alving's maid. Mrs. Alving had concealed all this for something like twenty years. She was following the advice of the conventional Pastor Manders and endeavoring to save Oswald from the horrors of the household: it was for this reason she had sent him away to school. But now, with her husband's death, she proposes to get rid of the Alving heritage in all its forms, in order to free herself and Oswald for the innocent, unconventional "joy of life." She wants to endow an orphanage with the Captain's money, both to quiet any rumors there may be of his sinful life and to get rid of the remains of his power over her. She encounters this power, however, in many forms, through the Pastor's timidity and through the attempt by Engstrand (a local carpenter who was bribed to pretend to be Regina's father) to blackmail her. Oswald wants to marry Regina and has to be told the whole story. At last he reveals that he has inherited syphilis from his father—the dead hand of the past in its most sensationally ugly form—and when his brain softens at the end, Mrs. Alving's whole plan collapses in unrelieved horror. It is "proved" that she should have left home twenty years before, like Nora in *A Doll's House*; and that conventional marriage is therefore an evil tyranny.

In accordance with the principles of the thesis play, *Ghosts* is plotted as a series of debates on conventional morality, between Mrs. Alving and the Pastor, the Pastor and Oswald, and Oswald and his mother. It may also be read as a perfect well-made thriller. The story is presented with immediate clarity, with mounting and controlled suspense; each act ends with an exciting curtain which reaffirms the issues and promises important new developments. In this play, as in so many others, one may observe that the conception of dramatic form underlying the thesis play and the machine-made Boulevard entertainment is the same: the logically concatenated series of events (intriguing thesis or logical intrigue) which the characters and their relationships merely illustrate. And it was this view of *Ghosts* which made it an immediate scandal and success.

But Ibsen himself protested that he was not a reformer but a poet. He was often led to write by anger and he compared the process of composition to his pet scorpion's emptying of poison; Ibsen kept a piece of soft fruit in his cage for the scorpion to sting when the spirit moved him. But Ibsen's own spirit was not satisfied by the mere discharge of venom; and one may see, in *Ghosts*, behind the surfaces of the savage story, a partially realized tragic form of really poetic scope, the result of Ibsen's more serious and disinterested brooding upon the human condition in general, where it underlies the myopic rebellions and empty clichés of the time.

In order to see the tragedy behind the thesis, it is necessary to return to the distinction between plot and action, and to the distinction between the plot as the rationalized series of events, and the plot as "the soul of the tragedy."* The action of the play is "to control the Alving heritage for my own life." Most of the characters want some material or social advantage from it—Engstrand money, for instance, and the Pastor the security of conventional respectability. But Mrs. Alving is seeking a true

*These distinctions are explained in the Appendix.

and free human life itself—for her son, and through him, for herself. Mrs. Alving sometimes puts this quest in terms of the iconoclasms of the time, but her spiritual life, as Ibsen gradually discovered it, is at a deeper level; she tests everything—Oswald, the Pastor, Regina, her own moves—in the light of her extremely strict if unsophisticated moral sensibility: by direct perception and not by ideas at all. She is tragically seeking; she suffers a series of pathoses and new insights in the course of the play; and this rhythm of will, feeling, and insight underneath the machinery of the plot is the form of the life of the play, the soul of the tragedy.

The similarity between *Ghosts* and Greek tragedy, with its single fated action moving to an unmistakable catastrophe, has been felt by many critics of Ibsen. Mrs. Alving, like Oedipus, is engaged in a quest for her true human condition; and Ibsen, like Sophocles, shows on-stage only the end of this quest, when the past is being brought up again in the light of the present action and its fated outcome. From this point of view Ibsen is a plot-maker in the first sense: by means of his selection and arrangement of incidents he defines an action underlying many particular events and realized in various modes of intelligible purpose, of suffering, and of new insight. What Mrs. Alving sees changes in the course of the play, just as what Oedipus sees changes as one veil after another is removed from the past and the present. The underlying form of *Ghosts* is that of the tragic rhythm as one finds it in *Oedipus Rex*.

But this judgment needs to be qualified in several respects: because of the theater for which Ibsen wrote, the tragic form which Sophocles could develop to the full, and with every theatrical resource, is hidden beneath the clichés of plot and the surfaces "evident to the most commonplace mind." At the end of the play the tragic rhythm of Mrs. Alving's quest is not so much completed as brutally truncated, in obedience to the requirements of the thesis and the thriller. Oswald's collapse, before our eyes, with his mother's screaming, makes the intrigue end with a bang, and hammers home the thesis. But from the point of view of Mrs. Alving's tragic quest as we have seen it develop through the rest of the play, this conclusion concludes nothing; it is merely sensational.

The exciting intrigue and the brilliantly, the violently clear surfaces of *Ghosts* are likely to obscure completely its real life and underlying form. The tragic rhythm, which Ibsen rediscovered by his long and loving attention to the reality of his fictive lives, is evident only to the histrionic sensibility. As Henry James put it, Ibsen's characters "have the extraordinary, the brilliant property of becoming when represented at once more abstract and more living": i.e., both their lives and the life of the play, the spiritual content and the form of the whole, are revealed in this medium. A Nazimova, a Duse, could show it to us on the stage. Lacking such a performance, the reader must endeavor to respond imaginatively and directly himself if he is to see the hidden poetry of *Ghosts*.

Mrs. Alving and Oswald: The Tragic Rhythm in a Small Figure

As Ibsen was fighting to present his poetic vision within the narrow theater admitted by modern realism, so his protagonist Mrs. Alving is fighting to realize her sense of human life in the blank photograph of her own stuffy parlor. She discovers there no means, no terms, and no nourishment; that is the truncated tragedy which underlies the savage thesis of the play. But she does find her son Oswald, and she makes of him the symbol of all she is seeking: freedom, innocence, joy, and truth. At the level of the life of the play, where Ibsen warms his characters into extraordinary human reality, they all have moral and emotional meanings for each other; and the pattern of their related actions, their partially blind struggle for the Alving heritage, is consistent and very complex. In this structure, Mrs. Alving's changing relation to Oswald is only one strand, though an important one. I wish to consider it as a sample of Ibsen's rediscovery, through modern realism, of the tragic rhythm.

Oswald is of course not only a symbol for his mother, but a person in his own right, with his own quest for freedom and release, and his own anomalous stake in the Alving heritage. He is also a symbol for Pastor Manders of what he wants from Captain Alving's estate: the stability and continuity of the bourgeois conventions. In the economy of the play as a whole, Oswald is the hidden reality of the whole situation, like Oedipus' actual status as son-husband: the hidden fatality which, revealed in a series of tragic and ironic steps, brings the final peripety of the action. To see how this works, the reader is asked to consider Oswald's role in Act I and the beginning of Act II.

The main part of Act I (after a prologue between Regina and Engstrand) is a debate, or rather agon, between Mrs. Alving and the Pastor. The Pastor has come to settle the details of Mrs. Alving's bequest of her husband's money to the orphanage. They at once disagree about the purpose and handling of the bequest; and this disagreement soon broadens into the whole issue of Mrs. Alving's emancipation versus the Pastor's conventionality. The question of Oswald is at the center. The Pastor wants to think of him, and to make of him, a pillar of society such as the Captain was supposed to have been, while Mrs. Alving wants him to be her masterpiece of liberation. At this point Oswald himself wanders in, the actual but still mysterious truth underlying the dispute between his mother and the Pastor. His appearance produces what the Greeks would have called a complex recognition scene, with an implied peripety for both Mrs. Alving and the Pastor, which will not be realized by them until the end of the act. But this tragic development is written to be acted; it is to be found, not so much in the actual words of the characters, as in their moral-emotional responses and changing relationships to one another.

The Pastor has not seen Oswald since he grew up; and seeing him now he is startled as though by a real ghost; he recognizes him as the very reincarnation of his father: the same physique, the same mannerisms, even the same kind of pipe. Mrs. Alving with equal confidence recognizes him as her own son, and she notes that his mouth-mannerism is like the Pastor's. (She had been in love with the Pastor during the early years of her marriage, when she wanted to leave the Captain.) As for Oswald himself, the mention of the pipe gives him a Proustian intermittence of the heart: he suddenly recalls a childhood scene when his father had given him his own pipe to smoke. He feels again the nausea and the cold sweat, and hears the Captain's hearty laughter. Thus in effect he recognizes himself as his father's, in the sense of his father's *victim;* a premonition of the ugly scene at the end of the play. But at this point no one is prepared to accept the full import of these insights. The whole scene is, on the surface, light and conventional, an accurate report of a passage of provincial politeness. Oswald wanders off for a walk before dinner, and the Pastor and his mother are left to bring their struggle more into the open.

Oswald's brief scene marks the end of the first round of the fight, and serves as prologue for the second round, much as the intervention of the chorus in the agon between Oedipus and Tiresias punctuates their struggle, and hints at an unexpected outcome on a new level of awareness. As soon as Oswald has gone, the Pastor launches an attack in form upon Mrs. Alving's entire emancipated way of life, with the question of Oswald, his role in the community, his upbringing and his future, always at the center of the attack. Mrs. Alving replies with her whole rebellious philosophy, illustrated by a detailed account of her tormented life with the Captain, none of which the Pastor had known (or been willing to recognize) before. Mrs. Alving proves on the basis of this evidence that her new freedom is right; that her long secret rebellion was justified; and that she is now about to complete Oswald's emancipation, and thereby her own, from the swarming ghosts of the past. If the issue were merely on this rationalistic level, and between her and the Pastor, she would triumph at this point. But the real truth of her situation (as Oswald's appearance led us to suppose) does not fit either her rationalization or the Pastor's.

Oswald passes through the parlor again on his way to the dining room to get a drink before dinner, and his mother watches him in pride and pleasure. But from behind the door we hear the affected squealing of Regina. It is now Mrs. Alving's turn for an intermittence of the heart: it is as though she heard again her husband with Regina's mother. The insight which she had rejected before now reaches her in full strength, bringing the promised pathos and peripety; she sees Oswald, not as her masterpiece of liberation, but as the sinister, tyrannical, and continuing life of the past itself. The basis of her rationalization is gone; she suffers the breakdown of the moral being which she had built upon her now exploded view of Oswald.

At this point Ibsen brings down the curtain in obedience to the principles of the well-made play. The effect is to raise the suspense by stimulating our curiosity about the facts of the rest of the story. What will Mrs. Alving do now? What will the Pastor do—for Oswald and Regina are half-brother and sister; can we prevent the scandal from coming out? So the suspense is raised, but the attention of the audience is diverted from Mrs. Alving's tragic quest to the most literal, newspaper version of the facts.

The second act (which occurs immediately after dinner) is ostensibly concerned only with these gossipy facts. The Pastor and Mrs. Alving debate ways of handling the threatened scandal. But this is only the literal surface: Ibsen has his eye upon Mrs. Alving's shaken psyche, and the actual dramatic form of this scene, under the discussion which Mrs. Alving keeps up, is her pathos which the Act I curtain broke off. Mrs. Alving is suffering the blow in courage and faith; and she is rewarded with her deepest insight: ("I am half inclined to think we are all ghosts, Mr. Manders. It is not only what we have inherited from our fathers and mothers that exists again in us, but all sorts of dead ideas and all kinds of old dead beliefs and things of that kind. They are not actually alive in us; but they are dormant all the same, and we can never be rid of them. Whenever I take up a newspaper and read it, I fancy I see ghosts creeping between the lines. There must be ghosts all over the world. They must be as countless as the grains of sand, it seems to me. And we are so miserably afraid of the light, all of us."* This passage, in the fumbling phrases of Ibsen's provincial lady, and in William Archer's translation, is not by itself the poetry of the great dramatic poets. It does not have the verbal music of Racine, nor the freedom and sophistication of Hamlet, nor the scope of the Sophoclean chorus, with its use of the full complement of poetic and musical and theatrical resources. But in the total situation in the Alving parlor which Ibsen has so carefully established, and in terms of Mrs. Alving's uninstructed but profoundly develop-

Ghosts, by Henrik Ibsen. Translated by William Archer.

ing awareness, it has its own hidden poetry: a poetry not of words but of the theater, a poetry of the histrionic sensibility. From the point of view of the underlying form of the play—the form as "the soul" of the tragedy—this scene completes the sequence which began with the debate in Act I: it is the pathos-and-epiphany following that agon.

It is evident, I think, that insofar as Ibsen was able to obey his realistic scruple, his need for the disinterested perception of human life beneath the clichés of custom and rationalization, he rediscovered the perennial basis of tragedy. The poetry of *Ghosts* is under the words, in the detail of action, where Ibsen accurately sensed the tragic rhythm of human life in a thousand small figures. And these little "movements of the psyche" are composed in a complex rhythm like music, a formal development sustained (beneath the sensational story and the angry thesis) until the very end. But the action is not completed: Mrs. Alving is left screaming with the raw impact of the calamity. The music is broken off, the dissonance unresolved—or, in more properly dramatic terms, the acceptance of the catastrophe, leading to the final vision or epiphany which should correspond to the insight Mrs. Alving gains in Act II, is lacking. The action of the play is neither completed nor placed in the wider context of meanings which the disinterested or contemplative purposes of poetry demand.

The unsatisfactory end of *Ghosts* may be understood in several ways. Thinking of the relation between Mrs. Alving and Oswald, one might say that she had romantically loaded more symbolic values upon her son than a human being can carry; hence his collapse proves too much—more than Mrs. Alving or the audience can digest. One may say that, at the end, Ibsen himself could not quite dissociate himself from his rebellious protagonist and see her action in the round, and so broke off in anger, losing his tragic vision in the satisfaction of reducing the bourgeois parlor to a nightmare, and proving the hollowness of a society which sees human life in such myopic and dishonest terms. As a thesis play, *Ghosts* is an ancestor of many related genres: Brieux's arguments for social reform., propaganda plays like those of the Marxists, or parables à la Andreev, or even

Shaw's more generalized plays of the play-of-thought about social questions. But this use of the theater of modern realism for promoting or discussing political and social ideas never appealed to Ibsen. It did not solve his real problem, which was to use the publicly accepted theater of his time for poetic purposes. The most general way to understand the unsatisfactory end of *Ghosts* is to say that Ibsen could not find a way to represent the action of his protagonist, with all its moral and intellectual depth, within the terms of modern realism. In the attempt he truncated this action, and revealed as in a brilliant light the limitations of the bourgeois parlor as the scene of human life.

The End of *Ghosts*: The Tasteless Parlor and the Stage of Europe

Oswald is the chief symbol of what Mrs. Alving is seeking, and his collapse ends her quest in a horrifying catastrophe. But in the complex life of the play, all of the persons and things acquire emotional and moral significance for Mrs. Alving; and at the end, to throw as much light as possible upon the catastrophe, Ibsen brings all of the elements of his composition together in their highest symbolic valency. The orphanage has burned to the ground; the Pastor has promised Engstrand money for his "Sailor's Home" which he plans as a brothel; Regina departs, to follow her mother in the search for pleasure and money. In these eventualities the conventional morality of the Alving heritage is revealed as lewdness and dishonesty, quickly consumed in the fires of lust and greed, as Oswald himself (the central symbol) was consumed even before his birth. But what does this wreckage mean? Where are we to place it in human experience? Ibsen can only place it in the literal parlor, with lamplight giving place to daylight, and sunrise on the empty, stimulating, virginal snow-peaks out the window. The emotional force of this complicated effect is very great; it has the searching intimacy of nightmare. But it is also as disquieting as a nightmare from which we are suddenly awakened; it is incomplete, and the contradiction between the inner power of dream and the literal appearances of the daylight world is unresolved. The spirit that

moved Ibsen to write the play, and which moved his protagonist through her tragic progress, is lost to sight, disembodied,
imperceptible in any form unless the dreary exaltation of the in-
human mountain scene conveys it in feeling.

Henry James felt very acutely the contradiction between the
deep and strict spirit of Ibsen and his superb craftsmanship on
one side, and the little scene he tried to use—the parlor in its
surrounding void—on the other. "If the spirit is a lamp within
us, glowing through what the world and the flesh make of us as
through a ground-glass shade, then such pictures as Little Eyolf
and John Gabriel are each a chassez-croisez of lamps burning,
as in tasteless parlors, with the flame practically exposed," he
wrote in *London Notes*.* "There is a positive odor of spiritual
paraffin. The author nevertheless arrives at the dramatist's great
goal—he arrives for all his meagerness at intensity. The meagerness, which is after all but an unconscious, an admirable economy, never interferes with that: it plays straight into the hands
of his rare mastery of form. The contrast between this form—so
difficult to have reached, so 'evolved,' so civilized—and the bare-
ness and bleakness of his little northern democracy is the source
of half the hard frugal charm he puts forth."

James had rejected very early in his career his own little
northern democracy, that of General Grant's America, with its
ugly parlor, its dead conventions, its enthusiastic materialism,
and its "non-conducting atmosphere." At the same time he
shared Ibsen's ethical preoccupation, and his strict sense of form.
His comments on Ibsen are at once the most sympathetic and
the most objective that have been written. But James's own
solution was to try to find a better parlor for the theater of
human life; to present the quest of his American pilgrim of culture on the wider "stage of Europe" as this might still be felt
and suggested in the manners of the leisured classes in England
and France. James would have nothing to do with the prophetic
and revolutionary spirit which was driving the great continental authors, Ibsen among them. In his artistry and his moral
exactitude Ibsen is akin to James; but this is not his whole story,
and if one is to understand the spirit he tried to realize in Mrs.

*Jan.-Aug., 1897.

Alving, one must think of Kierkegaard, who had a great influence on Ibsen in the beginning of his career.

Kierkegaard (in *For Self-Examination*) has this to say of the disembodied and insatiable spirit of the times: " . . . thou wilt scarcely find anyone who does not believe in—let us say, for example, the spirit of the age, the *Zeitgeist*. Even he who has taken leave of higher things and is rendered blissful by mediocrity, yea, even he who toils slavishly for paltry ends or in the contemptible servitude of ill-gotten gains, even he believes, firmly and fully too, in the spirit of the age. Well, that is natural enough, it is by no means anything very lofty he believes in, for the spirit of the age is after all no higher than the age, it keeps close to the ground, so that it is the sort of spirit which is most like will-o'-the-wisp; but yet he believes in spirit. Or he believes in the world-spirit (*Weltgeist*) that strong spirit (for allurements, yes), that ingenious spirit (for deceits, yes); that spirit which Christianity calls an evil spirit—so that, in consideration of this, it is by no means anything very lofty he believes in when he believes in the world-spirit; but yet he believes in spirit. Or he believes in 'the spirit of humanity,' not spirit in the individual, but in the race, that spirit which, when it is god-forsaken for having forsaken God, is again, according to Christianity's teaching, an evil spirit—so that in view of this it is by no means anything very lofty he believes in when he believes in this spirit; but yet he believes in spirit.

"On the other hand, as soon as the talk is about a holy spirit—how many, dost thou think, believe in it? Or when the talk is about an evil spirit which is to be renounced—how many, dost thou think, believe in such a thing?"[*]

This description seems to me to throw some light upon Mrs. Alving's quest, upon Ibsen's modern-realistic scene, and upon the theater which his audience would accept. The other face of nineteenth century positivism is romantic aspiration. And Ibsen's realistic scene presents both of these aspects of the human condition: the photographically accurate parlor, in the foreground, satisfies the requirements of positivism, while the empty but

[*]Kierkegaard, *For Self Examination and Judge for Yourselves* (Princeton University Press, 1944), p. 94.

stimulating scene out the window—Europe as a moral void, an uninhabited wilderness—offers as it were a blank check to the insatiate spirit. Ibsen always felt this exhilarating wilderness behind his cramped interiors. In *A Doll's House* we glimpse it as winter weather and black water. In *The Lady from the Sea* it is the cold ocean, with its whales and its gulls. In *The Wild Duck* it is the northern marshes, with wildfowl but no people. In the last scene of *Ghosts* it is, of course, the bright snow-peaks, which may mean Mrs. Alving's quest in its most disembodied and ambivalent form; very much the same sensuous moral void in which Wagner, having totally rejected the little human foreground where Ibsen fights his battles, unrolls the solitary action of passion. It is the "stage of Europe" before human exploration, as it might have appeared to the first hunters.

There is a kinship between the fearless and demanding spirit of Kierkegaard, and the spirit which Ibsen tried to realize in Mrs. Alving. But Mrs. Alving, like her contemporaries whom Kierkegaard describes, will not or cannot accept any interpretation of the spirit that drives her. It may look like the *Weltgeist* when she demands the joy of living, it may look like the Holy Ghost itself when one considers her appetite for truth. And it may look like the spirit of evil, a "goblin damned," when we see the desolation it produces. If one thinks of the symbols which Ibsen brings together in the last scene: the blank parlor, the wide unexplored world outside, the flames that consumed the Alving heritage and the sunrise flaming on the peaks, one may be reminded of the condition of Dante's great rebel Ulysses. He too is wrapped in the flame of his own consciousness, yet still dwells in the pride of the mind and the exhilaration of the world free of people, *il mondo senza gente*. But this analogy also may not be pressed too far. Ulysses is in hell; and when we explore the Mountain on which he was wrecked, we can place his condition with finality, and in relation to many other human modes of action and awareness. But Mrs. Alving's mountains do not place her anywhere: the realism of modern realism ends with the literal. Beyond that is not the ordered world of the tradition, but *Unendlichkeit*, and the anomalous "freedom" of undefined and uninformed aspiration.

Perhaps Mrs. Alving and Ibsen himself are closer to the role of Dante than to the role of Ulysses, seeing a hellish mode of being, but free to move on. Certainly Ibsen's development continued beyond *Ghosts*, and toward the end of his career he came much closer to achieving a consistent theatrical poetry within the confines of the theater of modern realism. He himself remarked that his poetry was to be found only in the series of his plays, no one of which was complete by itself.

But my purpose is, of course, not to do justice to Ibsen but to consider the potentialities of modern realism; and for this purpose Chekhov's masterpiece is essential. Chekhov did not solve the problem which Ibsen faced in *Ghosts*. He was not trying to show a desperate quest like Mrs. Alving's, with every weapon of the mind and the will. By his time the ambitious machinery of thesis and thriller had begun to pall; the prophetic-revolutionary spirit, grown skeptical and subtle, had sunk back into the flesh and the feelings, into the common beggarly body, for a period of pause, in hope and foreboding. Chekhov does not have Ibsen's force and intellect but he can accept the realistic stage much more completely, and use it with greater mastery for the contemplative purpose of art.

The Plot of *The Cherry Orchard*

The Cherry Orchard is often accused of having no plot whatever, and it is true that the story gives little indication of the play's content or meaning; nothing happens, as the Broadway reviewers so often point out. Nor does it have a thesis, though many attempts have been made to attribute a thesis to it, to make it into a Marxian tract, or into a nostalgic defense of the old regime. The play does not have much of a plot in either of these accepted meanings of the word, for it is not addressed to the rationalizing mind but to the poetic and histrionic sensibility. It is an imitation of an action in the strictest sense, and it is plotted according to the first meaning of this word which I have distinguished in other contexts: the incidents are selected and arranged to define an action in a certain mode; a complete action, with a beginning, middle, and end in time. Its freedom from the mechanical order of the thesis or the intrigue is the sign of the perfection of Chekhov's realistic art. And its apparently casual incidents are actually composed with most elaborate and conscious skill to reveal the underlying life, and the natural, objective form of the play as a whole.

In *Ghosts*, as I showed, the action is distorted by the stereotyped requirements of the thesis and the intrigue. That is partly a matter of the mode of action which Ibsen was trying to show; a quest "of ethical motivation" which requires some sort of intellectual framework, and yet can have no final meaning in the purely literal terms of Ibsen's theater. *The Cherry Orchard*, on the other hand, is a drama "of pathetic motivation," a theater-poem of the suffering of change; and this mode of action and awareness is much closer to the skeptical basis of modern realism, and to the histrionic basis of all realism. Direct perception before predication is always true, says Aristotle; and the extraordinary feat of Chekhov is to predicate nothing. This he achieves by means of his plot: he selects only those incidents, those moments in his characters' lives, between their rationalized efforts, when they sense their situation and destiny most directly. So he contrives to show the action of the play as a whole—the unsuccessful attempt to cling to the Cherry Orchard—in many diverse reflectors and without propounding any thesis about it.

The slight narrative thread which ties these incidents and characters together for the inquiring mind, is quickly recounted. The family that owns the old estate named after its famous orchard—Lyubov, her brother Gaev, and her daughters Varya and Anya—is all but bankrupt, and the question is how to prevent the bailiffs from selling the estate to pay their debts. Lopahin, whose family were formerly serfs on the estate, is now rapidly growing rich as a businessman, and he offers a very sensible plan: chop down the orchard, divide the property into small lots, and sell them off to make a residential suburb for the growing industrial town nearby. Thus the cash value of the estate could be not only preserved, but increased. But this would not save what Lyubov and her brother find valuable in the old estate; they cannot consent to the destruction of the orchard. But they cannot find, or earn, or borrow the money to pay their debts either; and in due course the estate is sold at auction to

Lopahin himself, who will make a very good thing of it. His workmen are hacking at the old trees before the family is out of the house.

The play may be briefly described as a realistic ensemble pathos: the characters all suffer the passing of the estate in different ways, thus adumbrating this change at a deeper and more generally significant level than that of any individual's experience. The action which they all share by analogy, and which informs the suffering of the destined change of the Cherry Orchard, is "to save the Cherry Orchard": that is, each character sees some value in it—economic, sentimental, social, cultural—which he wishes to keep. By means of his plot, Chekhov always focuses attention on the general action: his crowded stage, full of the characters I have mentioned as well as half a dozen hangers-on, is like an implicit discussion of the fatality which concerns them all; but Chekhov does not believe in their ideas, and the interplay he shows among his *dramatis personae* is not so much the play of thought as the alternation of his characters' perceptions of their situation, as the moods shift and the time for decision comes and goes.

Though the action which Chekhov chooses to show on-stage is "pathetic," i.e., suffering and perception, it is complete: the Cherry Orchard is constituted before our eyes, and then dissolved. The first act is a prologue: it is the occasion of Lyubov's return from Paris to try to resume her old life. Through her eyes and those of her daughter Anya, as well as from the complementary perspectives of Lopahin and Trofimov, we see the estate as it were in the round, in its many possible meanings. The second act corresponds to the agon; it is in this act that we become aware of the conflicting values of all the characters, and of the efforts they make (off-stage) to save each one *his* Orchard. The third act corresponds to the pathos and peripety of the traditional tragic form. The occasion is a rather hysterical party which Lyubov gives while her estate is being sold at auction in the nearby town; it ends with Lopahin's announcement, in pride and the bitterness of guilt, that he was the purchaser. The last act is the epiphany: we see the action, now completed, in a new and ironic light. The occasion is the departure of the family: the windows are boarded up, the furniture piled in the corners, and the bags packed. All the characters feel, and the audience sees in a thousand ways, that the wish to save the Orchard has amounted in fact to destroying it; the gathering of its denizens to separation; the homecoming to departure. What this "means" we are not told. But the action is completed, and the poem of the suffering of change concludes in a new and final perception, and a rich chord of feeling.

The structure of each act is based upon a more or less ceremonious social occasion. In his use of the social ceremony—arrivals, departures, anniversaries, parties—Chekhov is akin to James. His purpose is the same: to focus attention on an action which all share by analogy, instead of upon the reasoned purpose of any individual, as Ibsen does in his drama of ethical motivation. Chekhov uses the social occasion also to reveal the individual at moments when he is least enclosed in his private rationalization and most open to disinterested insights. The Chekhovian ensembles may appear superficially to be mere pointless stalemates—too like family gatherings and arbitrary meetings which we know off-stage. So they are. But in his miraculous arrangement the very discomfort of many presences is made to reveal fundamental aspects of the human situation.

That Chekhov's art of plotting is extremely conscious and deliberate is clear the moment one considers the distinction between the stories of his characters as we learn about them, and the moments of their lives which he chose to show directly onstage. Lopahin, for example, is a man of action like one of the new capitalists in Gorki's plays. Chekhov knew all about him, and could have shown us an exciting episode from his career if he had not chosen to see him only when he was forced to pause and pathetically sense his own motives in a wider context which qualifies their importance. Lyubov has been dragged about Europe for years by her ne'er-do-well lover, and her life might have yielded several sure-fire erotic intrigues like those of the commercial theater. But Chekhov, like all the great artists of modern times, rejected these standard motivations as both stale and false. The actress Arkadina, in *The Seagull*, remarks, as she closes a novel of Maupassant's, "Well, among the French that may be, but here with us there's nothing of the kind, we've no set program." In the context the irony of her remark is deep: she is herself a purest product of the commercial theater, and at that very time she is engaged in a love affair of the kind she objects to in Maupassant. But Chekhov, with his subtle art of plotting, has caught her in a situation, and at a brief moment of clarity and pause, when the falsity of her career is clear to all, even herself.

Thus Chekhov, by his art of plot-making, defines an action in the opposite mode to that of *Ghosts.* Ibsen defines a desperate quest for reasons and for ultimate, intelligible moral values. This action falls naturally into the form of the agon, and at the end of the play Ibsen is at a loss to develop the final pathos, or bring it to an end with an accepted perception. But the pathetic is the very mode of action and awareness which seems to Chekhov closest to the reality of the human situation, and by means of his plot he shows, even in characters who are not in themselves unusually passive, the suffering and the perception of change. The "moment" of human experience which *The Cherry Orchard* presents thus corresponds to that of the Sophoclean chorus, and of the evenings in the *Purgatorio. Ghosts* is a fighting play, armed for its sharp encounter with the rationalizing mind, its poetry concealed by its reasons. Chekhov's poetry, like Ibsen's, is behind the naturalistic surfaces; but the form of the play as a whole is "nothing but" poetry in the widest sense: the coherence of the concrete elements of the composition. Hence the curious vulnerability of Chekhov on the contemporary stage: he does not argue, he merely presents; and though his audiences even on Broadway are touched by the time they reach the last act, they are at a loss to say what it is all about.

It is this reticent objectivity of Chekhov also which makes him so difficult to analyze in words: he appeals exclusively to the histrionic sensibility where the little poetry of modern realism is to be found. Nevertheless, the effort of analysis must be made if one is to understand this art at all; and if the reader will bear with me, he is asked to consider one element, that of the scene, in the composition of the second act.

Act II: The Scene as a Basic Element in the Composition

M. Cocteau writes, in his preface to *Les Mariés de la Tour Eiffel*: "The action of my play is in images (*imagée*) while the text is not: I attempt to substitute a 'poetry of the theater' for 'poetry in the theater.' Poetry in the theater is a piece of lace which it is impossible to see at a distance. Poetry of the theater would be coarse lace; a lace of ropes, a ship at sea. *Les Mariés* should have the frightening look of a drop of poetry under the microscope. The *scenes* are integrated like the *words* of a poem."

This description applies very exactly to *The Cherry Orchard*: the larger elements of the composition—the scenes or episodes, the setting and the developing story—are composed in such a way as to make a poetry of the theater; but the "text" as we read it literally, is not. Chekhov's method, as Mr. Stark Young puts it in the preface to his translation of *The Seagull*, "is to take actual material such as we find in life and manage it in such a way that the inner meanings are made to appear. On the surface the life in his plays is natural, possible, and at times in effect even casual."

Mr. Young's translations of Chekhov's plays, together with his beautifully accurate notes, explanations, and interpretations, have made the text of Chekhov at last available for the English-speaking stage, and for any reader who will bring to his reading a little patience and imagination.* Mr. Young shows us what Chekhov means in detail: by the particular words his characters use; by their rhythms of speech; by their gestures, pauses, and bits of stage business. In short, he makes the text transparent, enabling us to see through it to the music of action, the underlying poetry of the composition as a whole—and this is as much as to say that any study of Chekhov (lacking as we do adequate and available productions) must be based upon Mr. Young's work. At this point I propose to take this work for granted; to assume the translucent text; and to consider the role of the setting in

---

*The quotations from *The Cherry Orchard* are taken from the translation by Stark Young (New York: Samuel French). Copyright, 1947, by Stark Young. All rights reserved. Reprinted by permission of the author and Samuel French.

the poetic or musical order of Act II.

The second act, as I have said, corresponds to the agon of the traditional plot scheme: it is here that we see most clearly the divisive purposes of the characters, the contrasts between their views of the Cherry Orchard itself. But the center of interest is not in these individual conflicts, nor in the contrasting visions for their own sake, but in the common fatality which they reveal: the passing of the old estate. The setting, as we come to know it behind the casual surfaces of the text, is one of the chief elements in this poem of change: if Act II were a lyric, instead of an act of a play, the setting would be a crucial word appearing in a succession of rich contexts which endow it with a developing meaning.

Chekhov describes the setting in the following realistic terms. "A field. An old chapel, long abandoned, with crooked walls, near it a well, big stones that apparently were once tombstones, and an old bench. A road to the estate of Gaev can be seen. On one side poplars rise, casting their shadows, the cherry orchard begins there. In the distance a row of telegraph poles; and far, far away, faintly traced on the horizon, is a large town, visible only in the clearest weather. The sun will soon be down."

To make this set out of a cyclorama, flats, cut-out silhouettes, and lighting-effects, would be difficult, without producing that unbelievable but literally intended—and in any case indigestible—scene which modern realism demands; and here Chekhov is uncomfortably bound by the convention of his time. The best strategy in production is that adopted by Robert Edmund Jones in his setting for *The Seagull*: to pay lip service only to the convention of photographic realism, and make the trees, the chapel and all the other elements as simple as possible. The less closely the setting is defined by the carpenter, the freer it is to play the role Chekhov wrote for it: a role which changes and develops in relation to the story. Shakespeare did not have this problem; he could present his setting in different ways at different moments in a few lines of verse:

> Alack! the night comes on, and the bleak winds
> Do sorely ruffle; for many miles about
> There's scarce a bush.

Chekhov, as we shall see, gives his setting life and flexibility in spite of the visible elements on-stage, not by means of the poetry of words but by means of his characters' changing sense of it.

When the curtain rises we see the setting simply as the country at the sentimental hour of sunset. Epihodov is playing his guitar and other hangers-on of the estate are loafing, as is their habit, before supper. The dialogue which starts after a brief pause focuses attention upon individuals in the group: Charlotta, the governess, boasting of her culture and complaining that no one understands her; the silly maid Dunyasha, who is infatuated with Yasha, Lyubov's valet. The scene, as reflected by these characters, is a satirical period-piece like the "Stag at eve" or "The Maiden's Prayer"; and when the group falls silent and begins to drift away (having heard Lyubov, Gaev, and Lopahin approaching along the path) Chekhov expects us to smile at the sentimental clichés which the place and the hour have produced.

But Lyubov's party brings with it a very different atmosphere: of irritation, frustration, and fear. It is here we learn that Lopahin cannot persuade Lyubov and Gaev to put their affairs in order; that Gaev has been making futile gestures toward getting a job and borrowing money; that Lyubov is worried about the estate, about her daughters, and about her lover, who has now fallen ill in Paris. Lopahin, in a huff, offers to leave; but Lyubov will not let him go—"It's more cheerful with you here," she says; and this group in its turn falls silent. In the distance we hear the music of the Jewish orchestra—when Chekhov wishes us to raise our eyes from the people in the foreground to their wider setting, he often uses music as a signal and an inducement. This time the musical entrance of the setting into our consciousness is more urgent and sinister than it was before: we see not so much the peace of evening as the silhouette of the dynamic industrial town on the horizon, and the approach of darkness. After a little more desultory conversation, there is another pause, this time without music, and the foreboding aspect of the scene in silence is more intense.

In this silence Firs, the ancient servant, hurries on with Gaev's coat, to protect him from the evening chill, and we briefly see the scene through Firs's eyes. He remembers the estate before the emancipation of the serfs, when it was the scene of a way of life which made sense to him; and now we become aware of the frail relics of this life: the old gravestones and the chapel "fallen out of the perpendicular."

In sharpest contrast with this vision come the young voices of Anya, Varya, and Trofimov who are approaching along the path. The middle-aged and the old in the foreground are pathetically grateful for this note of youth, of strength, and of hope; and presently they are listening happily (though without agreement or belief) to Trofimov's aspirations, his creed of social progress, and his conviction that their generation is no longer important to the life of Russia. When the group falls silent again, they are all disposed to contentment with the moment; and when Epihodov's guitar is heard, and we look up, we feel the country and the evening under the aspect of hope—as offering freedom from the responsibilities and conflicts of the estate itself:

(*Epihodov passes by at the back, playing his guitar.*)

LYUBOV. (*Lost in thought.*) Epihodov is coming—

ANYA. (*Lost in thought.*) Epihodov is coming.

GAEV. The sun has set, ladies and gentlemen.

TROFIMOV. Yes.

GAEV. (*Not loud and as if he were declaiming.*) Oh, Nature, wonderful, you gleam with eternal radiance, beautiful and indifferent, you, whom we call Mother, combine in yourself both life and death, you give life and take it away.

VARYA. (*Beseechingly.*) Uncle!

Gaev's false, rhetorical note ends the harmony, brings us back to the present and to the awareness of change on the horizon, and produces a sort of empty stalemate—a silent pause with worry and fear in it.

(*All sit absorbed in their thoughts. There is only the silence.* FIRS *is heard muttering to himself softly. Suddenly a distant sound is heard, as if from the sky, like the sound of a snapped string, dying away, mournful.*)

This mysterious sound is used like Epihodov's strumming to

remind us of the wider scene, but (though distant) it is sharp, almost a warning signal, and all the characters listen and peer toward the dim edges of the horizon. In their attitudes and guesses Chekhov reflects, in rapid succession, the contradictory aspects of the scene which have been developed at more length before us:

LYUBOV. What's that?

LOPAHIN. I don't know. Somewhere far off in a mine shaft a bucket fell. But somewhere very far off.

GAEV. And it may be some bird—like a heron.

TROFIMOV. Or an owl—

LYUBOV. (*Shivering.*) It's unpleasant, somehow. (*A pause.*)

FIRS. Before the disaster it was like that. The owl hooted and the samovar hummed without stopping, both.

GAEV. Before what disaster?

FIRS. Before the emancipation.

(*A pause.*)

LYUBOV. You know, my friends, let's go. . . .

Lyubov feels the need to retreat, but the retreat is turned into flight when "the wayfarer" suddenly appears on the path asking for money. Lyubov in her bewilderment, her sympathy, and her bad conscience, gives him gold. The party breaks up, each in his own way thwarted and demoralized.

Anya and Trofimov are left on-stage; and, to conclude his theatrical poem of the suffering of change, Chekhov reflects the setting in them:

ANYA. (*A pause.*) It's wonderful here today!

TROFIMOV. Yes, the weather is marvelous.

ANYA. What have you done to me, Petya, why don't I love the cherry orchard any longer the way I used to? I loved it too tenderly; it seemed to me there was not a better place on earth than our orchard.

TROFIMOV. All Russia is our garden. The earth is immense and beautiful. . . .

The sun has set, the moon is rising with its chill and its ancient animal excitement, and the estate is dissolved in the darkness as

Nineveh is dissolved in a pile of rubble with vegetation creeping over it. Chekhov wishes to show the Cherry Orchard as "gone"; but for this purpose he employs not only the literal time-scheme (sunset to moonrise) but, as reflectors, Anya and Trofimov, for whom the present in any form is alrea ... ne and only the bo iless future is real. Anya's young love ... Trofimov's intellectual enthusi sm (like Juliet's "all as b indless as the sea") has freed her from her ... tual childhood ne, made her feel "at home in the world" anywl ... e. Trofimov's als ... aspirations give him a chillier and more artificial, but equally complete, detachment not only from the estate itself (he disapproves of it on theoretical grounds) but from Anya (he thinks it would be vulgar to be in love with her). We hear the worried Varya calling for Anya in the distance; Anya and Trofimov run down to the river to discuss the socialistic *Paradiso Terrestre*; and with these complementary images of the human scene, and this subtle chord of feeling, Chekhov ends the act.

The "scene" is only one element in the composition of Act II, but it illustrates the nature of Chekhov's poetry of the theater. It is very clear, I think, that Chekhov is not trying to present us with a rationalization of social change *à la* Marx, or even with a subtler rationalization *à la* Shaw. On the other hand, he is not seeking, like Wagner, to seduce us into one passion. He shows us a moment of change in society, and he shows us a "pathos"; but the elements of his composition are always taken as objectively real. He offers us various rationalizations, various images and various feelings, which cannot be reduced either to one emotion or to one idea: they indicate an action and a scene which is "there" before the rational formulations, or the emotionally charged attitudes, of any of the characters.

The surrounding scene of *The Cherry Orchard* corresponds to the significant stage of human life which Sophocles' choruses reveal, and to the empty wilderness beyond Ibsen's little parlor. We miss, in Chekhov's scene, any fixed points of human significance, and that is why, compared with Sophocles, he seems limited and partial—a bit too pathetic even for our bewildered times. But, precisely because he subtly and elaborately develops the moments of pathos with their sad insights, he sees much more in the little scene of modern realism than Ibsen does. Ibsen's snowpeaks strike us as rather hysterical; but the "stage of Europe" which we divine behind the Cherry Orchard is confirmed by a thousand impressions derived from other sources. We may recognize its main elements in a cocktail party in Connecticut or Westchester: someone's lawn full of voluble people; a dry white clapboard church (instead of an Orthodox chapel) just visible across a field; time passing, and the muffled roar of a four-lane highway under the hill—or we may be reminded of it in the final section of *The Wasteland*, with its twittering voices, its old gravestones and deserted chapel, and its dim crowd on the horizon foreboding change. It is because Chekhov says so little that he reveals so much, providing a concrete basis for many conflicting rationalizations of contemporary social change: by accepting the immediacy and unintelligibility of modern realism so completely, he in some ways transcends its limitations, and prepares the way for subsequent developments in the modern theater.

Chekhov's Histrionic Art: An End and a Beginning

> Era già l'ora che volge il disio
> ai naviganti, e intenercisce il core
> lo dì ch'han detto ai dolci amici addio;
> e che lo nuovo peregrin d'amore
> punge, se ode squilla di lontano,
> che paia il giorno pianger che si more.
>
> —*Purgatorio*, CANTO VIII*

The poetry of modern realistic drama is to be found in those inarticulate moments when the human creature is shown responding directly to his immediate situation. Such are the many moments—composed, interrelated, echoing each other—when the waiting and loafing characters in Act II get a fresh sense (one after the other, and each in his own way) of their situation on the doomed estate. It is because of the exactitude with which

---

*It was now the hour that turns back the desire of those who sail the seas and melts their heart, that day when they have said to their sweet friends adieu, and that pierces the new pilgrim with love, if from afar he hears the chimes which seem to mourn for the dying day.

Chekhov perceives and imitates these tiny responses, that he can make them echo each other, and convey, when taken together, a single action with the scope, the general significance or suggestiveness, of poetry. Chekhov, like other great dramatists, has what might be called an ear for action, comparable to the trained musician's ear for musical sound.

The action which Chekhov thus imitates in his second act (that of lending ear, in a moment of freedom from practical pressures, to impending change) echoes, in its turn, a number of other poets: Laforgue's "poetry of waiting-rooms" comes to mind, as well as other works stemming from the period of hush before the first World War. The poets are to some extent talking about the same thing, and their works, like voices in a continuing colloquy, help to explain each other: hence the justification and the purpose of seeking comparisons. The eighth canto of the *Purgatorio* is widely separated from *The Cherry Orchard* in space and time, but these two poems unmistakably echo and confirm each other. Thinking of them together, one can begin to place Chekhov's curiously non-verbal dramaturgy and understand the purpose and the value of his reduction of the art to histrionic terms, as well as the more obvious limitations which he thereby accepts. For Dante accepts similar limitations at this point but locates the mode of action he shows here at a certain point in his vast scheme.

The explicit co-ordinates whereby Dante places the action of Canto VIII might alone suffice to give one a clue to the comparison with *The Cherry Orchard*: we are in the Valley of Negligent Rulers who, lacking light, unwillingly suffer their irresponsibility, just as Lyubov and Gaev do. The ante-purgatorio is behind us, and purgatory proper, with its hoped-for work, thought, and moral effort, is somewhere ahead, beyond the night which is now approaching. It is the end of the day; and as we wait, watch, and listen, evening moves slowly over our heads, from sunset to darkness to moonrise. Looking more closely at this canto, one can see that Dante the Pilgrim, and the Negligent Rulers he meets, are listening and looking as Chekhov's characters are in Act II: the action is the same; in both a childish and uninstructed responsiveness, an unpremeditated obedience to what is actual, informs the suffering of change. Dante the author, for his elaborate and completely conscious reasons, works here with the primitive histrionic sensibility, he composes with elements sensuously or sympathetically, but not rationally or verbally, defined. The rhythms, the pauses, and the sound effects he employs are strikingly similar to Chekhov's. And so he shows himself—Dante "the new Pilgrim"—meeting this mode of awareness for the first time: as delicately and ignorantly as Gaev when he feels all of a sudden the extent of evening, and before he falsifies this perception with his embarrassing apostrophe to Nature.

If Dante allows himself as artist and as protagonist only the primitive sensibility of the child, the naïf, the natural saint, at this point in the ascent, it is because, like Chekhov, he is presenting a threshold or moment of change in human experience. He wants to show the unbounded potentialities of the psyche before or between the moments when it is morally and intellectually realized. In Canto VIII the pilgrim is both a child, and a child who is changing; later moments of transition are different. Here he is virtually (but for the Grace of God) lost; all the dangers are present. Yet he remains uncommitted and therefore open to finding himself again and more truly. In all of this the parallel to Chekhov is close. But because Dante sees this moment as a moment only in the ascent, Canto VIII is also composed in ways in which Act II of *The Cherry Orchard* is not—ways which the reader of the *Purgatorio* will not understand until he looks back from the top of the mountain. Then he will see the homesickness which informs Canto VIII in a new light, and all of the concrete elements, the snake in the grass, the winged figures that roost at the edge of the valley like night-hawks, will be intelligible to the mind and, without losing their concreteness, take their places in a more general frame. Dante's fiction is laid in the scene beyond the grave, where every human action has its relation to ultimate reality, even though that relation becomes explicit only gradually. But Chekhov's characters are seen in the flesh and in their very secular emotional entanglements: in the contemporary world as anyone can see it—nothing visible beyond the earth's horizon, with its signs of social change. The fatality of the *Zeit-*

geist is the ultimate reality in the theater of modern realism; the anagoge is lacking. And though Ibsen and Chekhov are aware of both history and moral effort, they do not know what to make of them—perhaps they reveal only illusory perspectives, "masquerades which time resumes." If Chekhov echoes Dante, it is not because of what he ultimately understood but because of the accuracy with which he saw and imitated that moment of action.

If one thinks of the generation to which Anya and Trofimov were supposed to belong, it is clear that the new motives and reasons which they were to find, after their inspired evening together, were not such as to turn all Russia, or all the world, into a garden. The potentialities which Chekhov presented at that moment of change were not to be realized in the wars and revolutions which followed: what actually followed was rather that separation and destruction, that scattering and destinationless trekking, which he also sensed as possible. But, in the cultivation of the dramatic art after Chekhov, renewals, the realization of hidden potentialities, did follow. In Chekhov's histrionic art, the "desire is turned back" to its very root, to the immediate response, to the movements of the psyche before they are limited, defined, and realized in reasoned purpose. Thus Chekhov revealed hidden potentialities, if not in the life of the time, at least in ways of seeing and showing human life; if not in society, at least in the dramatic art. The first and most generally recognized result of these labors was to bring modern realism to its final perfection in the productions of the Moscow Art Theater and in those who learned from it. But the end of modern realism was also a return to very ancient sources; and in our time the fertilizing effect of Chekhov's humble objectivity may be traced in a number of dramatic forms which cannot be called modern realism at all.

The acting technique of the Moscow Art Theater is so closely connected, in its final development, with Chekhov's dramaturgy, that it would be hard to say which gave the more important clues. Stanislavsky and Nemirovitch-Dantchenko from one point of view, and Chekhov from another, approached the same conception: both were searching for an attitude and a method that would be less hidebound, truer to experience, than the cliché-responses of the commercial theater. The Moscow Art Theater taught the performer to make that direct and total response which is the root of poetry in the widest sense: they cultivated the histrionic sensibility in order to free the actor to realize, in his art, the situations and actions which the playwright had imagined. Chekhov's plays demand this accuracy and imaginative freedom from the performer; and the Moscow Art Theater's productions of his works were a demonstration of the perfection, the reticent poetry, of modern realism. And modern realism of this kind is still alive in the work of many artists who have been more or less directly influenced either by Chekhov or by the Moscow Art Theater. In our country, for instance, there is Clifford Odets; in France, Vildrac and Bernard, and the realistic cinema, of which *Symphonie Pastorale* is a recent example.

But this cultivation of the histrionic sensibility,* bringing modern realism to its end and its perfection, also provided fresh access to many other dramatic forms. The Moscow technique, when properly developed and critically understood, enables the producer and performer to find the life in any theatrical form; and before the revolution the Moscow Art Theater had thus revivified *Hamlet, Carmen*, the interludes of Cervantes, Neoclassic comedies of several kinds, and many other works which were not realistic in the modern sense at all. A closely related acting technique underlay Reinhardt's virtuosity; and Copeau, in the Vieux Colombier, used it to renew not only the art of acting but, by that means, the art of play-writing also. I shall return to this development in the last chapter, when I discuss Obey's *Noah*, a play based upon Chekhovian modes of awareness but transcending the limitations of modern realism by means of the Biblical legend.

After periods when great drama is written, great performers usually appear to carry on the life of the theater for a few more generations. Such were the Siddonses and Macreadys who kept the great Shakespearian roles alive after Shakespeare's theater was gone, and such, at a further stage of degeneration, were the mimes of the Commedia dell'Arte, improvising on the themes of

*"Histrionic sensibility" is explained in the Appendix.

Terence and Plautus when the theater had lost most of its meaning. The progress of modern realism from Ibsen to Chekhov looks in some respects like a withering and degeneration of this kind: Chekhov does not demand the intellectual scope, the ultimate meanings, which Ibsen demanded, and to some critics Chekhov does not look like a real dramatist but merely an overdeveloped mime, a stage virtuoso. But the theater of modern realism did not afford what Ibsen demanded, and Chekhov is much the more perfect master of its little scene. If Chekhov drastically reduced the dramatic art, he did so in full consciousness, and in obedience both to artistic scruples and to a strict sense of reality. He reduced the dramatic art to its ancient root, from which new growths are possible.

But the tradition of modern realism is not the only version of the theater in our time. The stage itself, belying the realistic pretense of artlessness and pseudo-scientific truth, is there. Most of the best contemporary play-writing accepts the stage "as stage," and by so doing tries to escape realistic limitations altogether. In the following chapters I propose to sample this effort in several kinds of modern plays.

CHAPTER VI

THE THEATRICALITY OF SHAW AND PIRANDELLO

On Shavian Theatricality: The Platform and the Drawing-room

THE curious convention-of-no-convention of modern realism is often described as that of the fourth wall: we pretend, as audience, that we are not present at all, but behind the invisible fourth wall of the parlor which the stage accurately reproduces. This is a pretense which it is difficult to maintain; and side by side with modern realism many dramatic forms have flourished which frankly accepted the stage as such and the audience as extremely present. Opera, ballet, and many kinds of comedy do so, in modern times, on the plea that they are not quite serious—"only" music, or distraction, or jokes.

Comedy in any period assumes the presence of the audience, and so cannot as such pretend to the strict modern realism of Ibsen and Chekhov. It is certainly true that Chekhov reveals comic aspects of his action and expects the laughter of the audience; but his convention does not admit that relationship between stage and house, and the pretense of unarranged and untheatrical actuality is never broken. Comic genres, on the other hand, accept some sort of limited perspective, shared with the audience, as the basis of the fun; they show human life *as* comic just because they show it as consistent according to some narrowly defined, and hence unreal, basis. They fit Mr. Eliot's definition of a convention: they are agreed-upon distortions, forms or rhythms frankly imposed upon the world of action. When we understand a comic convention we see the play with godlike omniscience; we know what moves the puppets; but we do not take them as real—when Scaramouche gets a beating, we do not feel the blows, but the idea of a beating, at that moment, strikes us as funny. If the beating is too realistic, if it breaks the light rhythms of thought, the fun is gone, and the comedy destroyed. Hence comedy has provided one of the chief clues to the development of unrealistic forms in the modern theater. And hence the purpose, in this inquiry, of considering the Shavian comic inspiration.

I say "the Shavian inspiration," because Shaw's peculiar comic sense, brilliant, theatrical, and unmistakable as it is, never found a consistent comic convention, comparable to Molière's for instance, in which it could be completely realized. He obviously assumes the audience, he plays to the gallery, from the very beginning; yet in the early part of his career he did not distinguish his aims from the realism of Ibsen. Later he seemed to identify his purposes with Brieux's—in the preface he wrote to Brieux's *Three Plays;* but he never propounds a simple thesis as Brieux, with perfect logic and consistency, always does. In this same preface he pays his respects to the machine-made boulevard entertainment in such scornful terms as would lead one to suppose that he would never use it himself; yet his plays written before the first World War are usually (among other things) sentimental parlor comedies of the boulevard type, "stirred to the tune of perpetual motion" and topped with "the bread sauce of the happy ending," as Henry James describes them. At the same time they have the quality called Shavian, which means something as definite as "quixotic." As Shaw survives from epoch to epoch, however, his thinking and his reading as active as ever, he becomes more and more self-conscious; and though the theater for which he started writing is nearly gone, he himself is brilliantly revealed, sparring upon the bare platform; and so the nature of his comic inspiration comes clear. In this development one may learn something about the peculiar difficulties of modern comedy, and something about the ways in which modern realism is superseded by other and subsequent forms.

Mr. Eric Bentley, in his very useful study *George Bernard Shaw,* has pointed out that Shaw's comedy in its beginnings is based upon the same enlightened drawing room as Oscar Wilde's. *Major Barbara* is an example of this early period in his development. Lady Brit's drawing-room feels as stable and secure as the traditional cosmos of the Greeks or Elizabethans, but it is as clear and small as a photograph; the London version of the bourgeois world. And the story of the play may be read as a typical sentimental parlor comedy for the carriage-trade. Lady Brit is an absurd but likeable pillar of society; her estranged husband, Undershaft, a fabulously wealthy munitions-maker of great wisdom and kindliness; her daughter Barbara a sincere but misguided major in the Salvation Army. She is in love with Cousins, a professor of Greek, a character suggested by Professor Gilbert Murray. The main issues are between Barbara and her father: the relative merits of the Salvation Army and munitions-making as ways to be saved. Cousins disapproves both of the Salvation Army and the Undershaft industry of destruction, but at the end he marries Barbara and places his Greek-trained intellect together with her revivalistic fervor in the service of bigger and better bombs. Shaw apparently wants us to believe in Barbara as a real human being in the round, instead of a caricature, and to take her dramatic conversion to her father's business seriously. At any rate he rejoices, and bids us sentimentally rejoice, at the end of his fable when the girl, the man, and the money are at last brought together. The audience may go home (in spite of the witty dialectics it has heard) in laughter, tears, and complacency, spiced, at most, with a touch of the shocking—for the secure basis of their little world, the eternity of the drawing-room, is never seriously questioned. Where, in all this, is the Shavian quality?

The play may be read as a thesis, a proof that munitions-making is the way to be saved; and this is in fact one of the bases of the many witty debates. It is a wonderfully farcical idea, but Shaw is far from offering it as Brieux offers his theses. As he uses it, it has depths of irony which Brieux never dreamed of: Shaw neither believes nor disbelieves it; its relation to reality is never digested—nor its relation to the sentimental story that Shaw puts with it. Its usefulness lies in its theatrical fertility: it is a paradox which may be endlessly debated, but it is in no sense the truth as Brieux thought he was proving the truth. The characters are conceived on a similar basis of paradox—except Barbara, who, as I have said is supposed to be real. But Lady Brit, Undershaft, and each of the minor characters clearly has his paradoxical platform. Lady Brit's is that she must have both the Undershaft money and the creed of the Church of England. The two are logically incompatible; but granted this non-Euclidean postulate, everything she does follows with unanswerable logic. And so for Undershaft, who presents himself as wise, kind, and completely dedicated to destruction. These platforms no doubt represent clarifications or schematizations of real attitudes in contemporary society. In the play, the rationalized platforms, as they are debated and developed, constitute the brisk mental life which we enjoy; but the relation of this life of the mind—this farce of rationalizing—to the human reality is no more defined than that of the paradoxical thesis to truth. Thus the play is a parlor-game, based upon the freedom of the mind to name and then to rationalize anything, without ever deviating from the concept to the thing—the British Empire and Original Sin as light and portable as the blueprints of the social planners and human engineers. Shaw the moralist invites us into this brisk exchange for therapeutic reasons, as gymnasium-instructors instigate boxing or softball: not to win, not to prove anything, but for the sake of a certain decent fitness in the moral void. But Shaw the clown sees his and our agility as a rather frightening farce.

If one thinks over these elements—the sentimental story, the farcical-profound paradoxical thesis, and the complacency of the audience—one may get spiritual indigestion. But if one sees a performance, one may understand how it all hangs together for those quick two hours: it is because its basis in the upholstered world of the carriage-trade is never violated. On this basis it is acceptable as a string of jokes which touch nothing. And Shavian comedy of this period still flatters and delights our prosperous suburbs. But Shaw himself, as the world changed and the London drawing-room appeared to be less than eternal, became dissatisfied with it. He first began planning *Heartbreak House* about thirty-five years ago.

In *Heartbreak House* the perpetual-motion machine of the dialogue is built on the same basis as in *Major Barbara*: each character has a paradoxical platform to defend, with epithet and logic, in the brisk free-for-all of the emancipated parlor. Hector, for instance, is unanswerable as a vain, erotic housecat and heroic man of action; Captain Shotover as omniscient, morally fit as a fiddle, and a futile old man secretly sustained by rum. The Shavian farcical inspiration is here to be found at its sharpest and deepest. But in this play Shaw comes very close to presenting it with the integrity and objectivity of art: to accepting the limited perspective afforded by his view of action as rationalizing, and to finding the proper dramatic form for its temporal development—neither the boulevard intrigue nor the thesis à la Brieux which he had tried to use in *Major Barbara,* but a "fantasia" as he calls it. This notion of dramatic form was derived from Chekhov, as he explains in the preface; and one way to understand the superior consistency and self-consciousness of this play is by comparing it with Chekhov's masterpiece. It was a performance of *The Cherry Orchard* which Shaw saw before the first World War that gave him his clue—precisely because Chekhov saw the prewar drawing room, "cultured, leisured Europe before the war," as Shaw puts it, not as eternal, but as dissolving before our eyes, and the significant mode of human action, not as rationalizing, but as the direct suffering of the perception of change. It was Chekhov's opposite perspective on the bourgeois theater of human life which made Shaw aware of the nature and limitations of his own.

Thus the ostensible scene is still the emancipated parlor; but in *Heartbreak House* this parlor is no longer felt as all reality: we feel around it and behind it the outer darkness, the unmapped forces of the changing modern world. The life of the play is still in the making of epithets and in logical fencing; but now we see that the emancipated mind, though omnipotent in its own realm, is helpless between the power of the wealth and war making business-industrial-financial machine one way, and the trivial or deathly passions of the faithless psyche the other way. And the parlor in which it is free to play its endless game is itself brought into focus as a thin insulating sheath.

Because of this added dimension—because Shaw now places his scene in a wider perspective—he understands the real shape, the temporal development of his action, far more accurately. In this play, as in *The Cherry Orchard,* nothing happens, and nothing is proved or disproved. The people come and go, their love affairs come and go with the pointless facility of the monkey-house; off-stage we are aware of their endless intrigues for money or power. But the interest is centered where it belongs: not on events or narrative sequences, not on what happens to any individual, but on the fateless fate and the bodiless farce of the emancipated mind itself. This, I think is what Shaw means by subtitling the play "A Fantasia in the Russian Manner on English Themes." Chekhov sees his people *as* suffering; Shaw, with his moral fitness, sees them *as* fully awake and sharply rationalizing. That the abstract form of these complementary versions of human action should be so similar is perhaps significant. In any case, the comparison between the two plays offers a good example of what I have called the partial perspectives of the modern theater.

But in spite of its greater artistry and self-consciousness, *Heartbreak House* has its blemishes. Ellie, like Major Barbara, is not quite objectified; the author has, and demands of us, a sympathy for her which violates the convention of farce. And at the end of the play, when the bombs fall and it is time to send the audience home, Shaw cannot resist a little preaching: he seems to wish to say that his farcical vision need not be accepted at all if we will only mend our ways; that we are all right, really. The therapist and drawing-room entertainer is even here not quite replaced by the inspired clown, with his disinterested vision of action as rationalizing in the void. Thus we are brought to the crux of our problem: why is it that the Shavian inspiration, so strong and lively, never quite finds a consistent convention and a completely accepted form?

Shaw never discovered a publicly acceptable, agreed-on basis in reality outside his peculiar comic perspective whereby it might have been consistently and objectively defined. All comedy is conventional and hence unreal; but Shaw does not make the distinction between the real and his own ironic perspective upon it. This is as much as to say that his perspective, or comic inspiration, is that of romantic irony: the basis of his theses, of his rationalized characters, and of the movement of his dialogue is the *unresolved* paradox. If the "emancipated mind" is to be really emancipated, its freedom must be that of the squirrel cage and its life (having neither beginning, middle, nor end) as formless as the squirrel's perpetual race.

In *The Magic Mountain* Hans Castorp and Settembrini are discussing irony. The only variety which Settembrini admits is what he calls "direct, classic irony," in which the ambiguity is a rhetorical device only, and the meaning of the ironist is unmistakable. I should prefer to call it Neoclassic, to distinguish it from Sophoclean irony, and because it is certainly the irony of Molière. For example, consider the platform of Molière's imaginary invalid, Argan: it is absurd as Lady Brit's. Argan is making a career of invalidism and (like a Shavian character) he is prepared to accept all the logical consequences of his position. But in the light of the sturdy common sense of Molière's *honnêtes gens*, to whom the story of Argan is presented, the absurdity and the impossibility are clear from the first. Thus the temporal form of the play is given: it will be a demonstration by *reductio ad absurdum* of Argan's untenable assumptions—i.e., by an appeal from logic to reality, from Argan's rationalizations to what Molière can assume that his audience directly sees. When the demonstration is complete, the play is over; both the comic convention and the dramatic form are objectified with reference to the *common* sense of the audience. It is this common or agreed-on basis which Shaw, like Hans Castorp, will not or cannot have—whether because he cannot rely on a common ground with his audience or because it would limit the freedom of the mind which he demands.

In the beginning of his career (in *Major Barbara*, for instance) the unmanageable depths of the Shavian irony were obscured by the clichés of the parlor comedy which he was ostensibly writing, and by the supposed security of the Edwardian parlor. And Shaw himself hid coyly and more or less successfully behind the pretense of the standard cast of characters. In *Heartbreak House* the parlor has lost its solidity, the rationalized "characters" are more frankly accepted as unreal, and the true Shavian sense of human life as rationalizing in the void almost finds its true form, the "fantasia" or the arbitrarily broken *aria da capo*. Moreover, in *Heartbreak House* we may observe the cognate process: the emergence upon the stage of the ironist himself. It is true that Shaw can be felt in all his plays behind the paper-thin masks of his characters; and it is true that there are representatives of the Shavian *persona* before Captain Shotover. But the Captain, probably Shaw's profoundest farcical figure, is also the most complete representative of Shaw himself. The drawing-room evaporates; the characters evaporate, and the prophet-clown himself appears upon a stage which is now accepted as a real platform before the modern crowd. The basis in reality of romantic irony is in the attitudes of the ironist; and just as everything in *The Magic Mountain* points to the shifting thoughts and feelings of Castorp-Mann, so Shavian comedy is not so much a consistent theatrical form as an extension of the author's own entertaining conceptual play.

Too True to Be Good is not one of Shaw's best plays; indeed he almost abandons the pretense that he is writing a play at all. But at the end, Audrey—the burglar-preacher who obviously represents the author—bursts forth in an impassioned monologue which presents an apocalyptic vision of the nature and destiny of the Shavian theater. As the other characters drift off the stage, bored with Audrey's preaching, he describes them as follows: "There is something fantastic about them, something unreal and perverse, something profoundly unsatisfactory. They are too absurd to be believed in; yet they are not fictions; the newspapers are full of them." He might be describing all of Shaw's characters: unbelievable as people, yet not defined as fictions either; unsatisfactory, now, even to their author. But the ironist's inspiration is unquenched. Alone on the lighted platform before the darkened house, Audrey continues: "And meanwhile my gift has possession of me; I must preach and preach no matter how late the hour and how short the day, no matter whether I have nothing to say." It is the voice of Shaw the genius of farce, at last aware of his real basis. But Shaw the moral therapist (though relegated to the final stage-direction) has still the last word. "But fine words butter no parsnips," he warns us; "the author, though a professional talk-maker, does not believe that the world can be saved by talk alone."

Action as Theatrical: *Six Characters in Search of an Author*

There is a kinship between what I have called the Shavian theatricality, especially as it emerges in the later plays, and the much deeper, more consistent and more objective theatrical forms of Pirandello. Shaw as theater artist seems to have been feeling for something which Pirandello achieved: the restoration of the ancient magic of "two boards and a passion," frankly placed in the glare of the stage lights and the eye of the audience. In both theaters, the human is caught rationalizing there in the bright void. But Pirandello, having the seriousness of the artist, presents this farcical-terrible vision with finality and in an integral theatrical form; while in Shaw's complex case the artist is always being thwarted by the drawing-room entertainer or dismissed as romantic by the Fabian optimist or the morally fit man of good will. It is therefore Pirandello that one must study in order to see how the contemporary idea of a theater (as held by its most accomplished masters) emerged from nineteenth century Realism and Romanticism, including and transcending those genres as well as Shaw's solitary farce-of-rationalizing.

Six Characters is a convenient example of Pirandello's art: his most famous work, and his first unqualified success. I here remind the reader of the main outlines of its plot.

When the play begins, the curtain is up, the set is stacked against the stage-wall, and a troupe of actors with their director is rehearsing a new play by Pirandello. The rehearsal is interrupted by the arrival of a family in deep mourning: Father, Mother, grown Daughter and Son, and two younger children. These are the "characters"—fictions of the imagination of an author who has refused to write their story—and they have come to get their story or their drama somehow realized. They ask the actors to perform it instead of the play by Pirandello which they had started to rehearse. From this point, the play develops on several levels of make-believe. There is the struggle of the "characters" against the actors and their director, who find the story confusing, or boring, or not good box-office. There is the more savage struggle between the various characters, who cannot agree about the shape, the meaning, or even the facts of their story, for each has rationalized, or mythicized it, in his own way. A few sordid facts emerge: the Father had sent the Mother away to live with another man, whom, he thought, she would love better, and the three younger children are hers by this other man. Hovering near the family, watching its life at a little distance, the Father had met his wife's Daughter at a house of assignation, Madame Pace's dress shop. Complicated jealousies had developed among the four children of the double brood, culminating in the suicide of the little boy. The crucial episodes are re-enacted by the tormented and disputing characters in order to show the actors what the story is. When the suicide of the little boy comes up again, by a sort of hellish eternal recurrence, all breaks up in confusion—the fictive characters more real, in their conscious suffering, than the flesh-and-blood acting company.

The story of the six characters, as we gradually make it out, is melodramatic and sensational. The disputes which break out from time to time about "idea and reality," "life and art," and the like, are based on paradoxes in the Shavian manner: romantically unresolved ambiguities. The whole work may seem, at first sight, to be shop-worn in its ideas and, in its dramaturgy, hardly more than a complex piece of theatrical trickery. When it first appeared, in 1921, some critics were disposed to dismiss it in this way. But the fine productions which it received all over the world gradually revealed its true power and interest, which is not in the literal story of the characters, nor in the bright, paradoxical play of ideas, but in the original sense of action underlying the whole play. Pirandello has explained all this with great clarity in the preface he wrote in 1930 for the ninth edition. This preface is almost as important as the play. It deserves to rank with Cocteau's *Call to Order* and Eliot's *Dialogue on Dramatic Poetry*, as one of the works which endeavor to lay the basis for a contemporary theory of drama.

The action of the play is "to take the stage"—with all that this suggestive phrase implies. The real actors and the director want to take it for the realistic purposes—vain or (with the box-office in mind) venal—of their rehearsal. Each of the characters want to take it for the rationalized myth which is, or would be, his very being. Pirandello sees human life itself as theatrical: as aiming at, and only to be realized in, the tragic epiphany. He inverts the convention of modern realism; instead of pretending that the stage is not the stage at all, but the familiar parlor, he pretends that the familiar parlor is not real, but a stage, containing many "realities." This is, of course, a narrow and violently idealist view of human life and action; but if held with Pirandello's strict consistency, it cuts deep—very much as the narrow idea of the Baroque theater, to which it is so closely akin, cuts deep, enabling a Racine to search and reveal the heart. Certainly it is a version of action which enables Pirandello to bring the stage itself alive at levels of awareness far beyond those of modern realism.

By the time Pirandello wrote the preface to his play, he had had time to read criticisms of it from all over the world, and to discover how its audiences had interpreted it. These audiences were trained in the modes of understanding of modern realism, and they almost automatically assumed that the point of the play was in the literal story of the characters, and that Pirandello's new idea therefore was simply a new way to present the sordid tale. If so, then the play would be only another melodrama on the edge of psychopathology. It is this interpretation which Pirandello is at pains to reject first of all. "Now it must be understood that for me it is not enough to represent the figure of a man or a woman, however special or strongly marked, for the mere pleasure of representing it," he writes; "to tell a story (gay or sad) for the mere pleasure of telling it; to describe a landscape for the mere pleasure of describing it." When the story of the characters first occurred to him, it was in this realistic form; and as such it did not seem to him to be, as yet, the material of art, which must be "more philosophical than history." He was, in fact, through with modern realism: the literal scene, the actual individuals, and the sensational events of individual lives, no longer seemed to have any form or meaning. But when he sensed the analogy between his problem as an artist and the problems of his tormented characters who were also seeking form and meaning, he had the clue to his new theatrical form, and to the peculiar sense of human action (as itself theatrical) which this form was to realize. His inspiration was to stop the film of his characters' lives; to play over and over again some crucial episode in this sequence; to dispute its form and meaning on the public stage. By this means he found a mode of action which he, and the actors, and the characters, and the audience could all share by analogy, and which could thus be the clue to formal relationships and a temporal order. And he lifted the action, as it were, from the realm of fact and sensation, of eavesdropping and the curious intrigue, to the more disinterested realm of contemplation. "Always on opening the book we shall find the living Francesca confessing her sweet sin to Dante," Pirandello explains; "and if we return a hundred thousand times in succession to reread that passage, a hundred thousand times in succession Francesca will utter words, never repeating them mechanically, but speaking them every time for the first time with such a living and unforeseen passion that Dante, each time, will swoon when he hears them. Everything that lives, by the very fact that it lives, has form, and by that same fact must die; except the work of art, which precisely lives forever, in so far as it is form." Francesca's life, as developing potentiality, is stopped at the moment when her peculiar destiny is realized. And it is the crucial moments in the tangled lives of his characters—the moment in Pace's dress-shop, the pistol-shot in the garden—which must be played over with the vitality of improvisation, "as though for the first time," yet because they are played *over*, lifted to the realm of contemplation—it is these moments which the characters must interrogate in the light of the stage, as we all must mull over (though in secret) the moments when our nature and destiny are defined.

I have explained that Chekhov, in his way, also to some degree transcended the limits of modern realism: by selecting only those moments of his characters' lives, to show on-stage, when they are most detached from the literal facts and the stultifying rationalizations of the daily struggle. But in Chekhov these moments are suffered in abstraction from thought and purpose, and so his image of human action may seem too pathetic. He lacks both Ibsen's powerful moral-intellectual will and Shaw's fitness-in-the-void. But Pirandello, by means of his fiction of unwritten characters, can show the human creature both as suffering and as willfully endeavoring to impose his rationalization. This fiction-of-fictive-characters enables him to play over his catastrophes; and it was this resource which the realistic stage denied to Ibsen. When his Mrs. Alving, in *Ghosts*, suddenly sees Oswald's infatuation with Regina as a return of her husband's infatuation with Regina's mother, she gets the passionate but disinterested intuition which is the material of art, and is rewarded with the poetic vision that "we are *all* ghosts." But her final catastrophe—Oswald's collapse—strikes her for the first time only, and so remains, when the curtain falls, undigested and sensational. Pirandello's inspiration is to stop the action with Mrs. Alving's scream, and to play it over, in the actual light of the stage, the imagined lamp- and dawn-light of Mrs. Alving's parlor, and the metaphysical light of her, and our, need for some form and meaning.

Pirandello is at pains to explain, in his preface, that his play transcends not only modern realism, but also the various romantic genres with which some critics had confused it. The characters may be romantic, he says, but the play is not. The Daughter, for instance, when she takes the stage with her song, her deep feeling, and her abandoned charm, would like to seduce us into her own world of passion, as "the old magician Wagner" does in *Tristan*. But the scene is the stage itself, not her inner world; and her action meets perforce the actions of other characters who also claim the stage. Pirandello might also have said, with equal correctness, that his play transcends the Shavian irony, and at the same time realizes the farce of rationalizing with a depth and a consistency beyond that of Shaw. The Father, for instance, has a taste for the paradoxical platform, the unresolved ambiguity, and the logical consistency on the irrational premise, which reminds one strongly of Shaw. But he is present as a "real Character" first, and a rationalized platform second; hence we can believe in his sufferings as well as in his conceptualizing—and see both in a scene wider than either. The basis in reality of the Shavian farce appears, at last, to be in Shaw's own "gift" of abstract fitness and verbal agility; but Pirandello, in the stage itself and in our need not only to rationalize but to mythicize, has found a wider basis, on which many versions of human action may be shown together to the eye of contemplation.

There would be much to say of the extraordinary theatrical fertility of Pirandello's plot. The basic situation—the characters claiming the stage for their incommensurable tragic epiphanies, the actors claiming it for the marketable entertainment they are trying to make—has both comic and tragic aspects, and Pirandello exploits both, shifting from one to the other with perfect mastery. The situation, fictive though it admittedly is, has the firmness and clarity, once we have accepted it, of Racinian tragedy or Molièresque comedy. And just because it is so firm and unmistakable there is great freedom within it: it may be explored and developed with the apparent spontaneity of circus-clowning, the alertness and endless surprises of the Commedia Dell'Arte, where the actors improvised a performance on the broad clear basis of the plots of Latin comedy. The scenes may break into confusion—into philosophical arias and disputes; into laughter; into violence—but we are never lost. The stage, and the need to take the stage, frame the action as a mirror might, which no amount of grimacing can destroy—or like the *ampulla* in which the sibyl hangs, wishing to die, in the epigraph to *The Wasteland*. It is the static quality of this basic situation which is both its triumph and its limitation; and in order to understand it more fully, one must also think of some of its limitations.

I have remarked that the play is always breaking down in disputes about the idea and the reality or, more generally, art and life. It is in these issueless disputes that the Pirandellesque brilliance most closely resembles the Shavian brilliance; and indeed the unresolvable paradox on which they are based is like the basis of the "free" Shavian irony. But Pirandello, unlike Shaw, transcends his paradoxes by accepting them as final—or rather (since he does not, like Shaw, see human action as rationalizing only, and the world as merely conceptualized) he accepts his paradoxes as various versions of a final split in human nature and destiny itself. In the same way Racine, accepting the split between reason and passion as final, thereby transcends it: i.e., transforms it into an object of contemplation. Pirandello's version of this tragic contradiction (after the endless explorations of modern realism and romanticism) is more general than Racine's, and his concept of art is (after modern idealism) deeper and wider than Racine's *raison*, which corresponds to it. Pirandello's utter darkness of unformed Life (or *elan vital*, or *Wille*, or libido) is perhaps even more savage and less human than Racine's passion. Pirandello is not limited, like Racine, to the rigid scene of the enlightened moral will; he can present characters of various degrees of heroism and enlightenment; and, as I have remarked, he can accept and exploit the comic as well as the tragic aspects of his basic contradiction. Nevertheless, his tragedy is a limited, an invented, an artificial tragedy, on the same principle as Racine's; and in the same way it offers to the eye of the mind the eternity of the perfect, and perfectly tragic artifact—the human damned in his realization—instead of the transcendence of the tragic rhythm, which eschews the final clarity and leaves the human both real and mysterious.

One may also understand the limitations of Pirandello's theater by thinking again of its relation to modern realism. I have said that he "inverts" the scene of modern realism, and thus vastly increases the suggestiveness and the possible scope of the stage itself. But of course he does not, by this device, provide the chaotic modern world with a "theater" of action in the ancient sense. One might justly say that his attitude is more "realistic"—more disillusioned and disbelieving—than simple-minded positivism itself, for he does not have to believe in the photograph of the parlor, and he can accept the actual stage for the two boards it is. But he is left, like Ibsen and Chekhov, with neither an artistic convention like the Baroque, nor a stable scene of human life like the Greek or Elizabethan cosmos; and, like Ibsen and Chekhov, he has only the plot as a means of defining his action. The inspiration of *Six Characters* is thus not only the view of action as theatrical but the plot-device whereby this vision may be realized: the brilliant notion of making his protagonists unwritten "characters" and setting them to invade a stage. This plot is so right, so perfect, that it almost exhausts, and certainly obscures, the deeper insights into life and the theater which it realizes. Hence the natural though unjustified tendency to think of the play as a brilliant plot idea, a piece of theatrical trickery only, and so miss its deep and serious content. The complete dependence of the play upon its plot-idea constitutes a limation; but it points to the fundamental problem of the modern theater, which no individual can solve alone.

Pirandello was quite right to think of his characters as being like Dante's Francesca. They too are caught and confined in the timeless moment of realizing their individual nature and destiny, and so imprisoned, damned, as she is. This vision has great authority. It develops naturally out of several diverse versions of the modern theater which I have mentioned, those of Ibsen, Wagner, and Shaw. At the same time it is deeply rooted in the Italian temperament and natural theatricality; and it revives crucial elements in the great theater of the Baroque. It is close to the author's place and to his times, which we share; yet one must remember that it takes as all-inclusive, as the whole story of human nature and destiny, a mode of action and understanding which Dante thought of as maimed, and which he presented in the realm of those who have lost, not the intellect, but the good of the intellect: *il ben dello intelletto.*

The most fertile property of Pirandello's dramaturgy is his use of the stage itself. By so boldly accepting it for what it is, he freed it from the demand which modern realism had made of it, that it be a literal copy of scenes off-stage; and also from the exorbitant Wagnerian demand, that it be an absolutely obedient instrument of hypnosis in the power of the artist. Thus he brought to light once more the wonderful property which the stage does have: of defining the primitive and subtle medium of the dramatic art. "After Pirandello"—to take him symbolically rather than chronologically—the way was open for Yeats and Lorca, Cocteau and Eliot. The search could start once more for a modern poetry of the theater, and even perhaps for an idea of the theater comparable to that of the Greeks yet tenable in the modern world. I shall explain how qualified the success of these authors has been; yet they have tried in various ways to tap the ancient sources, in myth, ritual, folk traditions, and theatrical forms outside the narrow scheme of modern rationalism. And they have all used the stage which Pirandello freed for the uses of the poetic imagination.

CHAPTER VII

POETRY OF THE THEATER AND THE POET IN THE THEATER

Poetry of the Theater after Wagner: Paris between the Wars

THE most considerable effort in our times to make a poetry of the theater comparable to that of the masterpieces of the tradition, centered in Paris during the 'twenties and early 'thirties. In that brief period, in the center of Western Europe, the theater lived "at the height of its times": it was contemporary with the thought of Bergson, Valéry, and Maritain, the "metapoetic" labors of Joyce, the painting of Picasso, the music of Stravinsky and Milhaud. It enjoyed the resources of the Russian and Swedish ballets, of the never-quite-broken French theatrical tradition, and of the patient labors of M. Jacques Copeau of the Théâtre du Vieux Colombier. This theatrical activity was centered in Paris but it was shared by many artists from other countries, some of whom did not even live and work there. Eliot, Lorca, and the later Yeats all belong in one way or another to this movement—this quest for a contemporary poetry of the theater. In our country the Gertrude Stein-Virgil Thompson operas, E. E. Cummings' *him*, many ballets, and the plays of Thornton Wilder, different though they are from each other, all take their start and get their clue from elements in this Parisian theater.

The three plays which I have chosen as samples, each the work of a very self-conscious artist, are quite different from each other: integral and incommensurable as works of art in their own right. But at this distance it appears that they accept certain problems and intentions in common. They are all strictly after Wagner, in the sense of having followed him to the end of his road, and then sought a further path beyond him. Like Wagner, they reject as meaningless and deathly the standard images and stereotyped dramaturgy of the commercial theater. Like him they seek a renewal of the dramatic art in the more direct modes of action and awareness associated in our time with poetry in the widest sense, and in other periods with myth, ritual, and traditional (as opposed to machine-made) popular art. But, having seen and experienced the finality of *Tristan*, they refuse, as it were, to join the cult: they all reject the prophetic, revivalistic, or hypnotic attitudes and strategies of Wagner, in the name of the intelligence, the classic spirit, or the integrity of Art. If the clichés of the tyrannical market are false, and the ever-present clue of passion—the nocturnal world, the different tyranny of *Tristan*—is illusory also, where, in the public consciousness of the commercial city, is the art of drama to be placed? The only plea upon which it may claim to exist would seem to be—on the analogy of music and painting—the plea of "art."

But in the case of the theater (even this most sophisticated of all theaters) it turns out, in practice, that the plea of art, though valid, is not enough. Whether this is because the theater is less pure than music, or because one cannot quite escape the fact that drama is in some sense an imitation of action, or because this art must live immediately in a public awareness or not live at all—the fact is that some basis in reality must be established. The audience must know, with reference to something it does believe, where its make-believe, or "suspension of disbelief," is to start. Or you may put it that behind every play which has lived (however small and knowing its audience, however perfect its form) some acceptable idea of a theater is implicit. Since Cocteau, Obey, and Eliot were seeking precisely to expand the awareness of the audience, to transcend the narrow shrewdness of the modern city, and to comprehend human life in the wider perspectives of ancient sources, the question of the scene of human life which they established on the modern stage as the basis of their art is of crucial importance. Each of them solves this problem and answers this question of the idea of a theater differently. And no wonder: for beyond the problem of tapping the roots of our culture for the revivification of the actual theater is the general cultural problem in its thousand forms, the preoccupation of Joyce, Mann, Yeats, and Eliot himself, in his essays and his verse. What is the relation between the divided modern awareness and that "organization of the sensibility" which we feel in Shakespeare, Dante, and Sophocles? We do not know; the context in which modern poetic drama struggles to be born is of unmanageable complexity.

But the art of drama, because it is so ancient, because the stage itself and the living performer before an audience never quite lose their primitive basis—this ancient art, however divided and undernourished, offers a unique means of access to the roots of the tradition, and thence an index of the present state of public awareness. If the Greeks, if Shakespeare and Dante are newly legible in our time, it is partly because of the efforts of poets and other artists to question and lend ear to the art of the theater. Thus the consideration of *The Infernal Machine*, of *Noah*, and of *Murder in the Cathedral* gives me an opportunity "orderly to end where I begun": with the idea of a theater underlying the art of the great periods, and its puzzling relation to the contemporary scene and the divided contemporary consciousness.

The Infernal Machine: The Myth behind the Modern City

Les Dieux éxistent—c'est le diable.
—Epigraph to the play

The Infernal Machine uses the Pirandellesque stage: i.e., the stage as an art-medium like that of the painter or musician; the stage as Pirandello's characters use it, to present a brilliant and final image of their tragedies. Thus Cocteau also finds his way back to some of the habits of mind of the Baroque, with its static scene, clear in advance to the eye of the mind. Racine is in his bones, and he assumes that the Neoclassic tradition may be in some sense reawakened in his audience. But at the same time he goes beyond Pirandello and the modernization of the

Baroque; he proposes to present upon this stage, acceptable in our time, a myth which was already ancient in the seventeenth century, embodying modes of awareness which Racine's generation could not accept.

At the beginning of the play we hear a Voice, which recounts the tale of Oedipus, and ends with these words:

> Regarde, spéctateur, remontée à bloc, de telle sorte que le ressort se déroule avec lenteur tout le long d'une vie humaine, une des plus parfaites machines construites par les dieux infernaux pour l'anéantissement mathématique d'un mortel.

> (Spectator, behold: completely mounted, set to unwind slowly during the whole course of a human life, one of the most perfect machines ever built by the infernal gods for the mathematical annihilation of a mortal.) *

The four scenes of the play are set and performed upon a small lighted platform in the center of the stage, which is hung with "nocturnal curtains." The first scene shows the ramparts of Thebes, on the night when the young Oedipus first approaches the City to meet the Sphinx. Two young soldiers are on guard; and (as in the first scene of *Hamlet*) we learn that they have seen the ghost of Laius, who has come to warn Jocasta against Oedipus. Jocasta herself, accompanied by the high-priest Tiresias, comes to investigate the rumor of the apparition; but the ghost cannot reach her; she departs unsatisfied, and the fated chain of events proceeds. The second scene, laid in the suburbs of Thebes where the Sphinx lies in wait, is supposed to occur at the same time as the first. It is the meeting of Oedipus and the Sphinx. The Sphinx tells him the answer to her riddles, hoping that he will fall in love with her; but he is more interested in fame and fortune; he proceeds to Thebes to claim his reward, while the Sphinx, leaving her dog's body with Oedipus, returns to the realm of the gods; and so the tale proceeds, as it were, behind a tenuous curtain of misunderstanding. The third scene shows Oedipus and Jocasta on their wedding-night. Here the curtain of mortal myopia is thinnest; but in spite of the cradle

*My translation.

beside the bed the wedding proceeds, sleep-walking, to its consummation. The last scene (which follows most closely Sophocles' plot-scheme) shows Oedipus, at the end of his reign, with the City under the plague, receiving at last, from the Corinthian messenger and the ancient shepherd, the truth of his situation. He is like a gambler who knows he has lost; but at the end, after Jocasta has hanged herself with her scarf and he has put out his eyes, Jocasta's maternal ghost reappears with the young Antigone, and the family departs like Pirandello's Characters upon its eternal mythic journey, in the steady "gloire" of the legend beyond life.

The scenic strategy which Cocteau uses to bring the myth into relation with contemporary life is similar to that which Joyce used in *Ulysses*. Modern life, with its disabused clarity, its small shrewdnesses, occupies the foreground, while the different reality of the mythic pattern is in the surrounding darkness. The visible arrangement of the stage itself presents this scene-within-a-scene: all that goes on upon the lighted platform in the center feels as contemporary as the newspaper, while the infernal machine slowly unrolls behind the "nocturnal curtains." The "Thebes" which is established in the first scene by the slangy gossip of the soldiers: its cafés throbbing with popular music, hot or blue; its rising prices and its threat of revolution or war—even the menace of the "Sphinx" which the authorities cannot deal with—might be any demoralized Balkan or Mediterranean commercial city of our time or any time. Its modernity is generalized, in the manner of Picasso's illustrations for Ovid. And so for the characters: Jocasta is at home with the superstitions of any period, and at the same time she is a café-society Queen *à la* Elsa Maxwell. The young Oedipus, impatiently cross-questioning the Sphinx, might be the winner of a bicycle marathon, or an ambitious politician who achieves the worldly *gloire classique* by stabilizing the franc for a day.

When Cocteau thus fixes the contemporary modes of action and perception in the eye of the mind, accepting the literal scene with hellish and timeless finality, he is returning to the very basis of rationalistic drama: a new version of Bergson's "closed soul" and "closed society." As in Racine and Pirandello, both the little scene of human reasoned purpose, and the wider scene of surrounding darkness, are accepted in advance as permanent and permanently separate. And the drama which the characters consciously act on their lighted platform is a little intrigue for pleasure and power like that of the commercial theater. Cocteau has accepted the histrionic basis (the rationalizing action) of the sophisticated comedies and triangles of the Boulevard theaters; and *The Infernal Machine* could be acted in the light and agile style of Guitry. The *poésie de théâtre* which he nevertheless contrives, is a matter of the scene behind the literal scene, and of the plot behind the intelligible intrigue.

Anyone who reads the prefaces to his plays, and his *Call to Order*, a collection of critical obiter dicta, will understand how extremely conscious his dramaturgy is: he did in *The Infernal Machine* exactly what he had set out to do fifteen years earlier. In the beginning of his career, while he was working with the new French musicians, "Les Six," the problem seemed to him to be that of recovering from Wagner, whose "long funeral procession," as ·he puts it, prevented him from "crossing the street to get home." He did not wish to hypnotize the audience but to meet it on its own narrow terms, and on that ground to place his vision and his art. He wanted to oppose to the Wagnerian religion of art, a "poésie de tous les jours," something skeptical and French; an art which should subsist side by side with the common sense of daily life instead of denying and utterly replacing it. In Cocteau and his associates, the interaction between the complementary French and German versions of human life and action enters a new phase: this time it is the French spirit which seeks to recover from Germanic modes of awareness and find itself again. Accordingly he finds, behind the meaningless but intelligible machinery of contemporary careers and pleasures, the less intelligible but more significant machine of the mythic "gods." The machine of the gods and the machinery of human rationality resemble each other, and "resemblance is an objective force which resists all the subjective transmutations," he writes in *Call to Order;* "do not confuse resemblance with analogy." So he recovers the Neoclassic univocal sense of form, with its illustrative images, its coherence in the eye of the mind. He finds, at home, the resources of the rationalist tradition with all its dexterous craftsmanship, its weapons sharpened for the modern fight. But he wants more than that, he wants by such means to reaffirm the life of the myth itself.

In the last act of the play, when the maimed and ghostly family is departing, Tiresias prevents Creon from interfering with them. They no longer belong to him, to the realm of duty and worldly values, Tiresias says; now they belong "to the people, to the poets, to the pure in heart." Throughout the play, which presents itself so sharply and consistently to the wakeful mind, Cocteau also endeavors to address the unrationalized awareness, the direct sensibility which he attributes to the people, the poets, and the pure in heart—as though, through the din of a cocktail party, he were endeavoring in secret asides to tell a fairy story to a child. The naïve soldiers of the first scene for instance penetrate the veil between the City and the gods; they see the ghost which Jocasta cannot quite take in. In his theatric style—notably in his handling of the Sphinx and her transformations—he employs the simple-minded marvelousness of the stage-magician; and some of these sequences do in fact please children who have no idea of the play as a whole. And in the final act of the play, when Oedipus moves from the literal to the mythic, Cocteau endeavors to comprehend the two levels of his scene together. It is at this point that his dramaturgy meets its severest test: he would seem to require some sense of the analogy between the various beings of his dramatis personae, instead of the more mental "force of resemblance"; and accordingly it is in this last act that one may see most plainly both his extraordinary virtuosity and the limitations of his rationalistic esthetics.

At the beginning of the last act, the Voice reminds us that we have reached the fated end of the story, which it describes as follows:

> Après les faux bonheurs, le roi va connaitre le vrai malheur, le vrai sacre, qui fait, de ce roi de jeux de cartes entre les mains des dieux cruels, enfin, un homme.

(After false good fortune, the King is to know true misfortune, the true consecration, which makes, out of this
playing-card King in the hands of the cruel gods, at last,
a man.) *

That is, we are to be shown a profound and double-edged
peripety, a change in the moral being of the protagonist by the
discovery of the truth. Cocteau (like Corneille in *Polyeucte*)
would present, in the mirror of reason, a change of heart. He
contrives to accomplish this feat in two steps. He takes Oedipus
as doomed from the first, and as tacitly admitting that he is
doomed. Thus the last act like all the rest is, in form, the rational
analysis of a static situation; and the first part of the peripety,
the impact of the catastrophe, is not so much shown in Oedipus'
suffering as assumed in advance. The tense atmosphere at the
opening of the curtain is that of a poker-game when a daring
player, with everything in the pot, has been called: Oedipus,
as I remarked, is like a gambler who knows he is caught. Creon
and Tiresias, watching, also know, and let the audience know,
that the messenger will show Oedipus up: the card-board King
is already gone. But what of the second step—the new realization of Oedipus "as a man"?

To some degree this step has also been made in advance, for
we feel a new and bitter sobriety in Oedipus; but the actual
revelation (like Polyeucte's instantaneous santification) is accomplished by legerdemain and in the twinkling of an eye.
When the ghost of Jocasta appears, mother rather than wife
(there is no marrying in heaven), the effect is to remind us
with startling suddenness of a donné basic to the whole play,
but which we had forgotten in the analysis of the three static
situations of the first three acts: the story was over before it
began: its ultimate reality is in the divine-infernal machine, in
the characters as tragically fated, in the beautiful coherence of
the myth—and not in the myopic intrigues of Oedipus' and
Jocasta's daily life, or in their contingent roles as child, or
spouse, or parent. So Oedipus is surprisingly but consistently
revealed, like a Corneillian or Racinian hero, in the timeless
"gloire" of art and the mind, and like Pirandello's Characters,

*My translation.

201

in the clarity of the stage. Oedipus, whom we had accepted as a person, is made again into a legend; he enjoys, if not the natural sanctity of Oedipus at Colonus, the eternity of the perfect artifact. And the whole play comes together on the basis of the objective resemblances between its elements—especially that between the rational coherence of each of the static situations, and the esthetic coherence of the myth itself. But these effects, beautiful in their own right, are intended to indicate something deeper, a sense of human life and action closer to that of Sophocles' tragedy.

The Voice has warned us that Oedipus is to become, not a legend or a work of art, but "a man." And Cocteau has placed Tiresias on stage as chief reflector of the action; and Tiresias, throughout the play, has been established as to some degree knowing both worlds, the human situation as we see it, and the truth of the gods. In this scene he understands the calamity as it develops; sees Oedipus while still deluded, as subject to the truth; and, after he has reentered the legend, in the human terms of pity and terror. Thus Cocteau's Tiresias is modeled upon the Tiresias of Sophocles; he must perceive the unrealized and therefore unrationalizable human essence beneath the masks, the contingent beings which it assumes; discern, beneath the mental force of resemblance the deeper analogies between beings; and perceive moral change directly. In the character of Tiresias, in his attitudes and in his remarks, Cocteau invites us to see the action as tragic in the ancient sense.

Thus in presenting the myth of Oedipus on the modern stage, Cocteau has adopted many of the attitudes, methods, and formal principles of a Euripides or a Voltaire in their treatment of myths; but he meets the rationalists, as it were, going in the opposite direction. Instead of rationalizing the mythic insights, he starts with the accepted reduction to the terms of reason, and to the elegant artificiality of the illustrative anecdote; but he seeks to reveal the moral and anagogical reality behind them.

Cocteau's contemporary and extremely sophisticated theater lacks all of the traditional resources represented by the Sophoclean chorus. He cannot expect his audience to have any of that habitual faith in an unseen mythic and ritual order which informs the choric odes, makes possible the theatrical representation of a change of moral being, and the placing of the literal scene in a wider perspective. He can count on nothing but the wakeful mind. Yet on that basis (so much wider than anything an American playwright can assume) he has succeeded in building a drama of great depth and beauty, a masterpiece of the modern theater. It is only when one thinks of it in relation to the landmarks—to Sophoclean tragedy, for instance—that it may appear merely ingenious,

> "Music and Philosophy, curiosity,
> The purple bullfinch in the lilac tree,"

as Eliot's Thomas of Canterbury scornfully says of such pleasures and triumphs.

Obey's *Noah*: The Theater-Poetic Reality of the Myth

Andre Obey's *Noah*, produced only three years before *The Infernal Machine*, also presents an ancient myth upon the modern stage. The stage itself is accepted in much the same way for what it is: illusion is dispensed with, or playfully accepted as such. The play has that lightness and economical directness, that irony, and that alert willingness to see a joke, which we think of as French as apposed to German—one of the qualities which Cocteau meant by "every-day poetry." But beyond that point Obey's strategy as a dramatist, his whole use of the theatrical and histrionic medium, is quite unlike Cocteau's. Obey proposes to make-believe the story of Noah as though it were literally real, and therefore as if the whole mythic world of the Old Testament (with God hidden but available and omnipotent) were real in exactly the same way. Cocteau, as I have explained, meets the audience of the *Théâtre Louis Jouvet* where it lives; accepts the most up-to-date modern mind first, and hopes that the "people, the poets, and the pure in heart," if such there be, may be led to sense the reality of the myth also, where he hints at it behind the glittering artifact of the play. But Obey adopts the bold strategy of by-passing the sophistication of the Boulevards, and of addressing the audience directly as people, poets, and (at least in make-believe) pure in heart. This strategy has its disadvantages; no doubt it is possible only for certain temperaments; in this case it rests upon the company for which Obey wrote, the Compagnie des Quinze, which was trained under Copeau and the heir of his Théâtre du Vieux Colombier. But by these means Obey shows one fundamental way of opening the modern theater to the wisdom of the tradition.

The play presents the story of the Flood in chronological order, like a simple fairy-tale, and in five scenes. In the first scene Noah is finishing the Ark, trying to talk to God (who is apparently as hard to reach as though He were on the other end of a poor telephone connection) and trying to imagine the Flood which he vaguely forsees. The beasts assemble, two-by-two; and then Noah's family, for whom the whole episode is like a rather pointless house-moving, which Father has decided upon in his usual eccentric way. The excitement rises rapidly with the embarkation, as the sky darkens, the rain begins to fall, and one of the savage humans whom God has decided to drown curses Noah the "magician," and his little family. The next three scenes show contrasting moments in the voyage of the Ark. The first of these shows the forty-first morning, when the family finds that the rain has stopped, the sky is clear, and the sea full of small bright ripples. The second shows a hot afternoon after a long calm: an empty silent pause, in which the envies, lusts, and hatreds of Noah's three sons, and the three girls whom they will marry, have had a chance to sprout. The third shows a storm. The whole family takes the storm as an unmistakable sign that Noah was wrong in his whole plan for the journey; that either God is deceiving him or there is no God, and that Noah is mad; and even his wife takes the children's side against him. But the dove brings the olive sprig which means that land has appeared somewhere; and in the frantic anticipation of release all issues are forgotten. Except by Noah, that is: he feels at this moment that the whole journey was a failure, nothing has been learned; and he cries to God, "Throw us into the soup!" The last scene shows the Ark stranded on the top of Ararat. The children, after greeting the ground in a savage dance and a fight, descend the mountain on their diverging paths; Mrs. Noah, grown old and childish, cannot face the new life; and Noah is left to begin again in the chill damp of the mountain-top, with only the silent colors of the rainbow to go on with.

The play may be briefly described as a meditation on the allegorical, moral, and anagogical reality of the Noah story, by means of an imaginative-histrionic technique like that which Ignatius Loyola in *The Spiritual Exercises* calls "the composition of place." That is, each episode, each moment of the narrative, and all of the people, are imaginatively reconstructed in their sensuous and emotional immediacy. The many-sided meaning of the story is sought, and brought home to us, by carefully and patiently building the fiction of its literal reality. Thus the appeal is to the full poetic or histrionic sensibility rather than to the mind. But to make this "poetic realism" acceptable on the modern stage, Obey adopts the rather coy attitude of the teller of fairy tales. Cocteau placed his imagined scene— "Thebes"—in the relentless modern city. Obey places his in a timeless countrified realm, the French equivalent of Grandma Moses' modern-primitive paintings of idyllic farm scenes. On this basis Noah is legible as the "old peasant" of a child's story; the animals may be mimed by skilled actors; the storm may be established, with all the imaginative lightness and scope of make-believe, by the rhythmic leaning and rushing of the actors on the heaving deck. Everything is consistent, every detail stylistically right. It is another instance of the French faculty for succeeding in their artistic efforts, coming off, every time, with something neat and pretty, concealing the depth and labor.

The fundamental difference between Obey's dramaturgy and that of Cocteau lies in Obey's fresh appeal to the histrionic sensibility, and his use of the refined and cultivated art of the actor. Cocteau assumes the skilled but narrow acting of the Boulevards; Obey demands a much greater imaginative effort on the part of the actor, and a much freer and more direct response from the audience. This he could do because he was writing for the highly trained ensemble of the Compagnie des Quinze. He was sustained by the idea of a theater which M. Copeau had realized in twenty years of patient labor.

The Vieux Colombier, like the Moscow Art Theater (whose methods Copeau carefully studied), was founded upon the cultivation of the histrionic sensibility and the performer's art. Like Chekhov, Copeau proposed to "undercut" the cliché responses of modern life and the commercial theater by studying the "movement of the psyche" before rationalization. He had, in fact, a very wide influence upon contemporary French acting; one can see some of it still in the refined naturalism of the better French films. But Copeau went a step beyond the Moscow Art Theater. He was interested in the histrionic as a means of revivifying play-writing, and from the first he studied dramatic forms which had developed before those of modern Rationalism: French popular comedy before Molière; the Elizabethan theater; the Commedia dell'Arte—forms which are closer to what I have called Ancient or Medieval Realism. The delicate realism of Vildrac and Bernard (so close to Chekhov's) owes much to Copeau; but it is in Obey's *Lucrece* and *Noah* that one may see, I think, the full fruit of the Vieux Colombier's idea of a theater—both its use of the trained acting company, and its cultivated sense of the older dramatic tradition. In *Noah* Obey uses the actor in a manner strongly reminiscent of Chekhov; but his stage is free from the limitations of modern realism, and he feels the vitality of the tradition back through the Medieval plays about Noah to the Bible story itself.

The sequence of short episodes in the last act, the departure of Ham, Shem, and Japhet with their wives, offers a good example of Obey's profound make-believe, and the realistic dramaturgy which he builds out of it. When the curtain rises, we see part of the Ark, now stranded on top of Ararat. The six young people, with their bundles, are lined up in silence on the deck. Noah descends, also in silence; and after kneeling to pray, starts to collect wood for an altar. He is followed by Mama Noah, with her cat in a little basket, querulously talking to herself. She has grown old, weak, and childish; she recognizes nothing on this misty mountain—neither the sea which she had grown used to, nor her own house which she had expected. Catching sight of Noah, all her bitterness comes out, and she curses him for a fool and a traitor, then shrinks back into the Ark in despair. All of a sudden the six young people throw their bundles to the ground, and leap after them with animal cries of pleasure: "Ah! . . . Cette vieille terre!" They do an improvised dance of savage gusto, tramping with their bare feet in the cold mud. The girls spit on the Ark, then scatter to explore the mountain, while Ham mounts a little hillock and yells in triumph, "Me! I! Ham!" The other boys climb up to push him off and a fight starts. We hear the girls calling in the distance; they return; and, each one pulling her man from the struggle, points out to him, far down the mountain, his destined realm: the south and the jungle for Ham; the east with its elephants and monkeys for Shem; and Europe, with its meadows and meadowy streams, for Japhet the shepherd—the pretty world, like a map in a first-grade geography book, theirs for the taking. They embrace briefly; and assuming their burdens, start the long trek, on their diverging paths, down the mountain with the descending streams, where the animals have gone already: "All the lives go down the mountain." Noah, who has suffered all this in silence, turns in fear to watch them go, thinking of them as children, putting his ear to the ground to catch the last sounds of their steps. Japhet's flute, fading out, measures their increasing distance for the ear.

The poetry of this sequence is very much like that of the second act of *The Cherry Orchard*, which I have analyzed in Chapter V: not a poetry of words, but a poetry of the rhythmic relationship and contrast of "scenes" established by the performers' make-believe, and appealing to the histrionic sensibility of the audience. As Chekhov plays upon our remembered sensations of sunset and evening and moonrise, so Obey plays upon remembered feelings: the damp chill of the mountain-top; the close sensations of trampling and struggling; the sense of distance in the landscape seen far off and heard far off in the faint cries and the diminishing sound of the flute. Chekhov has centered his realistic scene in a family and so has Obey: beyond the lingua franca of physical sensations is the language (also commonly understandable) of the rich and bitter emotional relationships of the family: the tragic complementariness of age and youth, of male and female, of memory and actuality. Thus we see and feel the return to earth reflected first by Mama Noah, in whose querulous weakness the circuit from cradle to grave is almost complete; then in the lusty hubris of the young adults; and finally in the more inclusive and tragic awareness, the richer chord of feeling, of Noah himself. All of this is the histrionic theater-poetry of the masters of modern realism. But Obey enjoys a further resource; he is realizing by such means the life of the Old Testament myth, tapping not only the riches of memories of childhood but as it were the childhood memories of the race. Chekhov shows us the passing of a particular family, and though he sees it so objectively that it becomes poetry his horizon is limited by the fatality of social change. But Obey envisages the ultimate horizon of the anagoge; his scene, or make-believe "theater" is not only the human world of history and moral effort, but "God's world" of the Old Testament. He offers, not only the realization of *a* change but, by these realistic means, a parable of the end (and the beginning) of the world:

> "Que le monde est grand à la clarté des lampes!
> Aux yeax du souvenir, que le monde est petit."

The dramaturgy of Noah depends of course upon the particular myth which Obey is here representing; in *Lucrece* his methods (equally self-conscious) are rather different. The Old Testament narrative, like the Medieval Noah plays, assumes the Family, which still survives into our own time: one of our few links, in habit and experience, with the pre-rational roots of our traditional culture. And the family provides the clue, not only to the present life of the Noah myth, but also to the form of the play, which consists of deeply felt analogical relationships entirely unlike the abstract resemblances which make the coherence of *The Infernal Machine.** The Oedipus story of that play depends upon the City, which Sophocles saw as dependent upon the divine order of Nature, but which Cocteau isolates from the natural world as a closed hell of discrete individuals

*Cornford has studied the relation between the order of the family and formal relationships in abstract thought and in art, in his very interesting book, *From Religion to Philosophy*. Mr. Kenneth Burke has considered the same point in another context in his *Grammar of Motives*, especially in Chapter II, "Familial Definition."

and mental machinery. But the Noah story assumes the human individual (male or female, child or parent) to be real in his relation to "God."* Cocteau's Oedipus cannot change before our eyes; the mind's eye freezes him into immutability; but Noah, whom we sympathetically take as real before his, or our, rationalization, is always changing. In short, if you grant Obey the theater which he makes-believe, the Old Testament world of God, he will show you there, in miniature, as it were in a colored stereoscopic view, the perpetual death and rebirth, the tragic rhythm, of human life.

But you must grant him the basis of his make-believe, and the question is what its relation may be to the industrialized community and rationalistic habits of mind in which we actually exist. From this point of view, *Noah* is harder to accept than *The Infernal Machine.* Cocteau demands only the perception of the Neoclassic art-form, and he carefully plots the relation between the life of the myth and the mental and spiritual life of the modern city. But Obey, working with childhood associations, appealing to the most complete and simple make-believe, asks us to forget the modern world altogether; and for this reason his play may look to some like a piece of fake primitivism, or "escapism" by way of false naïveté. It is probably true that the immediate audience appeal of *Noah,* which has been successfully performed all over this country in colleges and little theaters, is like that of *The Green Pastures* and *Our Town* which also try to reach back to the world of Old Testament legend by way of Sunday-school associations. But *Noah* has the beauty of the achieved and consistent art-form, and also a very sophisticated sense of the relation between the literal and the allegorical—between belief, make-believe, and "the willing suspension of disbelief." We feel behind it, not sentimental con-

---

*Professor Auerbach, in his *Mimesis, Dargestellte Wirklichkeit in der abendländischen Literatur,* has shown that the narrators of the Old Testament could present the human as real *apart* from convention and the order of the City—i.e., as having a place in history, a developing moral being, and a significant end—because of the ever-present "vertical" relation to God. He shows that this traditional view of the human situation, completed and transmitted by Christianity, was an essential component in the realism of Dante and also of Shakespeare, for whom the social order, at any moment, was not the whole theater of human life.

temporary fiction, but a theatrical folk-tradition going back to secular Medieval plays. It has some of the ancient force of the Hassidic stories about God, which are also childishly simple narratives with a very severe meaning.

However one may decide such questions of taste and judgment, it is clear that Obey has explored a fertile way, capable of other uses, of bringing the life of the myth to the contemporary stage. Cocteau accepts the consciousness of the modern city and its commercial stage, but *as* closed and damned. Obey disregards both, appealing to his audience *as* open to ancient modes of awareness outside the limits of modernity; seeking, like Chekhov, for those moments of our experience which are comparatively disinterested, comparatively free of the shrewd busyness of our usual lives.

Murder in the Cathedral: The Theological Scene

> You know and do not know, what it is to act or suffer.
> You know and do not know, that acting is suffering,
> And suffering action. Neither does the actor suffer
> Nor the patient act. But both are fixed
> In an eternal action, an eternal patience
> To which all must consent that it may be willed
> And which all must suffer that they may will it,
> That the pattern may subsist, that the wheel may turn and still
> Be forever still.
>
> —Thomas to the Women of Canterbury, and the
> Fourth Tempter to Thomas

Murder in the Cathedral, considered simply as a modern play, owes a great deal to continental theater-poetry, which I have sampled in the work of Pirandello, Cocteau, and Obey. It is most closely akin, in its dramaturgy and its formal sense, to *The Infernal Machine*: it has a similar coherence for the eye of the mind, a comparable esthetic intelligibility. It may be regarded as a work of art in the same way. But it is based upon a different idea of the theater; it seeks a different (and far more radical) basis in reality. It was written for the Canterbury Festival, June 1935, and it takes the audience as officially Christian. On this basis the play is a demonstration and expression of the "right reason" for martyrdom and, behind that, of the right doctrine of human life in general—orthodoxy. It is thus theology, a work of the intellect, as the continental plays are not. *The Infernal Machine* and *Noah* represent myths; *Murder in the Cathedral* represents (by way of the story of Thomas à Becket) a type of *the* myth, the central, the basic myth of the whole culture. Only after its performance at the Canterbury Festival did it enjoy an after-life in the commercial theater in London, in our Federal Theater, and in the limbo of the academic theaters all over the world.

The continental plays came out of the theater, and Cocteau's phrase *poetry of the theater* applies to them accurately; but *Murder in the Cathedral* (in spite of its theatrical dexterity) did not. In this play Eliot is not so much a poet of the theater as a poet and theologian who uses the stage for his own purposes; and though he seems to have benefited from the Paris theater, he has no connection with any theatrical arts actually practiced in English. The play has some of the abstractness of *Everyman,* which Eliot has called the one play in English "within the limitations of art"; but he does not seek to reawaken this sense of drama, in the manner of Cocteau, for example, who with his "gloire classique," seeks to echo the not-quite-lost Baroque theatricality. In its conception, its thought, its considered invention of a whole idea of the theater, *Murder* is unique in our time; and it is therefore more important to investigate what kind of thing it is (and is not) than to reach any judgment of its ultimate value as drama.

The basic plot-structure appears to be derived from the ritual form of ancient tragedy. The first part corresponds to the agon. The chief characters are the Chorus of Women of Canterbury, three Priests, four Tempters, and Thomas. The issue—whether and how Thomas is to suffer martyrdom for the authority of the Church—is most explicitly set forth in the scenes between Thomas and the Tempters, while the Priests worry about the physical security of the Church, and the Women suffer their premonitions of violation, a more metaphysical horror. The First Tempter, a courtier, offers pleasure, "kissing-time below the stairs." The Second, a Royalist politician, offers secular power, "rule for the good of the better cause." The Third, a baron, offers the snobbish comfort of acceptance by the best people, the security of the homogeneous class or tribe. These three echo motivations from Thomas's past, which he has completely transcended, and can now dismiss as "a cheat and a disappointment." But the Fourth Tempter offers Thomas the same formula ("You know and do not know, what it is to act or suffer") which Thomas had himself offered the Women when he first appeared; and he shows Thomas that his acted-suffered progress toward martyrdom is motivated by pride and aims at "general grasp of spiritual power." For the first time, Thomas nearly despairs: "Is there no way, in my soul's sickness / Does not lead to damnation in pride?" he asks. There follows a chorus in four parts, triumphant Tempters, Priests, and Women, envisaging and suffering Thomas's danger in their various ways; after which Thomas sees his way clear, the "right reason" for suffering martyrdom. This is the climax and peripety of Thomas's drama and the dramatic center of the play; and I shall consider it in more detail below. It concludes the first part.

There follows an Interlude: Thomas's Christmas sermon addressed directly to the audience. He sets forth the timeless theory of the paradox of martyrdom: mourning and rejoicing, living and dying in one: the bloody seed of the Church. From the point of view of the dramatic form, it corresponds to the epiphany following the agon and the choral pathos of Part I. It is also another demonstration, in another mode of discourse and another theatrical convention (the sermon), of the basic idea of the play.

Part II is, from the point of view of Thomas's drama, merely the overt result, the more extended pathos and epiphany, of his agon with the Tempters: he merely suffers (and the audience sees in more literal terms) what he had foreseen at the end of Part I. This part of the play is in broad, spectacular effects of various kinds. First there is the procession of the Priests with banners commemorating three saints' days: those of St. Stephen, St. John the Apostle, and the Holy Innocents. The four Knights (who replace the Tempters of Part I and, as a group, correspond to them) come to demand that Thomas yield to the King, and then they kill and sanctify him at once. The killing is enacted in several steps, including a chorus in English (one of the best in the play) while the Dies Irae is sung off-stage in Latin. After the killing the Knights advance to the front of the stage and rationalize the murder in the best British common sense political style. The immediate effect of the Knights is farcical—but, if one is following the successive illustrations of the idea of the play, their rationalization immediately fits as another instance of wrong reason. If it is farce, it is like the farce of the Porter in *Macbeth:* it embodies another aspect of the subject of the play. Part II as a whole, corresponding to a Shakespearean last act and to the catastrophe with chorus and visual effects at the end of a Greek tragedy, is rhythmic, visual, exciting, and musical—contrasting with Part I which is addressed essentially to the understanding.

Though the form of the play is derived from ritual tragedy, it is far more abstractly understood than any traditional ritual tragedy. It is based not only upon Dionysian but also upon Christian ritual, and upon the resemblance between them. The human scene, or social focus, is generalized in the same way: the Cathedral is neither Canterbury in 1935 nor Canterbury in 1170 but a scheme referring to both, and also to a social order like that which Sophoclean tragedy reflects; a three-part order consisting of the people, individuals with responsible roles in church or state, and the shepherd of the flock who is responsible for the tribal religion. Hence the dramatis personae are, in their initial conception, not so much real individuals as roles in the life of the schematic community: there are resemblances between Knights and Tempters, and between both and the Priests, which deprive all of them of complete individuality and point to ideas which the stage figures represent. The peculiar qualities of the play—its great intellectual scope and distinction as well as its allegorical dramatic style—rest upon the abstractness of its basic conception, so unlike that of ritual drama in a living tradition. The best place to study the scheme, or the dramatic machinery of the play, is Thomas's peripety at the end of Part I.

The ways which Eliot finds to represent Thomas at the crucial moment of his career are entirely unlike those by which Obey presents his Noah. Obey makes-believe Noah as a real man and "God's world" as real. He then shows Noah living moment by moment, in the alternation of light and darkness, and in the palpable effort to obey his *Deus Absconditus:* he appeals to our direct perception and to analogies in our own experience. Eliot does not seek to grasp Thomas imaginatively as a person; he rather postulates such a man, and places him, not in God's world but in a theological scheme. He then indicates both the man and his real, i.e., theological, situation indirectly by means of the significant elements which he assembles: Tempters, Priests, and Chorus of Women.

The first three Tempters do not tempt Thomas, because he is completely beyond the temptations they offer. They set forth three forms of temptation which are not so much realized in human character as expressed in the varied music and imagery of their verse. The Fourth Tempter does not really tempt Thomas either: he reveals a temptation to which Thomas is in danger of succumbing; but as soon as Thomas sees it, it ceases to be a temptation and becomes the instrument of purgatorial suffering. From this suffering come Thomas's desperate questions or appeals, ending with "Can I neither act nor suffer/ Without perdition?" To which the Fourth Tempter replies with the action-passion paradox which I have quoted. There follows a choral passage in four parts which, in its development, resembles what Thomas must be undergoing. The four Tempters chant their triumphant despair: "Man's life is a cheat and a disappointment." The Priests utter their very secular fright: "Should we not wait for the sea to subside?" The Chorus, the Priests, and the Tempters in alternation present a vision of horror: "Death has a hundred hands and walks by a thousand ways." The Chorus then appeals to Thomas: "God gave us always some reason, some hope," they chant, "but now a new terror has soiled us"; and the passage concludes,

> "O Thomas Archbishop, save us, save us, save your-
> self that we may be saved;
> Destroy yourself and we are destroyed."

To which Thomas answers (though, it seems, not directly to the Chorus):

"Now is my way clear, now is the meaning plain:
Temptation shall not come in this kind again.
The last temptation is the greatest treason:
To do the right deed for the wrong reason."

He then thinks over his career as he now sees it: his deluded pursuit of worldly triumphs, pleasures, and powers—talking to himself or the audience rather than to any of the figures onstage.

The difficulty of this passage is in grasping Thomas's peripety (or conversion) dramatically; and this is a matter both of the action Eliot is imitating and of the means he uses.

The chief means is the four-part chorus. *Murder* is the only modern play in which the chorus is an essential part of the dramatic scheme, and here the chorus plays a role similar in several respects to that of the Sophoclean chorus: i.e., it expresses, in the music and imagery of verse, if not what Thomas suffers, at least the suffering (depraved or painful) which results from Thomas's peril—a suffering similar to his yet on a completely different level of awareness, as the suffering of the Sophoclean chorus, in its real but mysterious world, is not. This chorus also reveals to Thomas the "right reason" (charity) for his martyrdom; but here again it does so without understanding anything itself, whereas the Sophoclean chorus, dim though its awareness is, to some degree shares a sense of the final good of all. We must suppose that Thomas hears their chanted appeal, and sees thereby the will of God (as distinguished from his own ambitious or suicidal will) in his progress toward martyrdom. Thus Eliot has arranged the elements of his composition in such a way that we may (like Thomas himself) deduce both his change of heart and his right reason at this point—but we may do so only in the light of the orthodox doctrine, the theological idea, of martyrdom.

But Eliot carefully does not show this change in Thomas himself at this point. If we attempt to imagine him as a real man in a real situation—as an actor would be impelled to do if he were trying to act the role—we may either say that he has found a new and better rationalization for the same deathly and power-mad impulse which drove him before, and thus achieved simply another intellectual feat, or else that the sudden intervention of Grace has removed him to a realm which is completely invisible to us. For Thomas himself remains invisible: he gives nothing, except the very interesting summary of his past and dead worldly career as the Tempters revealed it to him. Later—in the Christmas sermon—he will give his reasons at length and in very general terms; and after that, his life.

Before considering the allegorical dramaturgy and the peculiar theology underlying this passage, it should be pointed out that it cannot be understood apart from the whole play, which is all a demonstration and expression of Thomas and his sanctification. The sermon explains it, and Part ɪɪ of the play shows it in comparatively realistic terms. I have said that Part ɪ corresponds to the agon; and it does certainly complete Thomas's own drama: "I shall no longer act or suffer, to the sword's end," he says at the end of it. But if one thinks of the "drama" as the actual dispute with the drunken Knights, followed by the real killing, then Part ɪ may be considered a "Prolog im Himmel" which establishes the theological scene; and on this view its very abstract style is easy to justify. But the theological scene is presented as the sole reality; and in the realistic horrors of Part ɪɪ everything moves by its machinery—the drunken evil of the killers, the reflex fluttering of the Priests, the abandoned and Wagnerian somnambulism of the Chorus, and even Thomas, who goes through the motions without conviction, or rather with a conviction which is not literally represented at all:

> "It is out of time that my decision is taken
> If you call that decision
> To which my whole being gives entire consent.
> I give my life
> To the Law of God above the Law of Man.
> Those who do not the same
> How should they know what I do?"

as he puts it to the totally uncomprehending Priests. Realistic though Part ɪɪ is, in a way, its reality is at the same time denied; and it is composed according to the same formal principle, and in illustration of the same idea, as Part ɪ.

The purpose, or final cause, of the play is the demonstration of a particular theological idea which one must attempt to grasp if the play is to be understood. Mr. Eliot wrote of Pascal, in his introduction to the *Pensées:* "Capital, for instance, is his analysis of the *three orders:* the order of nature, the order of mind, and the order of charity. These three are *discontinuous;* the higher is not implicit in the lower as in an evolutionary doctrine it would be. In this distinction Pascal offers much about which the modern world would do well to think." This notion throws a good deal of light upon the schematic scene of *Murder in the Cathedral.* The Chorus would be in the order of nature; the Tempters, Priests and Knights in the order of the mind; and Thomas in the order of charity. Only the first two orders are visible to us, unless by Grace; but it is only in the order of Charity that Thomas and the form and meaning of the whole are finally intelligible. In the play, this order is represented by the doctrine which Thomas expounds in the sermon, and also by the abstract scheme of the play: the "three orders" and the three parts of society. Hence the mechanical feel of the play as a whole: the dramatis personae are as discontinuous from each other and from any common world as the parts of a machine, but they move according to the will of God as that is represented by (and deducible from) the theological doctrine. It is an idea of the divine plan, and of human experience as subject to it, which comes out of modern idealism: one is reminded of Leibniz's preestablished harmony. Is this the way in which we must now understand Christianity? I do not know. And I do not assume that Mr. Eliot himself would say so. But it is the doctrine which this play demonstrates; and in the play, therefore, the whole realm of experience represented by the *Purgatorio,* the direct sense of moral change (not to be confused with evolution), of natural faith, and of analogies which make the three orders not completely discontinuous—in short, the whole appeal to a real world which all may in some sense perceive—is lacking.*

*The reader is referred to Chapter i, Part i, "Analogues of the Tragic Rhythm" and to Chapter ii, Part i, "The Theater of Reason in Its Time and Place", where this view of the *Purgatorio* is somewhat elaborated.

On this basis one must understand the paradoxical notion of action which the play presents, and thence its dramatic form. The formal cause of the play (the clue to the plot, to the use of the stage, to the characterization, and to the verbal medium) is the idea of action expressed in the formula, "You know *and do not know* that acting is suffering/And suffering action."

In the play this formula works as a governing formal idea; but to avoid misunderstanding it is necessary to point out that this idea is itself poetic, and derived from experience—from that direct sense of human life which I have been calling histrionic. The histrionic basis of Eliot's verse has often been pointed out; it is the source of its unique and surprising vitality. He is a metaphysical poet by instinct; he imitates action by the music and imagery of his verse, or he defines it, or he does both at once:

"The child's hand, automatic . . ."

"My friend, blood shaking my heart,
The awful daring of a moment's surrender . . ."

"The lost heart quickens and rejoices
At the lost lilac and the lost sea voices . . ."

The action-suffering formula may be regarded as an achievement, in the medium of metaphysical poetry, for which all of Eliot's work up to that time had been a preparation. But part of this preparation must have been the study of the great dramas of the tradition; and the best way to grasp the scope of the formula is to compare it with the notions of action in three landmarks which I have studied: the tragic rhythm of Sophocles, the rational action of Racine, and the passionate action of Wagner.

The Sophoclean tragic rhythm spreads before us, in time, a spectrum of modes of action, from reasoned purpose, through suffering informed by faith, to a new perception of the human creature: the moment of the "epiphany." The whole movement occurs in time; and when, at the end of a figure, we see the human creature in a new light, it is still the human creature that we see, in a world continuous (by analogy) with that of common sense. It is only by means of this tragic rhythm repeated in varied figures that the action of the play as a whole is conveyed, also by analogy: and what is conveyed is not a verbal formulation but an action which we are invited to apprehend sympathetically and histrionically. Eliot's action-suffering formula is a generalization derived from the tragic rhythm; and it seeks to fix human action (beneath the "masquerades which time resumes") as it timelessly *is* in the hand of God. The tragic rhythm as such disappears when thus abstractly considered; and the elements of Eliot's composition are regarded not as imitations of the one action but as illustrations of the one eternal formula.

In this respect *Murder in the Cathedral* is closely akin to the "ideal" dramas of Racine and Wagner, which celebrate respectively action as rational, and action as passion (or suffering). The action-suffering paradox comprehends the complementariness of reasoned purpose and mindless passion which I endeavored to point out in Chapter IV, when considering Racine and Wagner. But though the notion of action in *Murder* seeks to comprehend and transcend Racine's and Wagner's visions, it implies, like them, the univocal sense of form and the idealist principles of composition. Thus the ideal perfection of the chorus is due to the fact that it exists primarily (like *Tristan*) as the expression, in music and imagery, of a mode of suffering, and only secondarily as "The Women of Canterbury": the performers would make it come alive by understanding the music rather than by understanding poor old women. And so for the Priests, Tempters, and Knights: they are demonstrations, and expressions in imagery, of rationalizations first, and men second, as though by an afterthought. The dramatis personae (essences of discontinuous worlds of experience) have nothing in common but the blank and meaningless fact of the killing—except Thomas. He knows what he act-suffers as the rest do not. The "basis in reality," which Mr. Eliot says every convention must have, is in Thomas's invisible moment of illumination, "the occupation of a saint." Thus a unique relation between author, performers, and audience is established: they are as discontinuous (and "perfect") as the dramatis personae. The perfection of the choral music, the elegance of the reasoned demonstrations by

Tempters, or Priests, or by Thomas in his sermon, is gained by accepting completely the limitations of a super-idealist convention. Hence the nightmarish feel of the play: all is explicit and expressed, yet all moves by unseen machinery and speaks by ventriloquism. This sense of dramatic form is akin both to the "despotic ideal" which Baudelaire felt in Wagner's orchestration, and to the a priori and almost actor-proof perfection of the Racinian Alexandrines.

If one considers, not the perfection of the discontinuous parts of the play but the perfection of the whole, it appears that all the parts are instances of the action-suffering, knowing-unknowing formula. It is in this way that the play as a whole coheres in the eye of the mind: the general scheme has the beauty of the perfectly formed and aptly illustrated thought. In Mr. Eliot's three orders, the realm of the mind would appear to be in some sense higher than that of nature, where his Chorus suffers in complete mindlessness. And he seems to have proposed to himself a dramaturgic problem like that which Corneille tackled in *Polyeucte,* and Cocteau in *The Infernal Machine*: to show, in the mirror of reason, a change of heart. He might have taken as his motto and principle of composition Cocteau's suggestive remark, "Resemblance is an objective force which resists all the subjective transformations. Do not confuse resemblance with analogy." Thus the form of the play is most closely akin to the masterpieces of the Rationalist tradition.

But Mr. Eliot parts company with this tradition, even more radically than Cocteau, by explicitly denying the reality of that "order of mind" in which the art of the play is legible:

> "Those who do not the same,
> How should they know what I do?"

asks Thomas. To this question there can be no reply. The play does not rest upon direct perception or natural faith; it does not base itself upon analogies in common experience. It does not assume that reason and the "mirror of reason" capture the truth of the human situation: it rests upon revealed truth, which can only reach us here below in the form of the paradoxical formulas of theology, at once reasoned and beyond reason. From the concepts of theology all is deduced: the very idea of a theater as well as the clue to the form of the play and the selection of illustrations. One might put it that the purpose, or final cause, of the play, which distinguishes it from any other drama, is precisely to demonstrate and express the priority, the sole reality, of this same final cause.

But, while recognizing the unique purpose of the play, I wish to study its formal rather than its final cause: to consider it as drama rather than theology. And I wish to offer two observations upon it as an example of the art of imitating action.

The first is that, whatever one may think of its theology and its epistemology, it cannot be dismissed as simply "unreal." It almost completely eschews photographic or modern realism; but the sense of human action which it conveys is very much like that which we get from other first-rate modern drama with a strong intellectual and ethical motivation, Ibsen's and Pirandello's for example. If one learns to understand the extremely consistent conventions of *Murder in the Cathedral*, one may read it as an imitation of that human action which we know from a thousand other sources: human life divided by the machinery of the mind, and confined by the greedy idolatries of the sensibility. The theological "basis in reality" which Eliot accepts may be regarded as an interpretation reached inductively through this common experience, even though Eliot presents it as the truth from which all is deduced.

The second observation follows from the first: in spite of its absolute finality and its ideal perfection, *Murder in the Cathedral* should be regarded as employing only one of many possible strategies for making modern poetic drama—which is as much as to say that the problem has not been solved in the sense of Sophoclean or Shakespearean drama. Mr. Eliot himself has explored other modes of action and awareness, other, less idealized relationships between poet and audience, both in his verse and in his other plays. I have quoted some of the explicit imitations of action to be found in his verse. In *The Rock*, the reality of time and place, of the historic moment, is explored as it is not in *Murder in the Cathedral*. In *Family Reunion* Mr. Eliot seems to be seeking a more realist type of dramaturgy; and he seeks it (like Obey in *Noah*) in the complex and prerational relationships of the Family. In short, Mr. Eliot's own practice in his other works invites us to consider *Murder in the Cathedral*, in spite of its perfectionism, not as the drama to end all dramas but as one example of the art in our confusing times.

Hence the purpose of placing it in relation to Cocteau's and Obey's poetries of the theater. As imitations of action, the three plays are comparable; three attempts to bring the light of the tradition to bear upon the contemporary human; three partial perspectives of great value and suggestiveness. A contemporary idea of the theater, if we had it, would leave room for them all as well as for some of the values of modern realism which modern poetry of the theater, or in the theater, has to do without.

The Unrealized Idea of a Theater

The impression which the Paris theater of the 'twenties and early 'thirties makes at this distance is that of extraordinary imaginative freedom and luxury. There must have been in the air, if not the idea of a theater in the ancient sense, at least a sophisticated awareness of all the arts. There must have been enough people with cultivated sensibilities and the mysterious means, both technical and financial, to indulge them—not only in painting and music and philosophy but in opera, ballet, and drama. Mr. Eliot's play, as theology, is the opposite of this Paris theater-art; for in it he renounces the absolute freedom of the artist as romantic and illusory. Yet insofar as this play exists as drama and enjoys a continuing life on the stages of the faithless modern world, it is on the same basis as *The Infernal Machine*: the "pure" and disinterested plea of art. This notion of art is proving less and less satisfactory, especially when it is taken as the one way in which to understand serious or poetic drama.

Some of the deathly connotations which the notion of art has acquired are undeserved. Those who proclaim that modern art is unintelligible have usually not bothered to acquire any of its languages. If one pays attention to the plays of Cocteau, Obey, and Eliot, for example, one may clearly see that on their own terms, on the particular basis of make-believe which each consistently maintains, they are extraordinarily intelligible: it is this very quality which gives them their beauty and distinction. They show more technical competence, more grasp of the formal resources of the tradition, than any successor is likely to know what to do with. They are also not open to the reproach of the "Ivory Tower"—by which is meant that modern art is somehow insulated from contemporary experience. It is insulated, like modern science, modern theology, or modern political theory, from any common area of public awareness (which shows that we lack such an area); but the freedom of modern art is precisely the freedom to respond, directly, and without premeditation, to any and every human experience. Is there any mode of action and awareness which has not been courageously or perversely accepted by some modern artist, and fixed in a form which is beautiful and pleasurable in itself? The Muse has a bad reputation, but it must be admitted that she has proved tougher and more resourceful than that protean *fille du régiment* whom Mr. Thornton Wilder found in *Finnegan's Wake*. She has been able to set up her shelter and (with a little cooperation from her devotees) to provide her infallible pleasures in every ruinous scene yet encountered on the road to chaos. If one were looking for a device for modern art, one would select, not the Ivory Tower, but a motto from World War II: "Kilroy was here."

If the notion of art is proving unsatisfactory, it is not because we lack art but because art when thus abstractly understood and freely practiced does not provide what we instinctively demand of it. The artistic triumphs of the Paris school do not perform the same function (even for us who are contemporary) as the dramas of Sophocles and Shakespeare. Their conventions are not defined with reference to any common, central idea of a theater. Their artistic freedom and integrity has been gained at a price which now appears too high.

The last living theater we had was that of modern realism. Ibsen and Chekhov, accepting the bourgeois parlor and its narrow awareness of the human situation, could think of their plays as mirroring nature, "abstracts and brief chronicles of the time." Some contemporary playwrights try to continue this tradition.

Odets and Tennessee Williams appear to be feeling for a theater-poetry based on modern realism. Mr. Noel Coward shows us a parlor, continuous with bedroom and bar, which has lost countenance. Socially conscious writers of every description offer photographic labor-union meeting-halls, proletarian kitchens, army camps. But none of these scenes is any more central or significant than the others: they are as arbitrary as facts, the spreading "desert of exact likeness" which Mr. Eliot described. But for Ibsen and Chekhov the bourgeois parlor was actually the focus of the life of the times, and therefore significant in however sinister a sense: it offered what James called a "social *point de repère*"; to its blank elements some symbolic significance could be attributed, and in that little scene a hidden theater-poetry could be evolved. We have seen, in the work of Shaw and Pirandello, some of the ways in which the bourgeois parlor lost its meanings. Thus the way was open for modern poetic drama. But as theater-poetry was freed from the limitations of modern realism, it lost its place in an actual society, its publicly perceptible and acceptable status as the mirror of human nature. The modernity of Cocteau's Thebes, the timeless peasantry of Obey's *Noah*, the schematic society of *Murder in the Cathedral* are derived from and throw light upon contemporary experience, as one may see if one learns to understand their art first. But this reference is oblique; the literal moorings are cut, and the resulting drama is arbitrary in its own way. Each poetic dramatist platonically discerns his own beautiful, consistent, and intelligible dramatic idea while the formless population, looking the other way, is engrossed in the commercially profitable shadows on the cave-wall.

This result of course was not intended by the authors I have studied: they have done their part, as dramatists, to place their visions in the public eye—Mr. Eliot in the most radical way of all. The problem, when looked at in this light, seems to be quite outside the realm of dramaturgy however *it* be understood. The founders of the Vieux Colombier, the Moscow Art Theater, and the innumerable repertory theaters of the last forty or fifty years have tackled the same problem from the other end—empirically and inductively. They have tried to appeal to the perennial appetite for drama and to establish centers, outside the entertainment industry but with their own audiences and support, where the theater arts could be cultivated and modern drama experimentally sought. These efforts have born fruit, as I have explained above. But, in the long run, the lesson to be learned from the art theaters is the same as that which we learn from the poets of the theater. Drama can only flourish in a human-sized scene, generally accepted as the focus of the life or awareness of its time; and such a focus no longer exists.

The hectic lives of the American art theaters (the only ones of which I have any first-hand knowledge) are instructive in this respect. In the 'twenties we had the Provincetown Theater, the Neighborhood Playhouse, the American Laboratory Theater, the Civic Repertory Theater, and a number of others both in New York and in other parts of the country, heroically endeavoring to establish theaters like the art theaters of Europe. None of them survived the depression; but in the 'thirties there were renewed efforts, notably the Federal Theater—which Mrs. Hallie Flanagan Davis was fortunately chosen to direct—and the Group Theater. The Federal Theater came and went with insane rapidity as the moods of Congress shifted.* The Group Theater, which inherited a good deal of the wisdom and skill of its predecessors, did not fade away until the approach of World War II. These theaters between them developed a large proportion of the ideas and theater-artists upon which the entertainment industry, in its improvident and predatory way, has fed. This is success, as we habitually understand the word; yet none of them succeeded in their aim of establishing an actual theater. It now appears that, in spite of their achievements, the more ambitious aims of these theaters were somehow deluded. They began with some change in the mood of the times, when the omnipotence of our market regime was being challenged, not only in the theater but in a thousand other contexts: with the humanitarian idealism of the New Freedom, or the popular-crusading idealism of the New Deal. But these sanctions proved (at least for the theaters) both brief and insubstantial. The "inspiration," the sense of the significant public role, leaked away

*Mrs. Davis has written its history in her important book, *Arena*.

after the first few years; *La toile était levée, et j'attendais encore* as Baudelaire put a similar experience. In the sober light of our recurrent normalcy it was clear that the non-committal dogma of the entertainment industry—the Broadway show-shops, the Hollywood daydream factories—truly embodied the authority of the market, arbiter both of our lives and of our images of life, the one idea of a theater which we can really count on. Mr. Harold Clurman, one of the directors of the Group Theater, has written a very candid and illuminating history of its struggles, *The Fervent Years*, and his conclusions may serve as epitaph for the whole movement: "The Group could not sustain itself as such because it was isolated. The Group Theatre was a failure because, as no individual can exist alone, *no group can exist alone*. For a group to live a healthy life and mature to a full consummation of its potentiality, it must be sustained by other groups. . . . When this fails to happen, regardless of its spirit or capacities, it will wither just as an organ that is not nourished by the blood's circulation through the body [will wither]."*

One of the speakers in Eliot's *Dialogue on Dramatic Poetry* makes the following rather wistful speech: "Aristotle did not have to worry about the relation of drama to religion, about the traditional morality of the Hellenes, about the relation of art to politics; he did not have to struggle with German or Italian aesthetics; he did not have to read the (extremely interesting) works of Miss Harrison or Mr. Cornford, or the translations of Professor Murray, or wrinkle his brow over the antics of the Todas and the Veddahs. Nor did he have to reckon with the theatre as a paying proposition." The speech is wistful because we cannot escape the unanswerable questions which Aristotle did not have to ask. The analysis of the art of drama leads to the idea of a theater which gives it its sanction, and its actual life in its time and place. And when the idea of a theater is inadequate or lacking, we are reduced to speculating about the plight of the whole culture. Unless the demoralizing power of modern industry is understood in some perspective, how can human life

The Fervent Years by Harold Clurman, p. 281. New York: Alfred Knopf, 1945.

itself be seen as anything more than a by-product (marketable or unmarketable, proletarian or capitalist) of its developing and collapsing machinery? Unless the cultural components of our melting-pot are recognized, evaluated, and understood in some sort of relationship—our religious, racial, and regional traditions, and our actual habits of mind derived from applied science and practical politics, seen as mutually relevant—how can we get a perspective on anything? And how can we hope for a public medium of communication more significant than that of our movie-palaces, induction-centers, and camps for displaced persons?

The ultimate questions about the theater of human life in our time, and the drama of the modern world, are interdependent, theoretical and practical at once; and therefore unanswerable. We do not have a theater in the classic sense nor do we see how we could have one. But we may still study the cultural landmarks—the drama of Sophocles and Shakespeare, the *Divina Commedia* of Dante—in which the idea of a theater has been briefly realized. So we may learn to recognize and appreciate the fragmentary perspectives we do have; collecting the pieces, keeping the idea alive in the tentative, fallible, and suggestive light of analogy.

For this purpose, the *Divina Commedia*, especially the *Purgatorio*, is the most useful: it is the most comprehensive and consciously elaborated pattern we have. It includes in rhythmic relationship the modes of action and awareness which in modern theatrical forms are absolute and isolated. Dante presents his contemporaries with the photographic accuracy of Ibsen and Chekhov; and he presents all of the social and political issues of his time. But the literal realities are also seen in the round: with all the dimensions of meaning, historical, moral, and final—the allegory, the trope and the anagoge, as they were called—which his fourfold symbolism was intended to bring out. The perspectives of dream, of myth, and of the most wakeful reason, which we think of as mutually exclusive, succeed each other in the movement of his poem but do not cancel each other out. His eye is always directly upon the life of the psyche in its shifting modes of being, its thought, its suffering, and its contemplation;

and it is this circumstance which makes his poem legible and living still. Dante's time is not our time; his terms are different; his beliefs must be different from our beliefs. Moreover, such a spirit rarely appears under any circumstances. Yet his work can show us, not the contemporary possibility, but the perennial idea, of a theater of human life and action.

PART III

CERTAIN TECHNICAL CONCEPTS
USED IN THIS STUDY

APPENDIX

ON CERTAIN TECHNICAL CONCEPTS USED IN THIS STUDY

THE few technical concepts used in this study are to be understood in relation to the plays themselves, which qualify them and give them their meaning. The medium and the forms of drama are so protean, and have been used in so many ways, that it is impossible to devise a technical vocabulary and system of notation comparable to that of music, for example. But there are a few terms I have used throughout the book which may suggest a general and analogical notion of the dramatic art; and it may be useful to indicate where I got them and how I understand them abstractly.

Aristotle made the most ambitious effort to describe the nature of the dramatic art and the concepts described below are derived in one way or another from the *Poetics*. My purpose, however, is not to invoke Aristotle's authority (if it still exists), nor to tackle once more the vexed question of what he really meant, but to assist the reader to understand the concepts themselves as I use them.

Plot and Action

The distinction between plot and action is fundamental, but it is very difficult to make in general terms. I have pointed it out explicitly in most of the plays studied, but the actions and the plots of these plays are all different. Aristotle does not explain the distinction, but in the first nine chapters of the *Poetics*, where he is concerned with tragedy in itself, and before he studies its purpose, or distinguishes the kinds of tragedies, he seems to me to assume it. I have collected a few passages which I think cannot be understood unless this distinction is admitted. The translation is Butcher's, and the page references are to the fourth edition of his *Aristotle's Theory of Poetry and Fine Art*.

"The plot is the imitation of the action—for by plot I here mean the arrangement of the incidents. . . . But most important of all is the structure of the incidents. For Tragedy is an imitation, not of men, but of an action and of life, and life consists in action, and its end is a mode of action, not a quality."—p. 25.

"The plot, then, is the first principle and as it were the soul of a tragedy."—p. 27.

"Unity of plot does not, as some persons think, consist in the unity of the hero. For infinitely various are the incidents in one man's life which cannot be reduced to unity. . . . But Homer . . . seems to have happily discerned the truth. . . . He made the Odyssey, and likewise the Iliad, to center round an action that in our sense of the word is one. As therefore, in the other imitative arts, the imitation is one when the object imitated is one, so the plot, being an imitation of an action, must imitate one action and that a whole."—p. 33.

"It clearly follows that the poet or 'maker' should be the maker of plots rather than of verses; since he is a poet because he imitates, and what he imitates are actions."—p. 37.

Aristotle offers a general definition of plot—the arrangement, or synthesis, of the incidents—but he offers no definition of action. I have already recorded my view that "action" is an analogical concept and that it can therefore only be understood with reference to particular actions. In this study the word refers to the action of which the play is an imitation; to the mimetic acts of the dramatist—plot-making, characterization, and speech—whereby he makes the play; and to the mimetic acts of the performers who reproduce, in the medium of their own beings, individual or characterized versions of the action the author had in mind. Thus the whole book is a study of action in some of its many modes; and at this point I propose to let the instances stand in place of a general definition. If the reader wishes to consider the difficulty of a univocal definition of this term, he is invited to read the symposium entitled "What is Action?" held in 1938 by the British Aristotelian Society. Professors Macmurray, Franks and Ewing read papers; they all saw the distinction between action and the events in which it is manifested; and they all agreed upon the fundamental importance of the concept. But they did not produce a definition which would help us much. It is interesting to note that none of them mentioned the art of imitating action.

If action cannot be abstractly defined, of what use is the concept in the study of the dramatic arts? It is to be used to indicate the direction which an analysis of a play should take. It points to the object which the dramatist is trying to show us, and we must in some sense grasp that if we are to understand his complex art: plotting, characterization, versification, thought, and their coherence. For this purpose practical rules may be devised, notably that of the Moscow Art Theater. They say that the action of a character or a play must be indicated by an infinitive phrase, e.g., in the play *Oedipus*, "to find the culprit." This device does not amount to a definition but it leads the performer to the particular action which the author intended. Thus whether one is interested in the arts of the dramatist or the arts of the performer, the distinction between plot and action is essential.

Two Aspects of the Plot: Form and Purpose

In the remarks quoted above, tragedy is considered as a species of art, and the plot is described as its first principle—its "soul," on the analogy of the soul of the living creature as the form of its body: in other words, as formal cause. But the purpose, or final cause, of tragedy is to produce a certain effect upon the audience; and the plot may be studied from this point of view also. In any given tragedy (if it is good) action, form, and purpose are one; yet the conceptual distinctions may be made; and for criticism and technical analysis they are very important.

Most of Aristotle's discussion of plot is concerned with its purpose, or final cause. He is showing how the dramatist produces the desired effect upon the audience. This is the part of the *Poetics* which has attracted most attention: the playwrights have gone to Aristotle in search of recipes for moving, diverting, or instructing their audiences. But Aristotle has a particular audience in mind, that of Athens in his day; and he assumes the "idea of a theater" which that audience assumed. For this reason it is a mistake to try to take his recipes literally, as the theorists of Racine's time tended to do. Moreover, Aristotle described the purpose of tragedy (its effect upon the audience) in at least two ways, which imply two views of what the audience expected or would accept.

The first of these is the famous formula of purgation: "Tragedy is an imitation not only of a complete action, but of events inspiring fear or pity."—p. 37.

"Tragedy, then, is an imitation of an action . . . through pity and fear effecting the proper purgation of these emotions."—p. 23.

I do not wish to join the discussion of this formula, or to attempt to limit its fertility, beyond pointing out that the aim of purgation, however understood, is certainly different from the aim of diversion which our commercial theater assumes. It seems to be connected with the ritual origin of tragedy, and with the "ritual expectancy" which the audience must still to some degree have had in Aristotle's time. Mr. George Thomson, in his very interesting book, *Aeschylus and Athens*, points out this connection, and interprets it according to a curious combination of Freud and Marx: "The actor who spoke the part composed for him by the poet was descended from the poet-actor; and the poet-actor, who spoke the words which he had been inspired to compose, was descended through the leader of the dithyramb from the priest at the head of the *Thíasos*, who, since the god had entered his body, *was* the god."*

Mr. Thomson's Freudian-Marxian interpretation (which I do not

---

*Aeschylus and Athens (London: Lawrence and Wisaart, 1946), chapter xIx, p. 382.

quote) seems to me unsatisfactory, but the connection which he affirms between the purgative function of tragedy and the ritual basis of that theater is unmistakably there. Tragedy, in this view, celebrates the mystery of human nature and destiny with the health of the soul in view.

But Aristotle also describes the purpose of tragedy in far more rationalistic terms, for instance in the following diagnosis: "It is not the function of the poet to relate what has happened, but what may happen—what is possible according to the law of probability or necessity. . . . Poetry, therefore, is more philosophical and a higher thing than history: for poetry tends to express the universal, history the particular."—p. 35.

In this passage it is assumed that the audience is enlightened, skeptical, and in need of reasons, satisfactions for the mind; the faith in ritual order, and in the revelatory and purgative properties of the ritual is not here in question—though Aristotle apparently feels no contradiction between the two versions of the tragic poet's purpose. Perhaps we must conclude that, at the mysterious moment when tragedy was formed, the audience had a free use of the reason without having lost the habits of feeling, and the modes of awareness, associated with the ancient tribal religion. However that may be, this second and more rationalistic view of the purpose of tragedy and the function of the plot is more acceptable than the first view in periods like ours when no guide except abstract reason is generally accepted. The notion of poetry as expressing the universal underlies the ideal theater of Racine, as well as the opposite, but equally ideal, theater of Wagner.

But what is probable or necessary? What is abstractly true? Aristotle, in the *Poetics*, is not worried about these questions as contemporary poets are, because he was describing a drama which in fact was accepted by its audience as sufficiently probable or necessary, and as expressing the universal. When Aristotle then proceeds to give his recipes for various kinds of recognition scenes, or for making a good man, a woman, a slave, or a king, he is simply analyzing and comparing techniques and attitudes which worked in actual practice, more or less well. From this distance it appears that they worked because of the whole complex culture of that time and place. That is why they will not work in the same way for us. In short, though it is still true that the purpose of any play is to have some effect upon the audience, and to mean something to it, Aristotle's analysis of the nature of this effect and this meaning cannot be directly applied to subsequent forms of drama. His detailed analysis of plot applies directly only to the tragedy he knew.

The question then arises, how we are to understand the plot; does this notion have any general validity at all?

The architects of the well-made plays have their answer to this question. They developed their very general lore of the plot by reducing the whole conception of drama to an empirically determined least common denominator. Sarcey committed himself to the view that the one constant purpose of drama was to hold an audience for two hours; hence the art of plot-making is the art of making an exciting arrangement of incidents with carefully controlled and mounting suspense. On this view, the action, its primary form (plot in Aristotle's first sense), the nature of the pleasure intended, and the meaning of the play need not be considered at all in our conception of the dramatic art. They are dismissed as subjective, mere matters of personal taste, or of passing fashions, incidental to the one constant purpose. Many playwrights of talent or genius have proved that the principles of the well-made play work; but they have also proved that they assume all the aspects of a drama which Sarcey refused to consider in his general definition: i.e., a certain very reduced view of human action, of the kind of pleasure best calculated to hold a crowd, and of the kind of meaning which anyone at any time is willing to attribute to a picture of human life. In other words, it has turned out in practice that the principles of the well-made play define, not all drama, but a very limited form of drama; and when an Ibsen or a Shaw tries to use them for his deeper purposes, there is a contradiction between this superficial form and the action which the author is trying to imitate.

The "well-made-play"—doctrine of the plot is as empirical as Aristotle's: it generalizes the techniques of the playwrights of the time, and takes the audience which they excited and diverted as determining the final cause of all drama. But Aristotle has a better philosophy and a better drama to study; and his doctrine of the plot is valuable precisely because it recognizes as essential the elements which Sarcey rejected as subjective. In the masterpieces of Greek tragedy which Aristotle examined, the action, the first form of the action, its ritual meaning, and its abstract intelligibility, were one; but Aristotle, in accordance with his careful principles, starts with those aspects of tragedy which make it what it is: first the species and then the actual individual tragedies, with their particular purposes and their particular appeal to the audience.

The most general definition of tragedy (which applies to all drama) is "the imitation of an action." And the most general definition of the plot is "the first principle and as it were the soul of the tragedy"; and this applies to all plots. After that comes the question of the playwright's purpose in the particular work, which depends upon the idea of the theater which the audience accepts or can be made to accept.

Though the distinctions between action and plot, and between the plot as the "soul of the tragedy" and the plot as the means of reaching the audience, seem to be in the *Poetics*, it is not clear that these distinctions were as important to Aristotle as they must be to us, if we wish to use his principles for the analysis of subsequent forms of drama and for understanding the ritual origins of Greek tragedy itself. Aristotle lacks our gloomy sense of the contingency of all cultural forms; he does not try to take account of the shifting perspectives of history as modern inquirers do. He explains that tragedy developed out of ritual, but he does not see (as the Cambridge Classical Anthropologists do) that the very existence of that tragedy depended upon the ritual order of that culture. He did not have the *Purgatorio* to read, and so could not imagine its sublimed Aristotelianism, its imitation of action in many modes, completely freed from the cultural forms of the Greek City. He did not foresee the ideal theaters of modern times, which seek some sort of substitute for a traditional cultural order. And for that reason, the parts of the *Poetics* in which he studies the effect of drama upon its audience are of limited value for other forms of drama. But his most general descriptions of the art of drama, and the principles of his investigation, are still the best we have and may be used with caution to bring out the analogies between various forms of drama in the varying theaters which the culture provided.

The Notion of Analogy

In this study I have used the term *analogy* again and again, hoping that the meaning would be reasonably clear in the context. But "analogy" is a very slippery concept. It has a disconcerting way of meaning all things to all men. Perhaps it is desirable to explain where I got it and, if not define it, describe the use I wish to make of it.

Thomas Aquinas distinguishes between univocity, equivocation, and analogy, for example in his discussion of terms applied to God, in *Selected Writings*, ed. by Father D'Arcy, pp. 148-153. Father Penido's book, *De L'Analogie*, is an extended study of this notion, chiefly as it is used by St. Thomas. He shows that the term itself is an analogical, and not a univocal concept; and he distinguishes so many kinds of analogy that one might well be afraid to use the term at all. But he also offers the following general description which I think is useful: "D'une manière très générale, toute analogie suppose deux conditions ontologiques: 1° une pluralité réelle d'êtres, et donc entre ces êtres une diversité essentielle—le Monisme est l'ennemi-né de l'Analogie; 2° au sein de cette multiplicité, de cette inégalité, une certaine unité." It is in that sense that I consider the plays I have studied as analogous: actually they are all different, each with its own action and its own form; yet they have "a certain unity" in that they may all be regarded as imitations of actions.

Father Penido offers a more extended list of the bases of what he calls true analogy, as follows: "Bases ontologiques de proportionalité-propre: une perfection doit exister objèctivement, qui réponde aux trois conditions suivantes: 1° participation intrinsèque en chaque analogué; 2° selon des modes essentiellement divers et gradués; 3° tels cependant que rien en eux ne soit extrinsèque à la perfection analogique où ils s'unissent." This seems to me to apply to the relationships between the elements in realist drama of all kinds, that of Ibsen or Chekhov as well as that of Sophocles or Shakespeare. The "objective perfection" is the action of the play as a whole, which "participates" in the parts of the composition—plot, characters, diction, and so forth, each regarded as "real" in itself and, in our acquaintance with the play, as prior to its unity or objective perfection.

This formula does not apply to the structure of the "ideal" dramas of Racine or Wagner, for in them the unity—reason or passion—is assumed as it were a priori, and the process of composition is felt, not as a succession of acts of imitation, but as a deduction from the one idea—i.e., as demonstration or expression. And the parts of the composition are taken, not as real in themselves, but as corollaries or illustrations of the central idea. Thus the dramas of Racine and Wagner are not only different from each other: in the "univocal sense of form" which they share they are different kinds of com position from all realist drama. In order to see any analogies between them, one must recur to the most general definition of drama and consider demonstration and expression themselves as forms of action, close imitations of their respective single objects.

Thus the notion of analogy which I am using is derived from Thomist realism. But Aquinas, and after him Father Penido, use this idea for the purposes of metaphysics and epistemology and I wish to use it merely for the formal analysis of drama. They are investigating Being, and the nature of our knowledge of Being; while my investigation is confined to the make-believe world of the imitation of action. In what sense is the Oedipus of Sophocles' play, with his mask and buskin, his versified speech, and his legendary background, real? Or Mrs. Alving, with her photographic surfaces? For my purposes it is unnecessary to inquire. In both cases the dramatist makes-believe their reality, while Racine and Wagner, in their different ways, use the characters and the other elements rather for metaphorical purposes; and "La métaphore ne rapproche pas des natures, mais simplement des éffèts," as Father Penido writes.

Though I make no attempt to study the epistemological, metaphysical, and theological questions, I do not deny for a moment that they "bristle" (Henry James's favorite word) whenever one attempts to study various forms of drama. Sophocles must have believed in the objective reality of the human situation which the tragic theater enabled him to mirror and celebrate. Dante must have believed that Being, Act Itself, dictated the form and content of his great fiction, for he writes, in explanation of his *dolce stil nuovo*:

> Io mi son un che, quando
> amor mi spira, noto, ed a quel modo
> che ditta dentro, vo significando.*

And I suppose that we shall not have a comparable form of the imitation of action unless a comparable sense of the reality of the human situation should again become available. But in the meantime, we may hope to get some light—if not upon what drama may be in our time, at least upon what it has been at its best—by studying the modes of awareness, and the structural principles, of the realist masters who worked with analogical relationships.

Father Penido points out that an analogical concept is not, like a univocal concept, completely abstracted. The many small actions in *Oedipus* are not related to a single idea but to a single action, that of the play as a whole. That is why one cannot get the coherence of the play at all unless one makes-believe its characters and events. That is what I mean by saying that it appeals primarily to the histrionic sensibility, just as a musical composition (in spite of its mathematical theory and abstract notation) can only be perceived by the ear. The concept of analogy (like that of action) is useful, not in making an abstractly intelligible scheme of the art of drama, or of a particular play, but in directing our attention to the relationships between concrete elements. And these elements—actions in various modes—we must perceive directly, "before predication."

The Histrionic Sensibility: The Mimetic Perception of Action

> "Poetry in general seems to have sprung from two causes, each of them lying deep in our nature. . . . Imitation is one instinct of our nature. Next there is the instinct for harmony and rhythm."
>
> —Aristotle's *Poetics*

"The histrionic sensibility" is another phrase which I have used so frequently that it has acquired an almost technical meaning: the dramatic art is based upon this form of perception as music is based upon the ear. The trained ear perceives and discriminates sounds; the histrionic sensibility (which may also be trained) perceives and discriminates actions. Neither form of perception can be defined

---

*"I am one who, when Love inspires me, take note, and go setting it forth after the fashion which he dictates within me."—*Purgatorio*, xxiv.

apart from experience but only indicated in various instances of its use. Perhaps it will help the reader to understand what I mean by the histrionic sensibility if I indicate a few of these instances.

Kittens, in their play, seem to be using something like our histrionic sensibility. They directly perceive each other's actions: stalking an imagined quarry; the bluff and formal defiance which precedes a fight; flight in terror; the sudden indifference which ends the play. Their perception of each other's actions is itself mimetic, a sympathetic response of the whole psyche, and may be expressed more or less completely and immediately in bodily changes, postures, and movements. The soul of the cat is the form of its body; but to some degree the soul is actual in different ways at different moments, depending upon what the cat believes, or makes-believe its situation to be; and to some degree the body instantly assumes these varied forms. When kittens perceive and imitate the action of grown cats, the histrionic sensibility is being used for educational, moral, or (by analogy) religious purposes: to explore the potentialities of the cat nature and the dimensions of the world in which the cat finds itself. When the kittens are only playing, their perception and imitation of action resembles art: they seem to enjoy something like the pleasure of the contemplation of form; and the actions of hunting or defiance, more rhythmic and harmonious than those of real hunting or fighting, approach the ceremonial or artistic disinterestedness of the hunting-dance or the war-dance.

Human nature has vaster potentialities for good or evil than cat-nature and our situation is far wider, more complex, and more unmanageable. But we also use the histrionic sensibility for education in many forms, as well as for the purposes of the dramatic art. When learning athletic skills we get as much from our direct sense of the instructor's action—the focus of his being upon the ball to be caught or the bar to be cleared—as we do from diagrams and verbal explanations. Spastics are trained histrionically—they are taught to concentrate, not upon the fork and the muscles being used, but upon the action of food-getting itself; and this focus of the psyche if repeated often enough gradually makes the proper neural and muscular patterns. It would appear that the same principle applies—the same appeal to the histrionic sensibility is made—when the skill to be communicated is not a physical skill at all. Good teachers, even of theoretical sciences, or of the arts of word and concept, teach by example: they reveal directly to the student the peculiar focus of psychic being, the kind of concentration, which their discipline requires. Hence the empirical wisdom of the apprentice-system, as it prevails in laboratories, studios, and schools of philosophy. *The Spiritual Exercises* of Ignatius Loyola would seem to be far removed from the play of kittens; yet their purpose is to reveal, through the techniques of make-believe, the potentialities of human nature and the realities of the human situation, as Loyola understood them. When he explains to the devout how to make present to their feelings and imaginations as well as their reason, scenes from the life of Christ, he sketches a technique like that which the Moscow Art Theater used to train actors. His immediate purpose is similar: to reveal a scene significant on many levels, and a mode of action capable of evoking a mimetic response of the whole being.

Because the histrionic sensibility is a basic, or primary, or primitive virtue of the human mind, it is difficult to describe in other terms; and it can only be cultivated by practice. For this reason there is little literature about it except drama itself, though from time to time a lore is developed, a traditional askesis, based upon a particular use of it for educational or therapeutic or moral purposes like those I mentioned. When the theater is cultivated, a lore of the art of acting is developed; and a few connoisseurs of the histrionic sensibility and of the art of acting have tried to write down their observations. Shakespeare's plays are full of obiter dicta on the acting art. Coquelin to some extent rationalized his own subtle practice as an actor. Henry James, a great admirer of Coquelin and of the French theater, became a connoisseur. And he has very revealing things to say about the actor's perception and imitation of action which he compares with his own as he practiced it in the different medium of the novel.

The technique of the Moscow Art Theater (which is cultivated here and there in this country by students of Moscow actors and directors) is a conscious and often highly developed method of training actors. Its purpose is to teach the actor to perceive and imitate *action* so that he can play accurately the roles which dramatists of all kinds have written. The actor must learn to free his mind, his feelings, and his imagination as far as possible, both from the clichés of his own time and from the special limitations of his own personality. He must make his own inner being "an instrument capable of playing any tune," as it is often put. To this end he practices the recall of sensory impressions (those of washing or shaving, for instance). He learns to make-believe situations, emotionally charged human relationships, and to respond freely within the imagined situation. This is as much as to say that he learns a certain kind of concentration, closely akin to that recommended by Loyola for a different purpose. When skilled actors improvise a playlet upon an imagined situation, they respond freely to each other's actions and words within it yet never violate its basic donnés. Thus the technique is intended to free the psyche, and then control it, for the purposes of playing; and the training of the body and voice, which is often supposed to be the only training an actor can receive, is merely ancillary. But it is necessary to emphasize the fact that a technique of acting, even so fundamental a one as this, merely leads to the literature of drama, just as the performer's technique of the violinist leads to the literature of the violin, where the possibilities of the instrument are explored.

The notion of action and the imitation of action is the connecting link between the art of the dramatist and the interpretive art of the actor. I cannot discover whether Stanislavksy and Nemirovitch-Dantchenko got their concept of action from Aristotle or not. Perhaps they merely rediscovered it empirically through a close study of the psychic content of many roles. In their system it is a technical-empirical notion, a convenient rule of thumb, which the actor needs in his study of the role he is to play: when he has discovered the "main action" and the many smaller actions of his character and can indicate them by an infinitive phrase, he knows what he has to reproduce in his stage-life. Because of their limited purposes, the masters of the Moscow technique did not explore the general possibilities of "action" as Aristotle did—it is one of the key notions in Aristotelian philosophies of Act and Potency, Form and Matter. But wherever they got this notion, the Moscow Art Theater's lore of action has, potentially, great value. It provides a kind of bridge between theory and practice; points to the pre-conceptual basis of the dramatic art; and offers a means of access to masterpieces of the tradition which our contemporary mental habits obscure.

I am aware that most contemporary theory—whether of art or of knowledge or of psychology—leaves no room for the notion of action or the imitation of action. Probably it is the primitive realism of this concept which is unacceptable, both to those who wish to reduce all knowledge to "facts" and abstract concepts, and to those who try to maintain the absoluteness of art.

The objections of the semanticists to Aristotle's epistemology with its basis in the *nous*, or "apperceptive intelligence," are not very convincing but they represent an important and stubborn contemporary habit of mind. Aristotle is not as *inaverti* as they think; "what he has that they haven't got" is not naïve credulity but a recognition that we are aware of things and people "before predication," as he puts it. The histrionic sensibility, the perception of action, is such a primitive and direct awareness.

Contemporary theories of art which omit or reject the notion of the imitation of action are more disquieting than pseudo-scientific theories because of the insight they give us into the actual work of artists in our time. They remind us how difficult it is—after three hundred years of rationalism and idealism, with the traditional modes of behavior lost or discredited—to see any action but our own. Eliot, for instance, probably the most accomplished poet alive, does not seem to find the Aristotelian formula useful or valid. Thus he suggests that the aim of the poet is to find objective equivalents for his feeling. The phrase "objective equivalent" seems to support Eliot's announced classicism. Yet it refers, not to the vision of the poet, but to the poem he is making; and it implies that it is only a *feeling* that the poet has to convey. Thus the formula is closer to the romantic notion of art as the expression of feeling or passion than to the doctrine of imitation. The emphasis on the poem and its form, to the exclusion of what it represents, recognizes only one of the instincts which Aristotle thought were the roots of poetry in general, the "instinct for harmony and rhythm." Perhaps this emphasis on the distinguishing feature of art—what separates it from other perceptions of action—is necessary in order to reaffirm the existence of art. Perhaps it is poor strategy for a poet at the moment of composition to worry about "truth" in any sense except truth to his feeling. And it may be that in our bewildered age the poet has only a pathetic inspiration; and that if he does not cling to the uniqueness of the mantic passion he is in danger of having nothing left to work with. "Poetry," says Aristotle, as though to recognize the limitations of his own theory, "implies either a happy gift of nature or a strain of madness. In the one case a man can take the mould of any character; in the other he is lifted out of his proper self." Such considerations remind us of the mystery of the creative act in any art; of our dependence upon the masters, and of their dependence upon the surrounding culture.

Yet the notion of drama as imitation of action is both possible for us and very valuable. We do actually in some sense perceive the shifting life of the psyche directly, before all predication: before we reach the concepts of ethics or psychology; even before imitating it in the medium of words or musical sounds. When we directly perceive the action which the artist intends, we can understand the objectivity of his vision, however he arrived at it; and thence the form of his art itself. And only on this basis can one grasp the analogies between acting and playwrighting, between various forms of drama, and between drama and other arts.